Paul's Use of the Old Testament

Paul's Use
of the Old Testament

E. Earle Ellis

BAKER BOOK HOUSE
Grand Rapids, Michigan 49506

PHOTOLITHOPRINTED BY CUSHING - MALLOY, INC.
ANN ARBOR, MICHIGAN, UNITED STATES OF AMERICA

To the Memory of
my Father,
who taught me from a child
to know and love
the Holy Scriptures

ACKNOWLEDGMENTS

THERE are many to whom the writer owes a debt of appreciation, but he desires to mention especially the helpfulness and advice of the following persons: Professors Matthew Black of St Andrews and James S. Stewart of Edinburgh, whose encouragement and insight were so instrumental in the completion of the book; Professor Otto Michel of Tübingen, who gave helpful suggestions regarding German works in the field, and whose own book, *Paulus und seine Bibel*, was *grundlegend* for the present study; Professor Krister Stendahl of Harvard, who so graciously made available at the earliest possible moment a copy of his important dissertation, *The School of St Matthew*; Rev. J. W. Wenham of Tyndale Hall, Bristol, who read the manuscript and offered instructive criticisms and suggestions.

REPRINTED EDITION

I am gratified that my study of Paul's use of the Old Testament has proved to be a useful tool for many colleagues and students. And I am grateful for the publisher's interest in issuing this reprint.

Research in this area, as in others, has moved on considerably since the volume first appeared, and any adequate revision would have to be extensive. It seems best, therefore, to republish the book in its original form. Those who are interested in my more recent studies bearing on the topic may refer to my *Prophecy and Hermeneutic* (Tübingen and Grand Rapids, 1978).

New Brunswick, New Jersey
Lent 1981   E. EARLE ELLIS

CONTENTS

ix

ABBREVIATIONS

BA	*Biblical Archaeologist*
BJRL	*Bulletin of the John Rylands Library*
CAP	Charles' *Apocrypha and Pseudepigrapha*
DSH	*Habakkuk Commentary, Dead Sea Scrolls*
DSS	*Dead Sea Scrolls*
ET	*Expository Times*
HDB	Hastings' *Dictionary of the Bible*
HDCG	Hastings' *Dictionary of Christ and the Gospels*
HTR	Harvard *Theological Review*
IF	Introductory Formula(s)
JBL	*Journal of Biblical Literature*
JQR	*Jewish Quarterly Review*
JTS	*Journal of Theological Studies*
KTW	Kittel's *Theologisches Wörterbuch*
LXX	Septuagint
MT	Masoretic Text
NT	New Testament
NTS	New Testament Studie.
OT	Old Testament
SBK	*Strack-Billerbeck Kommentar*
SBT	*Babylonian Talmud*, Socino Edition
SJE	Singer's *Jewish Encyclopedia*
SJT	*Scottish Journal of Theology*
SMR	*Midrash Rabba*, Socino Edition
VT	*Vetus Testamentum*
ZATW	*Zeitschrift für die alttestamentliche Wissenschaft*
ZFK	*Zeitschrift für Kirchengeschichte*
ZFST	*Zeitschrift für systematische Theologie*
ZNTW	*Zeitschrift für die neutestamentliche Wissenschaft*

TALMUD TRACTATES

Ab.	Aboth	Hag.	Hagigah	Shab.	Shabbath
'Ar.	'Arakin	Kid.	Kiddushin	Shebu.	Shebu'oth
'AZ	'Abodah Zarah	Mak.	Makkoth	Sot.	Sotah
BB	Baba Bathra	Meg.	Megillah	Ta.	Ta'anith
Ber.	Berakoth	Men.	Menahoth	Yeb.	Yebamoth
BK	Baba Kamma	Ned.	Nedarim	Yom.	Yoma
BM	Baba Mezia	Pes.	Pesahim		
'Er.	'Erubim	Sanh.	Sanhedrin		

INTRODUCTION

THE use of the OT in the New has long been recognised as an important field of research. Too often, however, the emphasis placed upon rabbinic and Hellenistic influences has tended to subordinate and obscure the unique place of the OT in the minds and theology of the early Christian writers. The trend of recent years to seek from the OT itself the source and meaning of NT thought has been an entirely proper one, as Hoskyns' words so well express: '[There are] grounds for supposing no further progress in the understanding of primitive Christianity to be possible unless the ark of NT exegesis be recovered from its wanderings in the land of the Philistines and be led back not merely to Jerusalem, for that might mean to contemporary Judaism, but to its home in the midst of the classical OT Scriptures—to the Law and to the Prophets.'[1]

The present study is not primarily textual, an area already well covered, but rather seeks the rationale underlying the Pauline usage both in its textual manifestation and in its theological application. Even where a variant text is apparently in view, Paul's textual aberrations in many cases have a hermeneutical purpose and often are closely tied to the immediate application of the citation. While rabbinic Judaism has influenced the mechanics of Pauline citation, one must look to the apostolic Church and to Christ Himself to find the primary source of the apostle's understanding and use of the OT. The emphases, applications and hermeneutics of Paul's quotations mark him as one with the apostolic Church in contrast to his rabbinic background.

---

[1] E. C. Hoskyns, 'Jesus the Messiah', *Mysterium Christi*, ed. G. K. A. Bell and A. Deissmann, London, 1930, p. 70. Cf. A. M. Hunter, *The Work and Words of Jesus*, London, 1950, p. 71: 'After ransacking all sorts of sources, Jewish and Greek (and, we may add, starting all sorts of "hares", some of which have not run very well) [scholars] are re-discovering the truth of Augustine's dictum, "The NT lies hidden in the Old, and the Old is made plain in the New".'

HISTORICAL SURVEY

The Reformation spurred a revival of interest in NT quotations and gave rise to the first systematic treatment of the subject.[1] In the Reformation, as in the early centuries, the prophetic element in quotation produced two schools of thought.[2] Reflecting the Alexandrian school were those favouring a double reference or allegorical view of prophecy; the reformers tended towards the historical emphasis of the Antiochene exegetes.[3] As for the more direct study of NT quotations, Drusius wrote (c. 1594) a series of critical notes which were published in London in 1660.[4] At about the same time Cappellus completed his *Critica Sacra*. Thirty-six years in the making, it contained variant NT textual readings and an appendix on NT quotations.[5] Alting, also in an appendix, compared OT citations in Matt. 1-12 with the Hebrew and LXX, with annotations.[6]

The following century saw the groundwork firmly laid for almost all of the important issues in this field of research, issues which have remained prominent even until the present, for example, textual variations, affinities with rabbinic practices and the propriety of NT exegesis. The Dean of Chichester concluded a course of lectures with the words, 'I conceived it seasonable, at a Time when the Argument from Prophecy was exposed to open ridicule, to suggest some proper Observations on the Subject, for the assistance of serious Minds disposed to consider . . . '.[7] But prophecy was not the only issue stirring the minds of scholars. In an argument strangely resembling

---

[1] The first listing of NT quotations appears to have been in Robert Stephens' Greek Testament, published in Paris in 1550. Cf. H. Gough, *The New Testament Quotations*, London, 1855, p. iii.

[2] Cf. F. A. G. Tholuck, *The Old Testament in the New*, trans. C. A. Aitken in *Bibliotheca Sacra*, XI (July 1854), pp. 568-616.

[3] e.g. Theodore of Mopsuestia. Cf. Calvin on Matt. 2.18; Rom. 10.6ff; Eph. 4.8f; Heb. 2.6ff; 4.4. Many such passages were viewed as the adaption of OT language and not as prophecies. So also Hengstenburg, *Commentary on the Psalms*, Edinburgh, 1846, I, pp. 264ff: Many Psalms are fulfilled in the Messiah inasmuch as they describe the righteous man according to his idea.

[4] J. Drusii, 'Notae in Parallela Sacra', *Tractatuum Biblicorum, Volumen Prius, sive Criticorum Sacrorum, Tomus VIII*, Londini, 1660, pp. 1262-326.

[5] L. Cappelli, 'Quaestio de Locis Parallelis Veteris et Novi Testamenti', *Critica Sacra*, Paris, 1650, pp. 443-557. He concluded that the apostles cited from the Greek and not the Hebrew, as commonly supposed.

[6] J. Alting, *Operum, Tome II*, Amstelaedami, 1685.

[7] T. Sherlock, *The Use and Intent of Prophecy*, London, 1726, p. 195.

some twentieth century discussions Whiston and Carpzov sought to resolve some of the textual problems of NT citation. Whiston argued that the NT was exact with first century Greek and Hebrew texts but that the latter were corrupted. Having 'shrewdly suspected some pernicious practices of the Jews in this case', especially with regard to the Hebrew Bible, Whiston sought to correct the present OT text with the Samaritan Pentateuch, the NT, Philo, Josephus and other sources.[1] Carpzov, in reply, defended the accuracy of the Hebrew text and attributed NT variation to hermeneutical purposes and literary convenience.[2] Later in the century Randolph tabulated, in columnar fashion, NT citations and their LXX and Hebrew parallels, giving notes of explanation; he judged that while NT writers were largely in agreement with the Hebrew, 'they sometimes quote the LXX, and perhaps other translations or paraphrases'.[3] Randolph's contemporary, Henry Owen, who contended that NT writers usually used the LXX, voices the sentiment which generally pervaded the study of the subject in his day: 'Objections of various kinds have been made to the truth of the Christian religion: but no objections of any kind seem to bear so hard upon it as those which are drawn from the *differences* that occur between the quotations in the NT and the passages to which they refer in the Old. On these differences therefore, Jews and Infidels particularly insist and largely expatiate.'[4]

Perhaps the most significant contribution of the period was that of Surenhusius, who demonstrated the extensive agreements in methodology between NT and rabbinic writers.[5] His epoch-making study supplied the foundation for the

---

[1] W. Whiston, *An Essay towards Restoring the True Text of the Old Testament*, London, 1722, p. 283.

[2] J. G. Carpzov, *A Defence of the Hebrew Bible*, London, 1729, pp. 104-83. The LXX was quoted when the sense corresponded to the Hebrew or 'well explained the Hebrew text' (p. 112).

[3] T. Randolph, *The Prophecies and other Texts Cited in the New Testament*, Oxford, 1782, p. 27. He found that 120 quotations followed the Hebrew, 119 the LXX. Randolph's 'paraphrases' are suggestive for later research.

[4] H. Owen, *The Modes of Quotation used by the Evangelical Writers*, London, 1789, p. 1.

[5] G. Surenhusio, ספר המשוה *sive* βιβλος καταλλαγης *in quo secundum veterum Theologorum Hebraeorum*, Amstelaedami, 1713. He especially deals with IF, merged quotations, and the practice of citing from the Law, Prophets and Hagiographa in succession.

investigations of Döpke[1] and all subsequent work in this field. Writers of the nineteenth century gave further attention to the critical problems of NT exegesis[2] and particularly intensified the study and comparison of textual data. Some writers such as Gough, Turpie, Toy and Dittmar were concerned chiefly with classification and comparison of NT citations with the LXX and MT.[3] The first and last are almost purely technical studies and compare apocryphal and rabbinic as well as OT parallels. Turpie and Toy give a commentary on each of the passages. The former seeks throughout to defend the propriety of NT texts and applications; (in a second volume he classified in similar fashion all the IF in the NT).[4] Toy's comments are of a more critical nature.

With particular reference to Pauline citations, Roepe concludes that the apostle quotes almost without exception from the LXX, and this is often from memory.[5] The valuable Leipzig dissertation of Kautzsch arrived at similar results: Paul always uses the Alexandrian version with the exception of the two Job citations (Rom. 11.25; 1 Cor. 3.19); in these, and perhaps a few others, Paul's text reflects the Hebrew because no LXX translation was available to him. Monnet and Vollmer generally follow Kautzsch in this regard.[6] In opposition to this trend, the ingenious theory of Edward Böhl sought to prove that the peculiarities of NT quotations should be attributed to

[1] J. C. C. Döpke, *Hermeneutik der neutestamentlichen Schriftsteller*, Leipzig, 1829.

[2] Cf. L. Woods, *The Objection to the Inspiration of the Evangelists and Apostles from their Manner of Quoting Texts from the Old Testament*, Andover, 1824; A. T. Hartmann, *Die Enge Verbindung des Alten Testamentes mit dem Neuen*, Hamburg, 1831; Tholuck, op. cit.; C. Taylor, *The Gospel in the Law*, Cambridge, 1869; A. Clemen, *Der Gebrauch des Alten Testamentes in den neuentestamentlichen Schriften*, Gütersloh, 1895; F. Johnson, *The Quotations of the New Testament from the Old*, London, 1896; J. Scott, *Principles of New Testament Quotation*, Edinburgh, 1877.

[3] E. Gough, op. cit.; D. M. Turpie, *The Old Testament in the New*, London, 1868; C. H. Toy, *Quotations in the New Testament*, New York, 1884; W. Dittmar, *Vetus Testamentum in Novo*, Göttingen, 1903. Cf. also E. Böhl, *Die Alttestamentlichen Citate im Neuen Testament*, Wien, 1878.

[4] D. M. Turpie, *The New Testament View of the Old*, London, 1872.

[5] G. Roepe, *De Veteris Testamenti locrum in apostolorum libris allegatione*, 1827. LXX variations are attributed to other Greek versions; combined quotations are the result of memory citation.

[6] A. F. Kautzsch, *De Veteris Testamenti Locis A Paulo Apostolo Allegatis*, Lipsiae, 1869. H. Monnet, *Les Citations de l'ancien testament dans les épitres de St Paul*, Lausanne, 1874; H. Vollmer, *Die alttestamentlichen Citate bei Paulus*, Freiburg, 1896. Monnet considers further Paul's hermeneutical method and his attitude towards the OT. Vollmer confines himself to the four *Hauptbriefe*; an appendix examines the literary relation between Paul and Philo.

an Aramaic *Volksbibel* current in the time of Christ, which in translation was almost identical with the LXX.[1] Although the idea never commanded a wide following and was often dismissed as quickly as it was heard,[2] the dominant views of the LXX protagonists were also to suffer considerable modification in subsequent investigations.

The problem of the LXX in contemporary study and other questions pertinent to Pauline quotations are examined in the following chapters.[3] Among the more important works on the subject are those of Thackeray, Harnack, Michel and Bonsirven.[4] Thackeray evaluates the influence of rabbinic ideas on Pauline theology and exegesis; Bonsirven compares and contrasts types of exegesis in rabbinic and Pauline literature. From the infrequent use of the OT in the shorter letters, Harnack gathers that Paul never intended that Gentile Christianity should become a 'book religion' based on the OT. Written almost thirty years ago, Michel's Halle dissertation is, in succession to Kautzsch and Vollmer, the most recent book on Paul's use of the OT.

THE PASTORAL PROBLEM

The present study includes the traditional Pauline corpus with the exception of Hebrews.[5] All these epistles are admittedly 'Pauline', whether they are written by the apostle himself or not; and one might, like Dodd, leave the question at that.[6] However, it may be in order to give some attention

---

[1] E. Böhl, *Forschungen nach einer Volksbibel*, Wien, 1873.

[2] Vollmer (op. cit., p. 8) regarded it as wishful thinking. However, L. Zunz (*Die gottesdienstlichen Vorträge der Juden*, Frankfurt, 1892, pp. 5ff, 330ff) argued that Palestinian Jews required an Aramaic translation; and Böhl's theory, though rejecting Böhl's theory, admits the extensive use of oral Targums. Cf. Toy, op. cit., p. xvi.

[3] In the field of NT quotation cf. also A. Schlatter, *Das Alte Testament in der johanneischen Apokalypse*, Gütersloh, 1912; T. Haering, 'Das Alte Testament im Neuen', *ZNTW*, 17 (1916), 213-27; L. Venard, 'Citations de l'ancien Testament dans le Nouveau Testament', *Dictionnaire de la Bible*, ed. L. Pirot, Supp. II (1934); R. Chasles, *L'ancien Testament dans le Nouveau*, 1937; M. Kähler, *Jesus und das Alte Testament*, Gütersloh, 1938; A. Oepke, *Jesus und das Alte Testament*, Leipzig, 1938; B.F.C. Atkinson, 'The Textual Background of the Use of the Old Testament by the New,' *The Victoria Institute*, LXXIX (1947), 39-70; T. W. Manson, 'The Old Testament in the Teaching of Jesus', *BJRL*, 34 (1952), 312-32; C. Smits, 'Oud-Testamentische Citaten in het Nieuwe Testament, I, Synoptische Evangelien', *Collect. Francisc. Neerlandica* 8.1 (1952); J. W. Wenham, *Our Lord's View of the Old Testament*, London, 1953; J. Dupont, 'L'utilisation apologétique de l'ancien Testament dans les discours des Actes', *Ephemer. Theol. Lovan.*, 29 (1953).

[4] H. St J. Thackeray, *The Relation of St Paul to Contemporary Jewish Thought*,

B

to the most pressing critical problem—the authenticity of the
Pastoral epistles. Their genuineness was first questioned by
Schleiermacher (1807) and Eichhorn (1812). A rapid development of this type of criticism led to the rejection by the 'Tübingen
School' of all the Pauline epistles except the *Hauptbriefe*; some
scholars, rejecting them all, concluded that 'Paul the apostle'
was a figment of second century imagination.[1] In the receding
tide of radical criticism over the past fifty years the Pastorals,
the first to be questioned, remain the only epistles still regarded
as spurious by most scholars; and even here the presence of
Pauline 'fragments' is generally recognised.[2]

The patristic testimony is about as good as for the other
epistles.[3] Isolated objections and their apparent absence from
p-46 and from Marcion's canon (because they were private
letters?) do not materially alter the total picture. Modern objections rest on other grounds: (1) the historical situation, (2) the
type of heresies present, (3) the stage of Church organisation,
(4) theological concepts, (5) vocabulary and style.[4] Lock, who
is undecided about the authorship of the Pastorals, considers
that it is only the last point which poses a difficult problem.[5]
As for the other points, Zahn contends that the false teaching
attacked in the Pastorals resembles nothing known in post-
apostolic times; it is definitely Jewish and appears to be related
to the Colossian heresy.[6] Jeremias, who gives a good summary

London, 1900; A. von Harnack, 'Das Alte Testament in den Paulinischen Briefen
und in den Paulinischen Gemeinden', *Sitzungsberichte der Preussischen Akademie der
Wissenschaften*, Berlin, 1928, 124-41; O. Michel, *Paulus und seine Bibel*, Gütersloh,
1929; J. Bonsirven, *Exégèse Rabbinique et Exégèse Paulinienne*, Paris, 1939.

[5] On this cf. B. F. Wescott, *The Epistle to the Hebrews*, 3rd ed., London, 1920,
pp. lxii-lxxix; O. Michel, *Der Brief an die Hebräer*, Göttingen, 1955, pp. 1f, 9ff.

[6] C. H. Dodd, *According to the Scriptures*, London, 1952, p. 30: 'For our present
purpose I shall treat the Pauline corpus (excluding Hebrews) as representing the
work of one author. Even if certain of the writings contained in it may not be
from the hand of the apostle, they all depend largely upon him.'

[1] Cf. A. Schweitzer, *Paul and His Interpreters*, London, 1948, pp. 7ff, 123ff.

[2] Cf. P. N. Harrison, *The Problem of the Pastorals*, Oxford, 1922, pp. 87-135;
R. Falconer, *The Pastoral Epistles*, Oxford, 1937, pp. 13-17. However, B. S. Easton
(*The Pastoral Epistles*, London, 1948, pp. 16f) finds no real evidence for the use of
sources; allowing for the influence of Pauline teaching, the letters are from a
single hand.

[3] Cf. J. D. James, *The Genuineness and Authorship of the Pastoral Epistles*, London,
1906, pp. 5-24.

[4] P. Feine and J. Behm, *Einleitung in das Neue Testament*, Leipzig, 1950, pp.
206-18. [5] W. Lock, *The Pastoral Epistles*, Edinburgh, 1924, pp. xxviif.

[6] Cf. 2 Tim. 3.6-9; Titus 1.10, 14. T. Zahn, *Introduction to the New Testament*.
Grand Rapids, 1953, II, p. 115; Feine-Behm, op. cit., p. 212.

of the whole problem, regards the theological peculiarities as stemming from the unique purpose and character of the letters; and they are not without parallels elsewhere in Paul.[1]

P. N. Harrison, in a most thorough and minute statistical analysis, argues that the type and frequency of vocabulary precludes Pauline authorship.[2] He found an extremely high proportion of *hapax legomena* and words used only infrequently elsewhere; and if his method is valid, his conclusions are well-nigh incontrovertible. However, Michaelis has shown that 'die statistische Methode Harrisons enthält im Ansatz einen Fehler der ihre Ergebnisse in Frage stellt'.[3] Two potent objections undermine the whole of Harrison's argument: First, any effective statistical argument must take into account both the subject matter and the literary character (e.g. doctrinal or paraenetic) of the text; the vocabulary is never independent of its situation and purpose. Words must be weighed as well as counted. By placing all words into one statistical tabulator Harrison omitted factors essential to a correct evaluation. Secondly, it is basic to all graph analysis that proper quantities of material are set in relation to each other. In general, the shorter a text the greater the proportional weight of elementary, indispensable vocabulary; as the text lengthens this vocabulary is repeated and its relation to the total drops. For example, Romans, with twenty-six pages, has a vocabulary of 993 words, or 38·2 words per page. However, 1 Tim. has 529:6 1/3 = 83·5; 2 Tim. 413:4 2/3 = 88·5; Tit. 293:2 2/3 = 109·9 words per page. Since the Pastorals have in any case an abundant vocabulary, any comparison with longer and less *wortreichen* texts is always heavily weighted towards the Pastorals. All of Harrison's tests produced the same results because, under the method, they had to produce the same results. The method, as Michaelis concludes,

---

[1] J. Jeremias, *Die Briefe an Timotheus und Titus*, 6th ed., Göttingen, 1953, p. 4. 1 Tim. 4.1, 6; Titus 1.13 equate faith with right doctrine, but cf. Rom. 6.17; 16.17; Gal. 1.23. Good works are stressed in 1 Tim. 2.10; 2 Tim. 2.21; Titus 2.14, but cf. 2 Thess. 2.17; 2 Cor. 9.8; Rom. 2.7; 13.3; Eph. 2.10. Most theological themes and some incidental allusions (e.g. to the Holy Spirit) are characteristically Pauline. Cf. Lock, op. cit., pp. xxvif; H. B. Swete, *The Holy Spirit in the New Testament*, London, 1909, p. 243.

[2] Harrison, op. cit.

[3] W. Michaelis, 'Pastoralbriefe und Wortstatistik', *ZNTW*, 28 (1929), p. 74: '... Harrison's statistical method contains an error at the outset which places its results in question.'

is incapable of showing either the genuineness or the spurious-
ness of the Pastorals.[1]

Stylistic differences, *hapax legomena* and the use of known words
in a different significance, structure and frequency remain a
problem for the Pauline authorship. Roller's valuable investigation into the nature and practice of ancient letter-writing
probably offers the best solution to it[2]: The writer often employed an amanuensis who copied first on a wax tablet and then
transcribed the contents onto papyrus; a variable degree of
freedom was involved in the process. The author then read
and corrected the material and added a closing greeting (cf.
Gal. 6.16). If Paul, because of age or infirmity (cf. 2 Tim. 2.9),
gave his amanuensis a greater degree of freedom than usual,
the stylistic peculiarities are suitably accounted for; and a conclusion to the problem of the Pastorals may be reached: 'auch
hinter diesen Briefen steht als ihr Schöpfer die Gestalt des
grossen Heidenapostels.'[3]

References to the OT in the Pastorals are, for the most part,
characteristic of the apostle Paul. The divine character and
contemporary application of the OT (2 Tim. 3.15; cf. Rom. 15.3;
1 Cor. 10.11), the ethical motivation in adducing Scripture
(1 Tim. 5.18f; cf. 1 Cor. 6.16; 9.9; 2 Cor. 6.16ff), and the
coupled or merged citation (1 Tim. 5.18; 2 Tim. 2.19; cf. Rom.
9.33; 11.34f; 1 Cor. 3.19f; 15.45)[4] are all found elsewhere in
the Pauline letters. The καί connective is unusual but not unknown (cf. Rom. 9.33). Also, no explicit quotation of a *verbum
Christi* as Scripture (1 Tim. 5.18b; cf. 1 Cor. 9.9, 14) occurs
elsewhere, but it is in keeping with his attitude toward Christ's
sayings.[5] The infrequent citation of Scripture (there is only
one formula quotation) follows the pattern of Paul's other short

---

[1] Michaelis, op. cit., p. 76. Cf. M. Dibelius, *Die Pastoralbriefe*, 2nd ed., Tübingen,
1931. For parallels to the Pastorals' *hapax legomena* in classical literature cf. E. K.
Simpson, *The Pastoral Epistles*, London, 1954, pp. 16ff. The small scope of extant
Pauline material (*c.* 120 pages, 3000 main vocables) is itself a hindrance to this
type of argument.

[2] O. Roller, *Das Formular der Paulinischen Briefe*, Stuttgart, 1933, pp. 4ff; cf.
Jeremias, op. cit., pp. 6f.

[3] Jeremias, op. cit., p. 7. 'Also behind these letters stands, as their creator, the
form of the great apostle to the Gentiles.' So also Feine-Behm (op. cit., p. 217),
who give further bibliography.

[4] On 2 Tim. 2.19; cf. also Phil. 2.12b-13.

[5] Cf. *infra*, pp. 28ff.

epistles[1]; and the tendency to cite pagan writers is reminiscent of earlier Pauline practice (Titus 1.14; cf. Acts 17.28; 1 Cor. 15.33).

All in all, the weight of evidence favours the genuineness of the Pastorals. For Jeremias, the unique situation and the intimate relation between writer and recipient stand as chief considerations. Certainly the difficulties surrounding a pseudepigraphal or fragment-redaction theory are considerable even for the historical situation: If attempted soon after Paul's death, his friends and Churches would have raised questions; if later, the Church at large would have subjected them to careful scrutiny. Early Christendom was not nearly so susceptible to 'pious fraud' in this regard as some modern writers would like to suppose; and the history of the Canon and of the 'Apocryphal NT' bears witness to this fact.

The textual sources in the following pages include Kittel, Swete and Nestle.[2] In quoting from the English Bible, the King James version has usually been followed; other versions are used as indicated, and on a few occasions the writer has given his own rendering. Abbreviations used in the text and footnotes are catalogued on p. xi f.

[1] Cf. *infra*, pp. 30ff. For a statistical analysis cf. H. K. Moulton, 'Scripture Quotations in the Pastoral Epistles', *ET*, 49 (1937-8), p. 94.

[2] R. Kittel, *Biblia Hebraica*, Stuttgart, 1937; H. B. Swete, *The Old Testament in Greek*, Cambridge, 1895; E. Nestle, *Novum Testamentum Graece*, Stuttgart, 1949.

CHAPTER I

PAUL AND HIS BIBLE

INTRODUCTION

THE writings of the apostle Paul reveal a person immersed in the content and teachings of the OT. H. A. A. Kennedy, after a study of Paul's religious terminology, found that practically every leading conception in this field of Paul's thought had its roots definitely laid in OT soil.[1] Whether he is giving a dogmatic proof,[2] an analogy[3] or an illustration,[4] or merely using language with which to clothe his own thoughts,[5] the OT appears frequently throughout the Pauline epistles.[6] The style and vocabulary of the apostle are such that it is often difficult to distinguish between quotation, allusion and language colouring from the OT.[7] This is not only the Word of God but also his mode of thought and speech; thus it is not unnatural that he should find in it vivid phraseology to apply to a parallel situation in his own day.[8]

The Pauline use of the OT appears in three distinct forms:

[1] H. A. A. Kennedy, *St Paul and the Mystery Religions*, London, 1913, pp. 154-60.
[2] e.g. Rom. 3.10-18.   [3] e.g. Rom. 2.24.   [4] e.g. Rom. 10.6-8.
[5] e.g. Rom. 12.20; 1 Cor. 15.32; 2 Cor. 10.17; 13.1.
[6] With these distinctions in mind writers have sought to measure Paul's fidelity to and departures from the sense of the OT passage; cf. B. Jowett, *The Epistles of St Paul to the Thessalonians, Galatians, and Romans: Commentary*, London, 1894, pp. 191ff; F. Johnson, op. cit. It is doubtful, however, whether the categories—proof, analogy, illustration—actually denote the rationale underlying the Pauline use of the OT, although they were appropriate in answering some critics who imagined the apostle finding 'proofs' at any cost; cf. Toy, op. cit., pp. xxi, xxxvi. However, quotations which seemingly are just analogy or rhetorical accommodations often prove to have a more profound significance in Paul's hermeneutic. See *infra*, pp. 114, 139ff.
[7] The non-formal character of the Pauline letters accords with this; cf. Roller, op. cit. Cf. A. Deissmann, *Light from the Ancient East*, London, 1927, p. 232; F. Prat, *The Theology of St Paul*, London, 1945, I, p. 18.
[8] The use today of such words as 'Munich', 'Dunkirk', 'blood, sweat and tears', follows in the same pattern. With this in mind Jowett framed his definition: 'Quotation, with ourselves, is an ingenious device for expressing our meaning in a pointed or forcible manner; it implies also an appeal to an authority. And its point frequently consists in a slight, or even great, deviation from the sense in which the words quoted were uttered by their author' (Jowett, op. cit., p. 190).

quotations proper, intentional and casual allusion, and dialectic and theological themes.[1] The task of defining 'quotation' in the Pauline literature is rather difficult, and the decision in the end is somewhat arbitrary. The apostle probably did not have our concept of quotation marks; he certainly did not give to it the sanctity which characterises our literary usage. Some references which are introduced with an explicit citation formula echo only the tenor of the passage[2]; others, not given even the dignity of an introductory conjunction, follow the OT text *verbatim ac litteratim*.[3] The gradation from quotation to allusion is so imperceptible that it is almost impossible to draw any certain line. The selection in Appendix I has taken into account three factors: the presence of an introductory formula or conjunction, the degree of verbal affinity with the OT text, and the intention of the apostle as judged from the context.

The Nature of the Quotations

General Analysis

Paul quotes the OT ninety-three times.[4] Reminiscences are found throughout the epistles (except Philemon), but quotations occur, apart from four in Ephesians and one each in First and Second Timothy, only in the four *Hauptbriefe*. Although the quotations are drawn from sixteen OT books, three-fourths of them are from the Pentateuch (thirty-three), Isaiah (twenty-five), and the Psalms (nineteen). The citations appear both singly and in combination.[5]

The texts appear in several forms. Most often they reproduce the OT passage with occasional variations in conformity with the new context.[6] A few times they are merely quotations of

---

[1] See Appendixes I and II.   [2] e.g. 1 Cor. 14.31.

[3] e.g. 1 Cor. 15.32. Neither the Westcott-Hort nor the Nestle text distinguishes between quotation and allusion. S. Johnson ('Biblical Quotations in Matthew', *HTR*, 36, April 1943, pp. 135-53) divides between the 'formula' quotations and the others. But this is not very effective; two texts in Paul are cited with and without a formula; cf. Jer. 9.24 (1 Cor. 1.31; 2 Cor. 10.17) and Hab. 2.4 (Rom. 1.17; Gal. 3.11).

[4] About one-third of all New Testament quotations are cited by Paul.

[5] See Appendix III. Paul combines texts in three ways: merged quotation (e.g. Rom. 3.10-18), chain quotation or *haraz* (e.g. Rom. 9.25-9), and looser midrashic commentary (cf. Rom. 9-11; Gal. 3). Cf. *infra*, pp. 49ff.

[6] e.g. Rom. 3.18 (αὐτοῦ to αὐτῶν); 10.5 (αὐτοὺς to αὐτῇ); 10.19 (αὐτοὺς to ὑμᾶς); 2 Cor. 6.18 (αὐτῷ ... αὐτὸς to ὑμῖν ... ὑμεῖς); Gal. 4.30 (υἱοῦ Ἰσαακ to υἱοῦ τῆς ἐλευθέρας).

substance whose source is conjectural.[1] The terse manner in which some texts are cited suggests that they may have been used as a teaching or catechetical device.[2]

Fifty-one of Paul's citations are in absolute or virtual agreement with the LXX, twenty-two of these at variance with the Hebrew.[3] In four passages Paul follows the Hebrew against the LXX; thirty-eight times he diverges from both.[4] Combined quotations show a much greater variation than the others[5]; there also seems to be a relation between the variations and the particular book cited.[6]

The priority of the LXX in Pauline quotations has long been recognised. As early a writer as Henry Owen noted the fact and ascribed it to the desire of early Christian missionaries to use a translation acceptable to Hellenistic Jews.[7] Kautzsch, in an oft-quoted dissertation,[8] concluded that the LXX had virtually an exclusive place in Paul's scriptural usage. Swete affirms that more than half of the Pauline quotations were taken from the LXX without material change and that, by any test, the LXX 'is the principal source from which the writers of the New Testament derived their Old Testament quotations'.[9] Even where the quotations vary from the LXX, parallel phraseology is often apparent.[10]

[1] e.g. 1 Cor. 2.9; Eph. 5.14; cf. Rom. 3.10.

[2] A familiar verse, quoted or summarised, could be utilised to bring the whole context before the reader's mind. Similarly, a 'pointer' or *lemma* text might recall a topical series previously taught them. Cf. Scott, op. cit., pp. 25-7; Dodd, *According to the Scriptures*, p. 126.

[3] These are chiefly from Genesis and Isaiah. See Appendix I. But in passages from Isaiah Paul also shows knowledge of the Hebrew. Cf. Rom. 10.15 (ὡραῖοι); 1 Cor. 14.21; 15.54.

[4] See Appendixes I and II.

[5] Almost all of them diverge. Of the merged quotations only two texts in Rom. 3.10ff follow the LXX. Among the chain quotations or *haraz* Rom. 9.12-13 and 9.25-9 each have one text in agreement with the Alexandrian text. Rom. 13.9, if included, should also be added.

[6] See Appendix I. All quotations from Kings, Job, Jeremiah and Hosea differ from the LXX, as do about half of those from Isaiah and Deuteronomy. Citations from Genesis and Psalms generally agree or vary only slightly.

[7] Owen, op. cit., p. 6.

[8] Kautzsch, op. cit., p. 5; cf. E. Schürer, *A History of the Jewish People in the Time of Jesus Christ*, 2nd ed. revised, Edinburgh, 1901, II, p. 285; W. Sanday and A. C. Headlam, *The Epistle to the Romans*, Edinburgh, 1895, p. 302. Monnet (op. cit.) follows and develops Kautzsch's theory.

[9] H. B. Swete, *An Introduction to the Old Testament in Greek*, Cambridge, 1900, pp. 392, 400ff.

[10] Cf. Rom. 2.27; 9.26; 1 Cor. 2.16; 6.16. See Appendix II.

Affinities with the LXX are not only evident in Paul's quotations but extend to his general style and vocabulary as well.[1] It was inevitable that, after the translation of the Hebrew Bible, words in the Greek version would acquire 'something of the value of the Hebrew words they represent'.[2] It was only natural that Paul, retaining in his mind Hebrew concepts and thought-forms, should frame his Greek on the analogy of the existing theological vocabulary of the LXX.[3] Even where the apostle quite evidently sees in a citation the underlying connotations of the Hebrew, the Alexandrian version remains his mode of expression.[4] 'The careful student of the Gospels and St Paul,' concludes Swete, 'is met at every turn by words and phrases which cannot be fully understood without reference to their earlier use in the Greek Old Testament.'[5]

The quotations show considerable distribution among the LXX text-forms, none of them being followed consistently. Sometimes they agree with LXX-B, more often with LXX-A and LXX-F.[6] There seems to be some relation between the text followed and the OT book quoted.[7] For example, in twenty-three quotations from Isaiah, Vollmer found seven in agreement with LXX-A against LXX-B. Leviticus, on the other hand, shows affinities with LXX-F.[8] There is no discernible connexion, however, between the OT text and the provenance of the Pauline letter. In general, LXX-A appears to

---

[1] e.g. 2 Cor. 3.4-18 (Exod. 34.29-35); Rom. 1.23 (Ps. 105 (106).20); cf. Vollmer, op. cit., pp. 10ff; Michel, op. cit., pp. 58-60. For terminology of LXX coinage see T. Nägeli, *Der Wortschatz des Apostels Paulus*, Göttingen, 1905, pp. 60-5. A. Deissmann perhaps overstates it: 'To understand the whole Paul from the point of view of the history of religion, we must know the spirit of the LXX' (*Paul*, 2nd ed. revised, London, 1926, p. 99).

[2] Reciprocally, Hebrew words acquired some new connotations, at least in the *diaspora*. C. H. Dodd, *The Bible and the Greeks*, London, 1935, p. xi; cf. N. H. Snaith, *The Distinctive Ideas of the Old Testament*, London, 1944, p. 159.

[3] Cf. H. A. A. Kennedy, *Sources of New Testament Greek*, Edinburgh, 1895, pp. 94f.

[4] A. D. Nock, 'The Style and Thought of Paul', *Contemporary Thinking about Paul: An Anthology*, ed. T. S. Kepler, Nashville, 1950, pp. 182-6.

[5] H. B. Swete, *Introduction*, p. 404; cf. W. O. E. Oesterley, *The Jews and Judaism during the Greek Period*, London, 1941, p. 54. The influence of the King James Version in the English-speaking world is a partial parallel. Cf. C. S. Lewis, *The Literary Impact of the Authorised Version*, London, 1950, pp. 15ff; W. M. Smith, *This Atomic Age and the Word of God*, Boston, 1948, pp. 44-57.

[6] e.g. Rom. 10.5; 2 Cor. 6.16; Gal. 3.10-12.

[7] This might be expected if different books were not allowed on the same roll. Cf. F. Buhl, *Canon and Text of the Old Testament*, Edinburgh, 1892, pp. 37f.

[8] Vollmer, op. cit., pp. 13-20, 48.

be more in accord with Paul's quotations than the other manuscripts.[1] It has been influenced in places by the NT,[2] but on
the whole it proves 'unusually trustworthy' in portions important for NT usage.[3]

As noted above, there are a considerable. number of variations from the LXX in Paul's quotations.[4] To account for
them several hypotheses lie at hand: a direct use of the Hebrew[5]
or its employment to correct the LXX,[6] citation from an Aramaic Targum or translation,[7] the use of other Greek translations,[8]
or free quotation from memory.[9] Paul often gives the impression
of quoting from memory, 'yet a memory which was the store-
house of more than one language, and one trained in Jewish
methods of bringing together passages from different books of
the Old Testament'.[10] From a psychological viewpoint it might
be expected that one who knew the Scripture in several languages and had a thorough knowledge of the sense of Scripture
would be less tied to any text-form. 'Memory quotation' should
be understood, however, as a free rendering in accordance with
literary custom[11] or for an exegetical purpose,[12] rather than as a

---

[1] Cf. Swete, *Introduction*, p. 403: 'In the Epistles, as in the Gospels, the text of
the LXX which is employed inclines to cod. A rather than to cod. B.' K. Stendahl
(*The School of St Matthew*, Uppsala, 1954) affirms that this relationship 'has more
solid foundations than Swete himself could have known . . .' (p. 176). Cf. also
W. Staerk, 'Die alttestamentlichen Citate bei den Schriftstellern des Neuen
Testament', *ZWT*, 35 (1892), pp. 464-85; 36 (1893), pp. 70-98.

[2] e.g. in adding Rom. 11.35 (Job 41.3) to Isa. 40.13 (Rom. 11.34) and probably
taking Ps. 13.1ff from Rom. 3.10ff. Cf. Swete, *Introduction*, p. 252.

[3] e.g. Isaiah and the Minor Prophets. Stendahl, op. cit., p. 172.

[4] Paul's vocabulary also, at times, reflects a usage distinct from the LXX. Cf.
Nägeli, op. cit., pp. 65-8. For a recent investigation of the Pauline text with
special reference to the Chester Beatty papyri cf. G. Zuntz, *The Text of the Epistles*,
Oxford, 1953.

[5] e.g. Rom. 9.17; 10.15 (ὡραῖοι); I Cor. 3.19; 14.21; 15.54; cf. E. Huhn, *Die
Messianischen Weissagungen*, Tübingen, 1900, II, p. 279.

[6] e.g. Rom. 9.17 הַעֲמַדְתִּי = ἐξήγειρά σε; Rom. 12.19, לִי נָקָם = ἐμοὶ ἐδίκησις.

[7] Toy, op. cit., p. xxxvi; Böhl, op. cit. Both, from partisan considerations, argue
against the idea of a reference to the Hebrew. F. H. Wood ('Quotation', *HDB*, IV,
1901) takes the variants εἰς νῖκος (I Cor. 15.54) and ἀγαπῶσιν (I Cor. 2.9) to be
from Aramaic interpretations of the Hebrew.

[8] Cf. H. Lietzmann, *An die Galater*, Tübingen, 1923, pp. 32-4.

[9] Perhaps the reason most often given, e.g. Swete, *Introduction*, p. 401; Sanday
and Headlam, op.cit., p. 302.

[10] Stendahl, op. cit., p. 159.

[11] For free quotation in the OT cf. the ten 'Words' in Exod. 20 and Deut. 5;
2 Sam. 23.17 (I Chron. 11.19); 2 Sam. 5.19-20 (I Chron. 14.9-11); I Kings 9.3-9
(2 Chron. 7.12-22). In the Apocrypha note the allusions in Baruch. 1.15-2.29 (Dan.
9.7-8; Deut. 9.7-19). For Philo's usage see H. E. Ryle, *Philo and Holy Scripture*,
London, 1895, pp. xxxv-vi. Examples from Greek and Latin writers and in the

result of 'memory lapse'. The importance of scriptural memorisation for the Jew, Paul's rabbinic training, and the verbal exactness of many of his quotations, militate against the latter explanation.[1] Moreover, the large measure of agreement with the LXX seems to reflect a conscious desire to reproduce a given text; it cautions against resorting to 'free quoting from memory' as soon as differences arise.[2]

One of Paul's quotations shows remarkable resemblance to Greek texts other than the LXX[3]:

Isa. 25.8	1 Cor. 15.54	Isa. 25.8 (LXX)	Theodotion	Aquila	Symmachus
בלע	κατεπόθε	κατέπιεν	καταπόθε	καταπόντισει	καταπόθηναι
המות	ὁ θάνατος	ὁ θάνατος	ὁ θάνατος	τόν θάνατον	τόν θάνατον
לנצח	εἰς νῖκος	ἰσχύσας	εἰς νῖκος	εἰς νῖκος	εἰς τέλος

Such noteworthy parallels are few, however,[4] and it is not certain that they reflect a common Greek version.[5] F. H. Woods points to εἰς νῖκος (לנצח) as a translation in accordance with the Aramaic meaning of the root. In some passages (e.g. Rom. 12.19) the same result is obtained if one posits an independent use of the Hebrew. It is probable that Paul was acquainted with other Greek texts[6]; however, the evidence is not sufficient to draw any final conclusions.

The theory of an Aramaic *Volksbibel* finds little, if any, support in Paul's variants; the apostle's fluency in both languages

early Fathers are cited by F. Johnson (op. cit., pp. 29-61) and J. Scott (op. cit., pp. 63-83, 87-91).

[12] e.g. σοφῶν for ἀνθρώπων (1 Cor. 3.20); ὁ πρῶτος ἄνθρωπος for ὁ ἄνθρωπος (1 Cor. 15.45); probably ἔδωκεν for ἐλαβες (Eph. 4.8); the addition of πᾶς (Rom. 10.11).

[1] J. Bonsirven (op. cit., p. 337) rejects the idea of memory failure: 'Infirmité humaine fort possible. Cependant cette explication est insuffisante à convaincre ceux qui ont vu des rabbins à l'ancienne récitant des livres entiers de la Bible et devenus de vivantes concordances de l'Ancien Testament.' ('Human weakness is quite possible. However, this explanation is insufficient to convince those who have seen some rabbis of the "Old School" who recited entire books of the Bible and became living concordances of the Old Testament.')

[2] Cf. Stendahl, op. cit., p. 158.   [3] Vollmer, op. cit., pp. 21-35.

[4] Paul's use of πανουργία (ערם) in 1 Cor. 3.19 as contrasted with the LXX's φρονήσις also agrees with Theodotion's translation of ערם in other places. Vollmer (p. 35) concludes that other versions of single OT books stand behind Paul, Aquila, Symmachus and Theodotion. Cf. Lietzmann, op. cit., pp. 32-4; A. Rahfl's 'Ueber Theodotion-Lesarten im Neuen Testament und Aquila-Lesarten bei Justin,' *ZNTW*, 20 (1921), pp. 182ff.

[5] The connexion may lie in a Targum. Note Aquila and Onkelos on Deut. 32.35; cf. Rom. 12.19. For the possible use of an Aramaic Targum by NT writers cf. the conclusions of M. Black, 'The Problem of the Old Testament Quotations in the Gospels', *Journal of the Manchester University Egyptian and Oriental Society*, 23 (1942), p. 4.   [6] So Lietzmann, op. cit.; Vollmer, op. cit., p. 35.

would make any accurate labelling in this regard difficult.[1] Nevertheless, Aramaic texts of some type probably lie behind some of the citations. Besides the instances given above, the variant in Eph. 4.8 may also reflect a Targum,[2] but its immediate source is more probably an interpretive rendering known to Paul and perhaps used in the early Church.[3]

The number and the character of Pauline variations from the LXX text give rise to questions which cannot be divorced from the wider context of the problem. Some appraisal of this wider context may be of assistance in drawing conclusions regarding the OT text in the epistles.

THE PROBLEM OF THE SEPTUAGINT

A generation ago the 'Letter of Aristeas',[4] for all its legendary accretions, was generally considered to be reliable in its most essential aspects, i.e. a third century B.C. Greek translation of the Pentateuch originating in the Jewish community in Alexandria. In addition, the Egyptian city was regarded as the probable later provenance of the rest of the Greek Bible, which became the *regula fidei* of most of the *diaspora* and later of the Christian Church. With this view of the LXX one would naturally treat it as any classical text: Seek the archetype behind the three major rescensions (Hesychius, Lucian, Origen) and other witnesses with the ordinary tools of textual criticism. Lagarde is a typical representative of this older school; Rahlfs, following in his train, bases the whole critical apparatus of his LXX on this view of LXX origins.[5]

[1] On Paul's bilingual ability see J. H. Moulton, *A Grammar of New Testament Greek*, Edinburgh, 1919, II, i, pp. 21-3; cf. Acts 21.40. Note such Semitic constructions as 'the light of the gospel of the glory of Christ' (2 Cor. 4.4).

[2] So Thackeray, op. cit., p. 182.

[3] On Eph. 4.8 see *infra* pp. 139ff. The Hebrew באדם may be rendered 'for men'. Meyer and Alford also note that the Hebrew verb (לקח) may have a proleptic significance, 'to fetch', i.e. to take in order to give. The fact that Paul's interpretation is found in the Syriac and the Targum shows that it is not merely arbitrary; it may point rather to his close acquaintance with the Aramaic and/or Hebrew. Cf. Rom. 9.7; 10.15; 1 Cor. 2.9. See T. K. Abbott, *The Epistles to the Ephesians and Colossians*, Edinburgh, 1897, pp. 111ff. Thackeray (op. cit., p. 182) notes a possible textual basis for the variant, i.e. a transposition of the letters in 'take' (לקח) and 'give' (חלק).

[4] See Swete (*Introduction*, pp. 1-27, 499ff) for a historical introduction and Greek text of the 'Letter'. An English translation is found in R. H. Charles, *The Apocrypha and Pseudepigrapha of the Old Testament*, Oxford, 1913, II, pp. 83-122.

[5] A. Rahlfs, *Septuaginta*, Stuttgart, 1935.

The theory of a third century B.C. proto-LXX, passing through various recensions and culminating in the Christians' Greek Bible, faced a problem in the textual variations of OT citations in Jewish writings (e.g. Philo), the NT and the early Fathers. These quotations often appeared to reflect, not *ad hoc* renderings of the LXX or even variant LXX recensions, but a different textual source. For a long time attempts to solve the problem were made within the framework of the traditional view of LXX origins, i.e. that it stems from one archetypal text. Aramaic Targums or versions, divergent LXX recensions and *ad hoc* translations were adduced to solve the problem of the variations. The 'testimony-book' hypothesis represents a special aspect of the same question.[1]

In a more recent attempt to solve the problem, advanced by Paul Kahle, the whole theory of LXX origins undergoes radical alteration.[2] In Kahle's eyes, the 'Letter of Aristeas' is a late second century B.C. propaganda piece designed to promote and standardise a recent Alexandrian revision of a Greek Torah. The legend was later attached to the Christian Greek Bible even though the Alexandrian Pentateuch was only one of the many roots of the resultant text. In short, 'the Letter of Aristeas has put us on a wrong track'[3]; the Greek Bible cannot be explained on the basis of an archetype at all. Its inception should be viewed rather as a development similar to the Aramaic Targums and Latin Vulgate. The Targums were at first oral renderings with a diversity of readings from synagogue to synagogue; later these were reduced to writing, and finally an official Targum evolved. In like manner the Vulgate arose out of many independent Latin texts. The Greek-speaking *diaspora* were no less in need of targumic paraphrases than their Aramaic-speaking brethren in Palestine. From these Greek Targums the first Greek texts were derived; and out of that diversity came the later uniformity of the Christian LXX.

---

[1] *infra*, pp. 98ff.
[2] P. E. Kahle, *The Cairo Geniza*, London, 1947, pp. 132-79. The theory of Sperber is similar: Transcriptions and translations were made, of which at least two Greek texts arising from two types of Hebrew texts are still identifiable. (A. Sperber, 'NT and Septuagint', *JBL*, 59 (June 1940), pp. 193-289; 'The NT and the Septuagint', *Tarbiz*, 6 (1934), pp. 1-29. See K. Stendahl, op. cit., pp. 174-82; B. J. Roberts, *The Old Testament Texts and Versions*, Cardiff, 1951, pp. 101-19.)
[3] Kahle, op. cit., p. 175.

In the NT, behind Origen's *Hexapla*, in the old Latin versions, and to a lesser extent in Philo[1] and Josephus,[2] one sees, according to Kahle, variant forms of the Greek texts in use at the time of Christ. Manson, in essential agreement with Kahle, views these texts as conforming to a regional pattern[3]; the large agreement of the NT with the LXX reflects the important place that one text-form enjoyed in the early Church. Much of what has come down to us, states Manson, 'is the debris of a primitive diversity only very imperfectly overcome rather than the record of sporadic lapses from a primitive uniformity.'[4] And so Kahle concludes: 'The task which the LXX presents to scholars is not the "reconstruction" of an imaginative Ur-text, nor the discovery of it, but a careful collection and investigation of all the remains and traces of earlier versions of the Greek Bible which differ from the Christian standard text.'[5]

Kahle presents his case in thorough fashion, but his handling of the Aristeas tradition[6] and the quotations of Philo is open to question; the lack of an extant Greek targumic tradition also militates against such a process on the scale which Kahle

[1] In a critique of Kahle's view of Philo's aberrant quotations P. Katz (*Philo's Bible*, Cambridge, 1950, p. 95) argues that the MSS-UF, upon which Kahle relies, actually reflects a lost recension of the Pentateuch which was interpolated into Philo's *lemma* text. Kahle, following A. Schroeder, accepted the variant MSS-UF as an accurate text and considered Philo's LXX uniformities to have been harmonised by Christian copyists. Cf. P. Katz, 'Das Problem des Urtexte der Septuaginta', *Theologische Zeitschrift*, 5 (1949), pp. 15-24; Stendahl, op. cit., p. 180.

[2] Against H. St J. Thackeray (*Josephus, the Man and the Historian*, New York, 1929, pp. 81ff), who divides Josephus' usage between Hebrew or Aramaic Targums (Pentateuch and probably Joshua, Judges, Ruth) and an ur-Lucianic recension of the LXX (rest of historical Books). Kahle assigns the variant texts to Greek Targums and the Lucianic affinities to Christian copyists. T. W. Manson ('The Cairo Geniza: A Review', *Dominican Studies*, 2 (April 1949), pp. 183-92) suggests that a Greek Targum may lie behind the Lucianic text itself.

[3] Ibid. For example, Theodotion (an Ephesian according to Irenaeus) finds parallels in 1 Cor. 15.54 and John 19.37, both of Ephesian origin. If behind Theodotion lies a Greek Targum of Asia, likewise there may lie Targums of Syria and Egypt behind Lucian and the LXX. Stendahl (op. cit., p. 160), however, finds Theodotion in Matthew and surmises that Paul's acquaintance stems from Greek studies under Gamaliel. Cf. Sotah 49 (*SBT*, pp. 265ff).

[4] Manson, 'The Cairo Geniza', p. 191.

[5] Kahle, op. cit., p. 179.

[6] See Swete's treatment (*Introduction*, pp. 1-27). Kahle does not mention the testimony of Aristobulus (second century B.C.) which Swete inclines to regard as genuine (pp. 12f, 18f). Assuming the 'Letter' to be a 100 B.C. propaganda piece, it does not follow that it was entirely baseless. Evidences of antiquity of the tradition both in the 'Letter' and in Philo (*de vita Mosis*, II, 25-44, trans F. H. Colson, London, 1935, VI, 461-70) are not easily dismissed.

envisions.[1] 'This [theory] is a most radical attitude to the relation of NT quotations to the Greek OT,' objects Stendahl, 'and Kahle has hardly faced its implications from the NT point of view. . . .'[2] Such a cleavage of opinion is not likely to be reconciled until many theoretical elements in the whole problem can be replaced by additional historical data; some recent evidence of this sort appears to favour an archetypal view of LXX origins.[3]

As the above observations indicate, the text behind Paul's quotations is a most difficult problem. While the Alexandrian version probably had the character of an official translation for the *diaspora* in certain areas[4] and plays an important part in Paul's usage,[5] it cannot be regarded as the apostle's sole textual source.[6] His fluency in Aramaic and Greek might, on first observations, favour an *ad hoc* rendering. However, affinities with other Greek texts and the familiar manner in which the quotations are often introduced suggest that Paul made use of variant translations or renderings known to his readers.[7] Whether these were independent texts or merely revisions within the LXX family cannot be determined with certainty, but the evidence does not point to any great number of independent textual traditions or to a great abundance of Greek

[1] Kahle admits the use of a revised Greek text in the *diaspora* c. 100 B.C. (cf. Schürer, op. cit., ii, II, p. 285). Yet Aramaic Targums do not appear until *c*. first century A.D., and the evolution of the text-form is much later. Assuming a parallel developmentary process (oral to written Targum to text) it is hard to imagine the Greek having gone to completion so much earlier, even granting the retarding effect of rabbinic proscriptions in Palestine.

[2] Stendahl, op. cit., p. 176; cf. B. J. Roberts, op. cit., pp. 101-19.

[3] Viz. Greek texts among the Qumram MSS. F. M. Cross ('The Manuscripts of the Dead Sea Scrolls', *BA*, 17, February 1954, pp. 2-21) regards them as 'decisive evidence' (p. 12) for the older view. D. Barthelemy ('Redécouverte d'un chainon manquant de l'histoire de la Septante', *Revue Biblique*, 60, January 1953, pp. 18-29) thinks they represent an old LXX revision which is a common denominator behind Aquila, Theodotion and Symmachus. They appear to be in close relation to some patristic quotations and to Origen's text (cf. Cross, op. cit., pp. 12ff).

[4] Philo's veneration for the LXX doubtless reflects the attitude of a great many Hellenistic Jews (Philo, *de vita Mosis*, II, 25-44; Colson, VI, 461-70).

[5] He probably possessed some rolls of Scripture (2 Tim. 4.13) and had access to texts in the synagogues.

[6] Paul's variant citations from Job are not, as Kautzsch thought, because of the lack of a LXX translation of that book; Philo (*de mut. nom.* 48, Colson, V, p. 167) quotes Job 14.4 from the LXX. Neither Kautzsch nor Vollmer settles the question of Paul's knowledge of Hebrew.

[7] As only one book was permitted on a roll, it was quite possible to have various text-forms in one collection. Cf. Buhl, op. cit., p. 38.

Targums.[1] Some of Paul's variants show the influence of the
Hebrew[2]; others can be traced to no text at all—they are Paul's
own rendering in which he interprets and applies as he quotes.[3]
The nature of the problem and the incomplete state of textual
evidence preclude any final adjudication of the matter; the
words of Sanday still remain relevant for several Pauline passages: '[There is] not sufficient evidence to say whether this
[variation] arises from a reminiscence of the Hebrew text . . . ,
or from an Aramaic Targum, or from the use of an earlier form
of LXX text.'[4]

The inconclusive character of results obtainable from textual
criteria leads one to consider a solution, or at least a partial
solution, on other grounds. There is always a temptation to
relieve oneself of textual difficulties by taking recourse in 'free
paraphrase' or 'interpretive rendering'. Nevertheless, several
factors, both in the textual analysis[5] and in the overall Pauline
hermeneutic,[6] indicate that the answer to many of these problems may lie in this direction.

PAUL'S ATTITUDE TO SCRIPTURE

GENERAL CONSIDERATIONS

Paul's use of the OT cannot be understood apart from his
attitude towards it.[7] To him the Scriptures are holy and
prophetic[8]; they constitute the very oracles of God ($\tau \grave{a} \lambda \acute{o} \gamma \iota a$
$\tau o \hat{v} \theta \epsilon o \hat{v}$),[9] and they 'were written . . . for our learning'.[10] All

---

[1] Deissmann, *Paul*, p. 100: 'It is not improbable that Paul made use of a text in
the LXX which had already undergone a Jewish revision.'

[2] See Appendix I.

[3] Cf. Bonsirven, op. cit., p. 377. See *infra*, pp. 139ff.

[4] Sanday and Headlam, op. cit., p. 302.

[5] Especially pertinent are variations in the citations of one epistle taken from
one OT book. Although, as Vollmer pointed out (*supra* p. 13), there is some relation
between the text-form and the book quoted, this is not uniformly true; in quotations
from Isaiah Rom. 9.27-8 varies from the LXX but v. 29 agrees; Rom. 10.15 varies,
v. 16 agrees; Rom. 3.15-17 varies, Rom. 15.21 agrees; 1 Cor. 2.16 varies, 1 Cor.
15.32 agrees; 2 Cor. 6.17 varies, 2 Cor. 6.2 agrees. It is impossible to reduce the
problem to the simplicity, 'What text of a given OT book was available to Paul in
a given city from which he wrote?'

[6] See *infra*, pp. 139ff.

[7] On the attitude of NT writers to Scripture see B. B. Warfield, *Revelation and
Inspiration*, New York, 1927, and the article 'Scripture' in *HDCG*.

[8] Rom. 1.2; 4.3.

[9] Rom. 3.1-2. That the phrase does refer to Holy Scripture against G. Kittel's
(*KTW*, Stuttgart, 1933, IV, pp. 143ff) contention that the reference is to
Heilsgeschichte in the OT and NT, see J. W. Doeve, 'Some Notes with reference to

his important doctrines are buttressed by an appeal to his Bible; to place the origin of Scripture in God, Paul's phrase 'God-breathed' (θεόπνευστος)[1] could hardly be improved upon. In his view of the OT the apostle is in agreement not only with Christ[2] and the other NT writers[3] but also with the whole of Judaism[4] and the early Church.[5]

Although the OT is sometimes referred to by Paul as 'the law',[6] 'the writings',[7] or 'the law and the prophets',[8] 'the scripture' (ή γραφή) is the prevailing usage.[9] These designations probably stemmed from the three divisions of the Jewish canon[10]; sometimes they were still applied in this distinctive sense.[11]

Lightfoot regards the singular γραφή in the NT as always indicating a particular passage of Scripture[12]; although this is generally true, Warfield's observation is more accurate: '[Often the] reference is to the Scripture as a whole, to that unitary written authority to which final appeal was made. In some of these passages it is no less than impossible to take it otherwise.'[13] In Warfield's opinion the anarthrous use of γραφή (1 Pet. 2.6; 2 Pet. 1.20; cf. 1 Tim. 3.16) is explicable only on this basis.

ΤΑ ΛΟΓΙΑ ΤΟΥ ΘΕΟΥ in Rom. III 2', *Studia Paulina, J. de Zwaan Festschrift*, Haarlem, 1953 pp. 111-123; Warfield, op. cit., pp. 351-407. T. W. Manson examines the word λόγια in the LXX, NT and patristic writings and concludes that it refers to divine utterances in Scripture, not Scripture itself ('The Life of Jesus', *BJRL* 29 (1945-6), pp. 392-428).   [10] Rom. 15.4.

[1] 2 Tim. 3.16. There is no basis in Pauline thought for constructing this passage to divide between γραφή which is God-breathed and other γραφή which is not.

[2] In Matt. 19.4f ('he who made them . . . said . . .') Christ attributes the text of the OT to the mouth of God. Cf. J. Hänel, *Der Schriftbegriff Jesu*, Gütersloh, 1919.

[3] Cf. 2 Pet. 1.21. The γραφή is not of its own 'breaking forth' (ἐπιλύσεως) but, carried along by the Holy Spirit, the prophets spoke ἀπὸ θεοῦ.

[4] H. Holtzmann, (*Die Pastoralbriefe*, p. 163, quoted in Warfield, op. cit., p. 272) writes: '[The writer] shares the Jewish conception of the purely supernatural origin of the Scriptures in its strictest form, according to which "theopneustic" is ascribed immediately to the Scriptures. . . .' Cf. W. O. E. Oesterley, *An Introduction to the Books of the Apocrypha*, London, 1935, p. 83.

[5] Cf. E. Reuss, *Canon of the Holy Scriptures*, Edinburgh, 1884, p. 210; E. Grafe, *Das Urchristentum und das Alte Testament*, Tübingen, 1907, p. 18; A. Harnack, *The Mission and Expansion of Christianity in the First Three Centuries*, 2nd ed. revised, London, 1908, I, pp. 279-89.   [6] e.g. 1 Cor. 14.21 (Isa. 28.11-12).

[7] Col. 2.14; cf. 2 Tim. 3.15 (ἱερὰ γράμματα).   [8] e.g. Rom. 3.21.

[9] As in the Fourth Gospel; αἱ γραφαί is more usual in Mark and Luke.

[10] Cf. Luke 24.44.   [11] e.g. Rom. 7.7; 16.26; 1 Cor. 9.9.

[12] J. B. Lightfoot, *The Epistle to the Galatians*, London, 1884, p. 147.

[13] Warfield, op. cit., p. 140; cf. Rom. 4.3; 9.17; 10.11; 11.2; Gal. 3.8, 22; 4.30; 1 Tim. 5.18. On the IF καθὼς εἶπεν ἡ γραφή (John 7.38) R. V. G. Tasker (*The Old Testament in the New Testament*, 2nd ed. revised, London, 1954, p. 58) concurs: 'The reference would seem to be to many Old Testament passages rather than to a single prophecy.' Cf. 1 Cor. 14.21; Jas. 4.5. See *KTW*, I, pp. 753-4.

THE INTRODUCTORY FORMULAS (IF)

One of the earliest examinations of IF was made in the seventeenth century by Surenhusius,[1] who sought to show that the IF supplied a clue to the purpose of the quotation and the reason for its textual variations. In 1789 Henry Owen, pointing to the fact that the same quotations, in the same words, to prove the same point, had different IF, discarded the theory as baseless.[2] Owen lays down the rule that the chief, if not sole purpose of the IF was to show that the words 'are either taken from, or have some reference to, books of the Old Testament'.[3] This precept still serves as a good foundation from which an investigation can proceed. In Rom. 4.17 καθὼς γέγραπται introduces a proof-text for an argument, but that is hardly its import in Rom. 8.36; in Rom. 4.17 the formula introduces a *verbatim* quotation, in 1 Cor. 1.31 the text is very free.[4] In Rom. 7.7 ὁ νόμος ἔλεγεν is used with a verbatim citation; but the virtually identical ὁ νόμος λέγει in 1 Cor. 14.34 concludes a very general reference to the teaching of various OT passages.[5] There is a tendency at times to use certain formulas for a specific purpose, but for the most part the wide variety of IF only illustrates the apostle's stylistic freedom.[6]

In the Pauline epistles an IF using 'it is written' (γέγραπται) is most common (twenty-nine times).[7] 'The scripture says' (ἡ γραφὴ λέγει) is second in frequency (six times). Other IF with λέγω are recurrent, for example, 'David says',[8] 'the law

---

[1] Surenhusio, op. cit.   [2] Owen, op. cit., pp. 12f.

[3] Ibid. Variations in IF were taken to reflect only the nature of the subject, cast of the discourse, the current idiom, and imitation of former writers. With the exception of ἵνα πληρωθῇ, which does not occur in the Pauline writings, and possibly διὸ λέγει, this classification is quite satisfactory. Cf. Rom. 1.17 (Gal. 3.11); 9.33 (Rom. 10.11); 10.5 (Gal. 3.12); 10.16 (John 12.38); 1 Cor. 1.31 (2 Cor. 10.17); 9.9 (1 Tim. 5.18); Gal. 3.6 (Jas. 2.23).

[4] Cf. also Gal. 4.22.

[5] Cf. Matt. 2.23; John 7.38; 8.17; Jas. 4.5. J. B. Lightfoot (*Notes on the Epistles of St Paul*, London, 1895, p. 263) and Thackeray (*Paul and Jewish Thought*, p. 188) take the postscript position of the IF in Rom. 2.24 to indicate that the quotation is deliberately disengaged from its OT context. But this occurs where the IF precedes the quotation also, e.g. Rom. 9.25. See *infra*, pp. 48f.

[6] Cf. especially Rom. 4.18; 7.7; 9.9; 11.4; 1 Cor. 15.54; 2 Cor. 4.13.

[7] Not including Gal. 4.22, where the general teaching of the OT is in view. See Appendix I. Cf. D. M. Turpie, *The New Testament View of the Old*, for a comprehensive tabulation of IF in the NT.

[8] Rom. 4.7, 8; 11.9, 10. Cf. 'Isaiah says' (Rom. 10.16, 20; 15.12); 'Moses says' (Rom. 10.19).

says',[1] 'God said'[2]; sometimes λέγει is used without a subject expressed but with God or Scripture probably to be understood.[3]

The IF are particularly important in showing Paul's attitude to the OT. Even in the Greek world the formula καθὼς γέγραπται was used with reference to the terms of an unalterable agreement[4]; for the Jew it signified much more—the unalterable Word of God.[5] 'The Scripture says', 'God says', and 'Isaiah says' are for Paul only different ways of expressing the same thing.[6] In two passages the Scripture is personified and viewed as speaking to someone or foreseeing certain events.[7] Weizsäcker has not put it too strongly: 'In short the written word is equivalent to Providence, so certainly is it the declaration of the Divine will.'[8] Often where the Scripture writer is named as speaker it is the words of God which are quoted[9]; once he apparently, as Christ,[10] quotes God as speaker when in the OT He does not so appear.[11] Perhaps the finality with which Paul uses the absolute γέγραπται supplies as good an indication as any of his view of Scripture. Regarding this formula, Warfield's words are apropos: 'No better index could be afforded of the sense of the unitary authority of the doctrine so cited which dominated the minds of the writers of the New Testament and of our Lord as reported by them.'[12]

To what extent do Paul's IF reflect his appreciation of the 'human element' of Scripture? Vollmer notes the manner in which Paul distinguishes between the Torah, Nebiim and Ketubim and cites the human author as the speaker; this is contrasted with the anarthrous λέγει prevalent in Hebrews.[13] Michel, in a similar vein, writes: '[Der] Verfasser immer unmittelbar an den göttlichen Ursprung des Orakels denkt, ohne irgendein Interesse für die menschliche Vermittlung des Wortes zu zeigen. Der tiefere Grund für diese stilistische Verschiedenheit liegt in der abweichenden Inspirationsvor-

---

[1] Rom. 7.7 (1 Cor. 14.34).
[2] 2 Cor. 6.16; cf. Rom. 9.15; 2 Cor. 6.2; Rom. 11.4.
[3] Cf. Rom. 15.10; Gal. 3.16; Eph. 4.8; 5.14. [4] Deissmann, *Paul*, p. 101.
[5] For the use of IF in Jewish literature see *infra*, pp. 48f.
[6] Cf. Warfield, op. cit., pp. 283-332. [7] Rom. 9.17.; Gal. 3.8; cf.v.22.
[8] C. von Weizsäcker, *The Apostolic Age*, 2nd ed., London, 1894, p. 132.
[9] Cf. Rom. 10.19f. [10] Matt. 19.4; 1 Cor. 6.16.
[11] The infrequency is not particularly significant; Paul seldom quotes God specifically as speaker in any case, viz. 2. Cor 6.16; 2 Cor. 6.2; Rom. 9.15.
[12] Warfield, op. cit., p. 147. [13] Vollmer, op. cit., p. 73.

stellung. Paulus hat für die menschliche Vermittlung des alttestamentlichen Gotteswortes Interesse; die alexandrinische Auffassung schaltet diese möglichst aus. Die philonische Inspiration wird durch das Wort characterisiert: "Ein Prophet sagt überhaupt nichts Eigenes, sondern er ist nur Dolmetscher, ein anderer gibt ihm alles, was er vorbringt, ein. So lange der Prophet in Begeisterung ist, ist er seiner selbst nicht bewusst, die Vernunft eilt fort und hat die Burg der Seele verlassen" (*de spec. leg.* IV, 49). Die paulinische Auffassung der Inspiration wird dagegen durch das Wort Rom. 10.20f gekennzeichnet: "Jesaia wagt es und sagt...". Für Paulus bleibt also der Prophet eine Persönlichkeit, die mehr bedeutet als ein blosses Gefäss oder ein Musikinstrument für den göttlichen Geist.'[1]

While it is true that Paul gives full recognition to the human personalities of the writers of the Scripture, it is questionable whether this is the purpose or even the main point reflected by Paul's IF. Actually the contrast between the apostle's formulas and those of Hebrews and Philo is one of frequency rather than of disjunction or antipody.[2] In Hebrews the human author is adduced in two formulas[3]; Philo too, for all his mechanical view of inspiration, occasionally mentions the human author in citing the OT.[4] Paul, on the other hand, has four IF in which God is the subject[5]: λέγει without a subject is found six

---

[1] Michel, *Bibel*, pp. 68, 69; '[The author of Hebrews] thinks immediately on the divine origin of the Oracle, without showing any interest in the human instrument communicating the Word. The deeper reason for this stylistic difference lies in their diverse view of inspiration. Paul has an interest in the spokesman of God's Word in the Old Testament; the Alexandrian view suppresses this as far as possible. Philonic inspiration is characterised by the saying "A prophet says absolutely nothing on his own but is only an interpreter. Another inspires him with all that he says. So long as the prophet is in the spirit, he knows nothing of himself; his reason withdraws and surrenders the citadel of the soul" (*de spec. leg.*, IV, 49; Colson, VIII, p. 37). The Pauline view of inspiration on the other hand, is seen in the expression of Rom. 10.20: "Isaiah makes bold and says...". For Paul therefore, the prophet remains a personality, more significant than a mere tool or musical instrument for the Divine Spirit.'

[2] W. Leonard (*The Authorship of the Epistle to the Hebrews*, London, 1939), who argues for the Palestinian background of Hebrews, points out some instances *contra* Michel (pp. 265-82).

[3] Heb. 9.20 (Μωϋσῆς λέγων); 12.21 (Μωϋσῆς εἶπεν); cf. Heb. 4.7. B. F. Westcott (op. cit., pp. 469-95) does not consider these passages as quotations in the strict sense.

[4] *de agric.*, 50 (Colson, III, p. 135): 'the writer of the Psalms says'; *de somn.*, II, 172 (Colson, V, p. 521): 'one of the ancient prophets ... said'; *de poster. Caini*, 12 (Colson, II, p. 335): 'But Moses will counsel'; (cf. *de gigan.*, 6, Colson, II, p. 449).   [5] Rom. 9.15; 11.4; 2 Cor. 6.2, 16.

times.[1] Moreover, the phrase 'saith the Lord' occurs a number of times within the quotation where it is not a part of the OT text,[2] even when God is not the speaker.[3] The Pauline formulas using the human author are found, with three exceptions,[4] in Rom. 9-11, a discourse of special character.

The adduction of the Scripture writer in the Pauline IF is probably designed to fix the place of citation.[5] Certainly Paul's usage gives due weight to the human aspect of Scripture and does not endorse Philo's mechanical explanation. But modern writers, in contrasting the 'human' and the 'divine' element in first century views of inspiration, are viewing the writers through twentieth century glasses and reflecting emphases of their own day. In Paul the 'human' and the 'divine' in Scripture appear as one inseparable whole, not as 'elements' to be contrasted. On his formula, 'Isaiah waxes bold and says', nothing would puzzle him more than Vollmer's remark 'how human'.[6]

In conclusion, Paul's IF do give important insights into his attitude toward the OT. The Scripture is adduced as a final authority and one divinely planned whole whose significance is bound up inseparably with the New Covenant Community of Christians. However, the use and frequency of certain IF is not a sufficient basis for defining Paul's view of inspiration in contrast to that of other first century writers.

Γραφή AND Γράμμα IN PAULINE USAGE

The notable NT scholar, Adolf Schlatter, was once approached by an ardent admirer who poured forth his praise: 'I've always

---

[1] Rom. 9.25; 10.21; 15.10; Gal. 3.16; Eph. 4.8; 5.14. Of the seven IF in Paul's discourses in the Acts (Acts 13.32, 33, 34, 35, 40, 47; 23.5; 28.25) only one mentions the human author (28.25). In three God is the speaker, in one the Holy Spirit, in one the Lord; two are passive. It may be that this phenomenon is editorial, but the other IF in Acts argue otherwise. Cf. Leonard, op. cit., p. 268: 'The book of Acts indicates that the omission of human names would have been more usual when quoting Scripture to Jews.'

[2] Rom. 12.19; 1 Cor. 14.21; 2 Cor. 6.17f.

[3] 1 Cor. 14.21 (Isa. 28.11f); cf. 2 Cor. 6.17.

[4] Rom. 15.12; 1 Cor. 9.9; Rom. 4.6.

[5] Cf. Acts 13.32, 35, 40; Rom. 9.15, 25; 1 Cor. 9.9. E. Lohmeyer (*Kyrios Jesus*, Heidelberg, 1928, p. 13) compares Rom. 11.2 (ἐν Ἠλείᾳ) with Phil. 2.5 (ἐν Χριστῷ Ἰησοῦ) and suggests that the Scripture is viewed as being in the prophet. Thackeray's (*Paul and Jewish Thought*, p. 182) explanation is much preferable: 'This was a common and indeed . . . the only mode of more nearly locating a quotation.'

[6] Vollmer, op. cit., p. 73. However, Vollmer goes on to say that his starting point of absolute-inspiration teaching is unmistakable.

wanted to meet a theologian who stands on the Word of God.'
Schlatter, in solemn mien, replied, 'Thank you, sir. But I don't
stand on the Word of God; I stand under it.'[1] This distinction
between standing *on* or *under* the Word of God is seen in Paul's
use of the OT. The essential difference between Paul and the
Jews in their employment of Scripture was an interpretive one[2];
and it is in this very area that the essence of γραφή lay. In Paul's
eyes the Jews stood *on* the Scripture; though they extolled it,
they erred because they did not know it.[3] Their interpretations
were only an eisegesis in which their own ideas were grafted
into Scripture; and its true meaning remained hidden from
them.

Paul's concept of γραφή is bound up with his use of two other
words, γράμμα and πνεῦμα.[4] Γράμμα is usually employed in an
uncomplimentary manner in the Pauline epistles.[5] Frequently
it is set in opposition to πνεῦμα and, sometimes, to νόμος:

'Through the *letter* and circumcision you break the *law*'
(Rom. 2.27).
'(True) circumcision is . . . in the *Spirit* not in the *letter*'
(Rom. 2.29).
'We are delivered from the *law* . . . that we might serve in
the newness of the *Spirit* not in the oldness of the *letter*'
(Rom. 7.6).
' . . . ministers of the New Covenant, not of the *letter* but
of the *Spirit* because the *letter* kills but the *Spirit* makes alive'
(2 Cor. 3.6).
' . . . ministry of death in *letters* . . . ministry of the *spirit*'
(2 Cor. 3.7).

For the most part γράμμα does not here signify merely letters
(*Buchstaben*) but the legal system seen only as 'written and
prescribed' ordinances.[6] In Rom. 2.29 circumcision 'by' the
Spirit is contrasted with circumcision 'by' the letter. Even in
2 Cor. 3.7, where the sense is 'in the form of letters', the wider

---

[1] Related to the writer in a conversation with Karl Heim.
[2] See *infra*, pp. 54-76.   [3] Cf. Matt. 22.29.
[4] On γράμμα and γραφή see G. Schrenk, 'Γράφω, Γραφή, Γράμμα, . . .' *KTW*, I,
pp. 749-69.
[5] An exception is seen in 2 Tim. 3.15: ' . . . from a child you have known the
ἱερὰ γράμματα.'   [6] Schrenk, op. cit., p. 765.

significance of his earlier usages is not negated. According to Schrenk, Paul is saying not only that 'das Judentum buchstäbelnde Auslegung der Schrift habe ... sondern das die ganze alte Phase der Offenbarung noch nicht durch Christus und seine Geist bestimmt ist'.[1] This is true in the sense of 'law versus grace', but the distinction should not be viewed merely as a temporal one.

Γραφή and νόμος both signify for Paul the revealed will of God.[2] But the law understood as a legal system apart from Christ could only bring death[3]; so also the whole OT understood and applied without the illumination of the πνεῦμα often resulted not in γραφή but only in γράμμα.[4] In Judaism this synthesis of Word and Spirit had been lost and the Scriptures had become mere 'letters'; the Law had become an end in itself rather than a means to evoke faith in God's grace; through their false interpretations the Word of God had been made ineffectual.[5] The issue of the Law versus Christ here passes into Paul's understanding of the nature of Scripture itself. Γραφή is the Spirit-carried letter, the Spirit-interpreted letter. Therefore, Paul does not hesitate to give his OT citations as interpretive renderings; and he is convinced that he conveys the true (i.e. the Spirit's) meaning best in this way. Thus Paul rejects the Law, yet he uses the Law; the apparent antinomy is resolved by distinguishing the Jewish and the spiritual understanding of it. In First and Second Corinthians Paul teaches expressly that a correct understanding of Scripture is impossible without the Holy Spirit.[6] In Michel's words: 'Die γραφή kann nur gesund bleiben, wenn sie mit dem πνεῦμα ganz eng verbunden bleibt. Das πνεῦμα muss aus der Schrift sprechen.'[7]

The place of the Spirit does not lessen the authority of the OT for Paul; nor is there any antithesis between the Scripture

---

[1] Ibid., p. 767: ' ... Judaism has a pedantic exegesis of Scripture ... but that the whole old phase of revelation is not yet channeled through Christ and his Spirit.'

[2] Cf. Rom. 7.14.   [3] e.g. Rom. 7.6.

[4] Paul, of course, considered the OT to be Divine revelation in an objective sense. The defect lay not in the writings but in the sin-clouded minds of the readers, and, in some cases, was God's judgment upon their sin. Cf. Acts 28.25ff (Mark 4.11f); Rom. 11.7ff; 1 Cor. 14.37f.

[5] Cf. Matt. 15.6.

[6] Cf. 1 Cor. 2; 2 Cor. 3.14.

[7] Michel, *Bibel*. p. 178. 'The γραφή can remain beneficial only if it remains entirely bound together with πνεῦμα. The πνεῦμα must speak out of the Scripture.'

and the Spirit.[1] The apostle does not answer the problem of two persons having the Spirit and yet differing as to the interpretation of Scripture. It may be that the Spirit's meaning is to be found through some such procedure as Acts 15; many answers may have to be qualified with a frank admission of uncertainty.[2] In any case, Paul thinks of the γραφή-πνεῦμα relationship as a whole and does not attempt to give a detailed application of the principles involved.[3]

THE RELATION OF Γραφή TO OTHER AUTHORITIES

Besides the Scripture there are several other authorities to which Paul appeals to support his assertions. There are the law of nature, the conscience of the individual, his own revelation from Christ or the Holy Spirit, and the teaching of Christ as received through oral or written apostolic tradition. Although the natural order is the source of many analogies,[4] it is evoked only a few times as an authority; in Rom. 1.18ff (cf. Rom. 2.14ff) God's power and Deity are declared to be taught by nature; distinction between the sexes in manner of appearance and dress is also in the very nature of things.[5] The authority of the individual conscience plays an important part for Paul: Regarding the eating of food offered to idols, one's own conscience is to be obeyed, and the consciences of others are not to be offended[6]; by disobeying the voice of conscience the faith of some has been made shipwreck.[7] Writing to the Gala-

---

[1] Michel, following Luther (see editor's preface in M. Luther, *Epistle to the Galatians*, London, 1953, pp. 1-15), views the relationship as a circle. One must have the Spirit to understand the Scripture; on the other hand it is through the Scripture that the Spirit is given (Michel, op. cit., p. 179.) Cf. G. W. Bromiley, 'The Authority of Scripture', *The New Bible Commentary*, 2nd ed., London, 1954, pp. 16, 18f, 22.

[2] So, 1 Cor. 7.40. But in 1 Cor. 14.37 Paul does not hesitate to ascribe a contrary opinion to a lack of spiritual discrimination in interpreting either the OT or a teaching of Christ.

[3] Cf. Michel, *Bibel*, p. 179. No solution, however, lies in Michel's suggestion that on particular Scriptures two Spirit-filled persons could interpret 'ganz anders'. The whole relationship cannot be so divorced from its concrete application.

[4] Analogies of law (Rom. 7.1-3; Gal. 3.15; 4.1ff), occupations (Rom. 9.21; 1 Cor. 3.7, 24ff) and natural phenomena (Rom. 11.16-24; 1 Cor. 12.14) are common. The OT is used in this manner as well, e.g. 2 Cor. 4.6, 13, as is the example of Christ, e.g. 2 Cor. 8.8-9. They serve only as illustrations, however, and not as an appeal to authority; their propriety depends upon the authority of the user or their appeal to the logic of the hearer.   [5] 1 Cor. 11.14.

[6] 1 Cor. 8.7ff; 10.25ff; cf. Rom. 14.23. Also Rom. 2.15; 13.5 may be viewed as referring to a sort of universal conscience.   [7] 1 Tim. 1.19.

tians, the apostle grounds the very nature of his Gospel in a personal revelation from Jesus Christ[1]; it is only after citing this authority and the witness of their own experience that the evidence of the OT is brought to bear.[2] The condemnation of the Corinthians for their desecrations of the Lord's Supper is founded upon Christ's own words as to the nature of that service[3]; Paul's command against divorce is similarly based upon the known teaching of the Lord.[4] These appeals to other authorities are not inconsistent with the apostle's appeal to scriptural authority.[5] They are complementary and, with some qualifications in the case of συνείδησις, are all different manifestations of the same Divine authority.[6]

This appeal to different authorities is at times found in close combination though there seems to be no consistent pattern of association. For example, in 1 Cor. 9.7-14 Paul proceeds from the analogy of nature to the witness of the OT; immediately he returns to another analogy, the practice of the temple, and clinches the whole argument citing the command of Christ directly bearing on the subject.[7] 1 Cor. 15.3-11 is even more noteworthy: Christ's resurrection is grounded in the OT, the apostolic tradition, and Paul's personal revelation. The ἐν Χριστῷ concept and OT evidence are then adduced to show that this necessitates the resurrection of believers.[8]

Paul's own authority plays a much larger rôle in his epistles than is usually assigned to it. A few times it is of a very much qualified nature,[9] but for the most part it is asserted with no

---

[1] Gal. 1.12, 16ff; 2.5 (but contrast Rom. 1.2); cf. 1 Thess. 4.15. The instances in Rom. 14.14 (cf. 1 Cor. 7.40) seem to be more in the nature of a 'witness of the Spirit' than specific revelation; cf. Col. 3.16.

[2] Gal. 3.1-5, 6ff.   [3] 1 Cor. 11.23ff.

[4] 1 Cor. 7.10 (Matt. 7.31); cf. 1 Cor. 9.14 (Matt. 10.10); Gal. 6.2 (John 13.34). See C. H. Dodd, 'ΕΝΝΟΜΟΣ ΧΡΙΣΤΟΥ', Studia Paulina, pp. 96-110; 1 Cor. 5.6; Gal. 5.9 (Matt. 16.6-12). Further, cf. C. H. Dodd, Gospel and Law, Cambridge, 1951, pp. 64-81.

[5] There are authorities inconsistent with Scripture which Paul condemns: any authority contrary to his Gospel (Gal. 1.8f) and the wisdom of this world (1 Cor. 1-3; cf. Rom. 1.22; Col. 2.23). The touchstone for judgment is not to go 'beyond that which is written' (1 Cor. 4.6).

[6] But Paul does not, as Test. Naph. 5.8 (CAP, II, p. 338), label as γραφή a revelation in a vision. Cf. Schrenk, op. cit., p. 751.

[7] Michel (Bibel, p. 164) sees the progression as analogy : Scripture :: anology: Word of Christ, i.e. the Scripture and the Herrenwort are equated.

[8] Viz. the Adam typology (1 Cor. 15.21f) and the promises to Christ (1 Cor. 15.25ff).   [9] Cf. 1 Cor. 7.12, 25, 40.

indication of being anything less than absolute. He does not often state its basis, but it appears to arise from his firm conviction of guidance from the Holy Spirit and from his authority as an apostle. Paul concludes his discussion of *glossolalia* with the words: 'If anyone thinks that he is a prophet, or spiritual, he should acknowledge that what I am writing to you is a command of the Lord.'[1] With reticence but firmness he warns the Corinthians in his second letter of the authority that he has from the Lord.[2] Instructions concerning the Christian's relation to the State are enjoined without citing an authority,[3] as are his commands regarding spiritual gifts.[4] Many other themes are developed at least in part without reference to any rule apart from his own. It is true that sometimes OT texts[5] and his former instructions[6] underlie the words, but they do not account for all of his paraenetic and doctrinal teachings. It is impossible, of course, to know just how much knowledge of the OT and the apostolic traditions Paul assumes on the part of his readers; but his own apostolic jurisdiction is unmistakable in a number of passages.

The important place which authorities other than the OT occupy in Paul's letters gave rise to Harnack's novel thesis that Paul never intended the OT to be the *Erbauungsbuch* of Christianity at all[7]: Paul's quotations are virtually confined to his four *Hauptbriefe*, and since they are dominated by a 'Law versus Gospel' dispute which necessitated the use of the OT, they cannot be regarded as the norm for Pauline teaching. An investigation of the five other Pauline letters (omitting Philemon as irrelevant and the Pastorals as non-Pauline) reveals an entirely different treatment of the OT.[8] Although covering a variety of subjects, there is in general no appeal to the Scripture;

---

[1] 1 Cor. 14.37. The verse may refer to a teaching of Christ; but the words imply primarily the guidance of the Spirit. Cf. Dodd, '*ΕΝΝΟΜΟΣ ΧΡΙΣΤΟΥ*', p. 105.
[2] 2 Cor. 10.8; 13.10. [3] Rom. 13.1-7 (but cf. Matt. 22.21).
[4] 1 Cor. 12-14. [5] e.g. Rom. 2.13; cf. Rom. 10.5; Gal. 3.12 (Lev. 18.5).
[6] Former instructions from Scripture or the apostolic traditions appear implied in the repeated use of οὐκ οἴδατε in 1 Cor. 6.3, 9, 15, 16; only the last instance is followed by an OT citation (cf. 1 Cor. 3.16; 2 Cor. 6.16). It may, however, only refer to their Christian commonsense.
[7] Harnack, 'Das Alte Testament in den Paulinischen Briefen', pp. 124-41.
[8] B. Weiss (*Biblical Theology of the New Testament*, Edinburgh, 1882, I, p. 381) had also noted that there were no quotations 'in the epistles to the purely Gentile-Christian churches of Thessalonica, Philippi, and Colossae'.

it is never cited under γραφή or γέγραπται, and only one of the
two formula quotations refers to the canonical writings.[1] In
these epistles it is to the 'Word of the Lord' (i.e. the Christian
Verkündigung, not the OT),[2] to the Gospel,[3] to Paul's own
authority, revelation or example,[4] and to their former teaching[5]
that appeal is made. In Colossians one looks in vain for an
invocation of the OT against the Gnostic influence; even the
theme of righteousness by faith in Philippians occasions no
reference to the OT.[6] In these epistles, according to Harnack,
one sees the real Paul[7]—an apostle for whom the Gospel and
the Spirit were primary, whose teaching of Christ, salvation
and ethics is developed independently of the OT, and whose
OT allusions were not even designed to be recognised as such
by his Gentile readers.[8] The question arises: If Paul subordinated the OT to the Gospel and the Spirit, how did Christianity
become a 'book-religion'? Harnack describes this development,
which was in firm mould after First Clement, as resulting from
two factors.[9] First, there was from the beginning a large faction
for which Christianity had two points of reference, the Gospel
and a 'holy book'. Secondly, Paul, though desiring a Christianity based upon the Spirit rather than upon a book, un-
wittingly aided this process by his typological exegesis and his
occasional appeal to the authority of the OT. 'Mit dem δι' ἡμᾶς
ἐγράφη [in 1 Cor. 9.10] beginnt die Geschichte des AT als
Erbauungsbuch in der Kirche aus den Heiden. . . .'[10]

Harnack's thesis is an important contribution to Pauline
studies in calling attention to questions formerly neglected. It
demonstrates, too, the weakness of the argument that Paul used

---

[1] Eph. 4.8; 5.14.   [2] 1 Thess. 1.6, 8; 2.13; 2 Thess. 2.15; 3.1.
[3] 1 Thess. 2.2, 8, 9; 3.2.
[4] 1 Thess. 4.15; 2 Thess. 3.6. In Colossians and Philippians also appeal to the
OT is passed over time and again as the apostle speaks in his own authority.
[5] 1 Thess. 1.4; 4.2; 5.2.   [6] Phil. 3.9.
[7] In Harnack's opinion even First Corinthians is not inconsistent with this
picture. The quotations in chapters 1-4, 9 are ad hominem, to satisfy the readers'
desire for ingenious exegesis. Other OT quotations (6.16, 15.27) are quoted not as
the γραφή of a holy book but simply as Gottesspruch (Harnack, 'Das Alte Testament
in den Paulinischen Briefen', pp. 129-37).
[8] It is doubtful to Harnack that Paul's churches had Scripture readings from the
beginning; διδαχὴν (1 Cor. 14.26) is not so taken by Harnack (ibid., p. 137). But
cf. O. Cullmann, Early Christian Worship, London, 1953, pp. 29f.
[9] Harnack, 'Das Alte Testament in den Paulinischen Briefen', pp. 138-41.
[10] Ibid., p. 138: 'With the δι' ἡμᾶς ἐγράφη [in 1 Cor. 9.10] begins the history of the
OT as Erbauungsbuch in the Church of the Gentiles. . . .'

OT proofs like patches from a ragbag—anything to fit the argument; he did not need to resort to such expedients. But the main issue raised turns on the interpretation of a fundamental component of Pauline thought. Does the place of the OT in Paul's teaching, especially as evidenced in his four *Hauptbriefe*, represent only an *ad hominem* usage or at best a subordinate authority suited to a particular argument? Harnack's position is modified by Lohmeyer, who contends that Paul can, equally well, use the OT as his Gospel source-book (Romans and Galatians) or establish his teachings entirely independent of it (the shorter epistles).[1] But even with this modification the question remains: Is the lack of citations in the smaller epistles so significant for Paul's attitude towards the OT as Harnack believes?

Michel, against Harnack, points to the use Paul makes of the OT in describing his own missionary labours; the discourses of the Acts also militate strongly against the view that Paul's attachment to the OT is only one of convenience.[2] The tendency in Harnack's thesis is to equate the Scripture with the γράμμα of the Jews and then to contrast this with the Spirit and the Gospel. But the OT was not one of those things which Paul counted loss for the sake of Christ; indeed, it could be understood only in the light of Christ.[3] There are many explanations for Paul's infrequent use of the OT in the shorter letters, and Harnack's is one of the least likely. The use of an authority other than the Jewish Scriptures may well have been more suitable for many questions which arose, especially in a young Gentile assembly. But it does not follow that thereby the OT was set aside or subordinated any more than a citation from Isaiah implies a lower view of Jeremiah. The shorter epistles, usually written with one or two specific and immediate questions in view, do not provide a comprehensive criterion for

[1] E. Lohmeyer, *Grundlagen der Paulinischen Theologie*, Tübingen, 1928, p. 104. H. Windisch (*Paulus und das Judentum*, Stuttgart, 1935, pp. 71-3) gives a similar view: One may, as Harnack does, play down Paul's use of the OT, or, as others do, exaggerate it; in truth Paul is both an OT Biblicist and a Christian teacher; and with a young Gentile Church he can do without the OT very well.

[2] Michel, *Bibel*, pp. 130f; cf. Acts 23.5; 24.14; 26.23; Rom. 8.36; 10.15-18; 14.11.

[3] Cf. Schrenk, op. cit., p. 768: Paul argues against a 'book-religion' to the extent of its being a mere occupation with the letters; but that does not mean that with the execution of the γράμμα the γραφή is also done away with.

Paul's teaching to his *Gemeinde* regarding regulative authorities. The variegated usage in the *Hauptbriefe* is much more representative in this respect.[1] For Paul, Jesus was above all the Christ; to divorce the Messiah from the 'book-religion' of the OT was hardly a task for a Jew—even one converted through personal revelation.

The Extent of Γραφή: Paul's Canon

It is a reasonable inference that the body of writings accepted as authoritative by the first century Jewish community serves as Paul's criterion of canonical authority as well. A problem arises, therefore, when in Paul's letters one finds quotations or references which are not to be found in the Jewish body of authority and yet which, from their context and IF, refer to authoritative writings. Several possible solutions to the dilemma present themselves:

1. Paul is freely paraphrasing one or several canonical passages or repeating a paraphrase in common use.
2. He is quoting a non-canonical writing, which itself makes use of a scriptural paraphrase, as an appropriate rendering of the OT and with no intention of vesting authority in the apocryphal document.
3. The apostle's canon differs from Palestinian Judaism in including oral and recorded sayings of Jesus, and psalms and oracles of the apostles and/or early Christian prophets. Certain of his quotations stem from this source.
4. His canon embraces certain apocryphal Jewish writings, and he uses these on occasion in an authoritative sense.

There is considerable evidence that the Jewish canon was in completed form in the first century and that it embraced the writings commonly received by Protestant Churches today.[2] The enumeration of Josephus—five books of Moses, thirteen of

---

[1] The writer's discussion of authorities for Paul other than γραφή was made with Harnack's dictum in mind and primarily considers the *Hauptbriefe* (cf. *supra*, pp. 28ff).

[2] Cf. J. Leipoldt, *Geschichte des neutestamentlichen Kanons*, Leipzig, 1907, pp. 5-27. W. Staerk, 'Der Schrift und Kanon-Begriff der Jüdischen Bibel', *ZFST*, 6 (1928), pp. 101-19.

the Prophets,[1] four of hymns and moral precepts[2]—reflects a current view of the extent and designated divisions of the Jewish OT.[3] These divisions, without enumeration, are cited in the prologue to Sirach (*c.* 132 B.C.)[4] and by the Lord.[5] Philo might be expected to reveal any Alexandrian accretions to or variances from the Palestinian canon. However, 'he makes no quotations from the Apocrypha, and he gives not the slightest ground for the supposition that the Jews of Alexandria of his time were disposed to accept any of the books of the Apocrypha in their canon of Holy Scripture'.[6] It is true that Philo is concerned almost exclusively with the Pentateuch and may simply never have had occasion to quote the Apocrypha.[7] But if there were a controversy between the *diaspora* and Palestine concerning the canon, one would expect some hint of it in Philo; and there is none.

There are a few quotations in the Pauline epistles which do not appear on first observation to be derived from the OT. The passages most often questioned in this regard are 1 Cor. 2.9 (IF: γέγραπται), Eph. 4.8 (IF: λέγει) and Eph. 5.14 (IF: λέγει). Probably 1 Cor. 15.45b (IF: γέγραπται) and 1 Tim. 5.18b (IF: ἡ γραφή λέγει) should be included in the same category. Each of these passages is introduced with an IF normally used in the NT and Jewish literature for citing Scripture,[8] although only one (1 Tim. 5.18)expressly uses the word γραφή.

---

[1] Judges-Ruth, Samuel, Kings, Chronicles, Ezra-Nehemiah, Jeremiah-Lamentations, and Minor Prophets were each on one roll and probably so counted. In Josephus' list Daniel seems to be included in the 'Prophets'.

[2] Probably Psalms, Proverbs, Ecclesiastes, Song of Solomon.

[3] Josephus, *contra Apion*, I, 40, trans. H. St J. Thackeray, London, 1926, I, p. 179; cf. Ta. 8a (*SBT*, p. 31). For the consistency of this testimony with other witnesses see Buhl, op. cit., pp. 18-32. The disputes arising in first century Jewry (e.g. at Jamnia) were not to establish a canon but to answer objections made against some of the received books (Buhl, p. 27). Such objections were recurrent in Jewish circles as late as the third century; cf. H. E. Ryle, *The Canon of the Old Testament*, London, 1892, pp. 177f.   [4] *CAP*, I, p. 293.   [5] Luke 24.44.

[6] H. E. Ryle, *Philo and Holy Scripture*, p. xxxiii: There is some affinity in subject matter and phraseology, particularly with the Wisdom literature, but it is not sufficient to suggest actual allusion.

[7] Some OT books are not quoted either: Ruth, Esther, Ecclesiastes, Song of Solomon, Lamentations, Ezekiel, Daniel (ibid., p. xxxi).

[8] Some hold that the anarthrous λέγει (cf. Eph. 4.8; 5.14) does not imply a scriptural citation (cf. Thackeray, *Paul and Jewish Thought*, p. 248); but it certainly has that significance in Hebrews, Philo, and the Mishnah; cf. A. Edersheim, *The Life and Times of Jesus the Messiah*, London, 1889, I, p. 187. And many commentators so view it here; cf. Toy, op. cit., p. 198; Clemen, op. cit., p. 220; Warfield, op. cit., p. 118. On διὸ λέγει cf. Heb. 3.7; 10.5; Jas. 4.6.

In the case of the first three citations the lack of a solution is not the result of a paucity of suggestions. 1 Cor. 2.9 has been attributed to an apocryphal writing,[1] an apocryphal phraseology of OT texts,[2] a Jewish anthology of OT passages[3] (and an apocryphal passage),[4] and a free paraphrase of the OT by Paul.[5] Eph. 4.8 is generally taken to be a Pauline use of a common Jewish interpretation of the OT passage.[6] As for Eph. 5.14, older commentators have generally assigned it to an exegetical paraphrase or summary of Isa. 60.1, 19ff (cf. Isa. 9.2; 26.19; 52.1)[7] or, with Jerome, to an apocryphal source.[8] Recent writers have suggested a *verbum Christi* or, more often, an early Christian hymn giving a messianic paraphrase of several OT passages.[9]

While no dogmatic answer can be given regarding these passages, at least some priority may be assigned to the several possibilities. The presence of an IF raises the inference of an immediate or ultimate OT source[10]; another factor pointing in this direction is the use by Paul in other places of paraphrastic renderings and merged quotations.[11] If Paul had a variant Greek text closer to his quotations, a textual solution is not improbable for 1 Cor. 2.9 and Eph. 4.8.[12] In the latter case the

---

[1] Ascension of Isaiah; So Origen (on Matt, 27.9); cf. B. Weiss, op. cit., p. 383; Huhn, op. cit., pp. 270f; Origen's suggestion is rejected by Jerome; if true, it was probably a Christian interpolation into the apocryphal writing; cf. Lightfoot, *Notes*, pp. 176f.   [2] F. B. Denio, 'Quotations', *HDCG*, II (1907).

[3] Thackeray, *Paul and Jewish Thought*, p. 244; cf. B. P. W. S. Hunt, *Primitive Gospel Sources*, London, 1951.

[4] Vollmer, op. cit., pp. 47f (Isa. 65.16 + Sirach 1.10).

[5] e.g. Isa. 64.4 + 65.16; cf. Jas. 1.12; J. B. Lightfoot, *Notes*, p. 176; J. Moffatt, *The First Epistle of Paul to the Corinthians*, London, 1938, p. 30; F. Johnson, op. cit., p. 149.

[6] So E. F. Scott, *The Epistle of Paul to the Colossians, to Philemon, and to the Ephesians*, London, 1930, p. 207; Abbott, op. cit., p. 112; Jerome on Isa. 64.4 and Epistula 57.9 'ad Pammachium'.

[7] Cf. B. Weiss, op. cit., p. 383; Toy, op. cit., p. 199; M. W. Jacobus ('The Citation Eph. 5.14 as affecting the Paulinity of the Epistle', *Theologische Studien*, B. Weiss *Festschrift*, Göttingen, 1897, pp. 9-29) argues at length that the reference is to Jonah 1.6, taken by Paul as messianic typology.

[8] Huhn, op. cit., pp. 270f; Lietzmann, op. cit., p. 33.

[9] Hunt, op. cit., p. 131; M. Dibelius, *An die Kolosser, Epheser, Philemon*, Tübingen, 1927, p. 69; A. M. Hunter, *Paul and his Predecessors*, London, 1940, p. 44; E. G. Selwyn, *The First Epistle to Peter*, London, 1952, p. 417; E. F. Scott, op. cit., p. 231.

[10] For IF in Jewish literature see *infra*, pp. 48f.

[11] See Appendixes II and III. Quotations giving the general tenor of Scripture are also found in Jn. 7.38 and Jas. 4.5.

[12] The text of 1 Cor. 2.9 in Clement of Rome (34.8) and the Martyrdom of Polycarp (2.3) lies between Paul and the LXX; cf. Lightfoot, *Notes*, p. 176. Paul's

problem lies in the interpretation of the Hebrew לָקַח (Ps. 67(68).19) as ἔδωκεν rather than the LXX ἔλαβες. The Syriac version and a Targum give the same interpretation as Paul.[1] The manner in which the two Ephesian citations are introduced does not suggest an *ad hoc* rendering; it is probable that the apostle follows an OT text or interpretive paraphrase familiar to his readers. The word Χριστός in Eph. 5.14 rules out any immediate citation of the OT. It may well be an early Christian paraphrase giving the import of several OT passages.[2]

The quotations in 1 Cor. 15.45 and 1 Tim. 5.18, both cited as Scripture, suggest another answer to the whole problem.[3] The latter clause in each of these passages seems logically and grammatically within the quotation,[4] yet neither is from the OT. 1 Tim. 5.18b is a saying of Jesus[5]; the former passage (1 Cor. 15.45b) is of undetermined origin.[6]

If early Christians had an extended concept of γραφή, it is not likely that it lay in the direction of Jewish apocryphal writings.[7] A departure of this kind surely would have aroused some vocal repercussions in canon-conscious first century Judaism. Yet there was an extension of the concept of γραφή in the apostolic community—an extension in another direction: The sayings of Christ were regarded as the Word of God by Paul,[8] and 2 Pet.

rendering is found in a Jewish collection (*Mikropresbutikon*, Basle, 1950, p. 316) suggesting its use in first century Jewish circles; cf. Thackeray, *Paul and Jewish Thought*, p. 243. Paul's order (seeing and hearing) is followed in First Clement and the Apostolic Constitutions (7.32). The LXX order appears in 2 Clement 11.7 and in the Martyrdom of Polycarp.

[1] Cf. *SBK*, III, pp. 596ff; supra p. 16n. [2] See *infra*, pp. 139ff.
[3] Cf. also 2 Tim. 2.11-13, 19; 2 Cor. 6.2; 1 Tim. 3.16.
[4] e.g. the argument in 1 Cor. 15 partly rests on that portion of the 'quotation'.
[5] Matt. 10.10; Luke 10.7; cf. Acts 20.35.
[6] That this properly belongs within the quotation is argued by M. Black, 'The Pauline Doctrine of the Second Adam', *SJT*, 7, (June 1954), pp. 170ff.
[7] Jewish apocalyptic literature often lends itself to an interpretation akin to NT eschatology, yet not once are these documents cited as Scripture. If the Ascension of Isaiah (cf. 1 Cor. 2.9) is post-apostolic, Jude 14 is the only NT citation with a certain apocryphal parallel. Although the IF in Jude does occur once in the NT introducing Scripture (Matt. 15.7), it more commonly signifies only the oracular saying (cf. Luke 1.6, 7; John 11.5; Acts 19.6; cf. I Cor. 14). The polyrhizal character of the Book of Enoch (cf. *CAP*, II, pp. 163ff) admits the possibility, at least, that the Enoch saying had an independent existence in Jewish tradition. If the Book of Enoch was Jude's source, it does not necessarily follow that he considered it Scripture. Contrast the IF in Barnabas 16.5.
[8] C. H. Dodd ('*ΕΝΝΟΜΟΣ ΧΡΙΣΤΟΥ*', pp. 96-110) argues convincingly that ὁ νόμος τοῦ Χριστοῦ (cf. Gal. 6.2) refers to specific teachings or commands of Christ and that they formed 'in some sort elements of a new Torah' (p. 107) for Paul and

3.16 appears to equate the Pauline writings with Scripture; furthermore, the exercise of the gift of prophecy was no less from the Holy Spirit than the oracles of the OT prophets.[1] If these observations are correct, and if Eph. 5.14 does not find its ultimate source in the OT, the most probable alternative source is a saying either of Jesus or of a Christian prophet.[2]

The influence of non-canonical Jewish writings in the Pauline epistles is discussed in the following chapter. Whatever the extent of their use by the apostle, it was in the nature of a vehicle or intermedium to the OT; they did not serve as a seat of authority in themselves. The only divergence from the Palestinian canon revealed by Paul's quotations lay within the tradition of the apostolic Church, from which was to emerge the γραφή of the New Covenant.[3]

the early Church. The use of διέταξεν (1 Cor. 9.14) favours such a view. Dodd here withdraws his former view (*The Bible and the Greeks*, p. 37) equating νόμος τοῦ Χριστοῦ with νόμος τοῦ πνεύματος.   The former, in distinction, conveys the idea of ἐπιταγαί or διατάγματα κυρίου.

[1] Cf. Acts 2.17ff; 19.6; 21.4, 9ff; 1 Cor. 14. These Spirit-inspired utterances evidently included hymns as well; cf. 1 Cor. 14.15.

[2] Cf. Rom. 13.11; John 5.25; cf. E. Lohmeyer, *Kyrios Jesus* on Phil. 2.5ff and 1 Tim. 3.16. κατὰ τὰς γραφάς in 1 Cor. 15.3ff has been attributed to an early Christian passion narrative. (Cf. V. Taylor, *The Formation of the Gospel Tradition*, London, 1949, pp. 48f.) Others relate it to Hos. 6.1ff. Cf. Dodd, *According to the Scriptures*, p. 103. However, it may refer only to the general teaching of the OT with 'the third day' given as a recitation of the fact, not covered by the κατὰ τὰς γραφάς.

[3] Paul's quotations from pagan writers (cf. Acts 17.28, Aratus; 1 Cor. 15.33, Menander; Tit.1.12, Epimenides) are of course not references to γραφή. For similar OT citations from various documents cf. Num. 21.14; Joshua 10.12; 1 Kings 11.41; 2 Chron. 12.15.

CHAPTER II

PAUL AND JUDAISM

INTRODUCTION

Tнıs and the following chapter consider Paul's use of the OT in the light of two significant elements of his environment, first century Judaism and the early Christian community. 'If God wished to give his people a series of letters like Paul's,' writes Warfield, 'he prepared a Paul to write them, and the Paul he brought to the task was a Paul who spontaneously would write just such letters.'[1] The Paul God prepared was a Jew, a Pharisee, and a rabbi; more than all, he was a slave of Christ whose heart and mind had been renewed to proclaim the Gospel of God.

Without doubt the apostle's understanding of the OT was completely revolutionised after his conversion; nevertheless his Jewish heritage remained of fundamental importance for his understanding and use of the Bible. His reverence for and study of the Scriptures long preceded his knowledge of Christ. Reading habits, methodology and hermeneutical norms were firmly implanted by his parents, his synagogue and, most of all, his teacher in rabbinics—Gamaliel. Indeed, apart from Christianity itself, it is most probable that Palestinian Judaism was the only determinative influence in Paul's life.[2] It is certainly adequate

---

[1] Warfield, op. cit., p. 155.

[2] W. C. van Unnik (*Tarsus of Jerusalem, De Stadt van Paulus' Jeugd*, Amsterdam, 1952), in a very acute argument, contends that Paul went to Jerusalem as an infant. His hypothesis rests basically upon Acts 22.3 and Acts 26.4, 5. In the former text Paul declares that he was 'brought up' (ἀνατεθραμμένος) in Jerusalem; van Unnik refers this, not to Gamaliel's teaching, but to Paul's parental 'upbringing'. The subsequent verb παιδεύω properly applies to the educational guidance of a teacher and follows (i.e. is not simultaneous with) the ἀνατρεφή at home. The assertion of Acts 26.4,5 retains its argumentative worth only on the supposition that Paul came to Jerusalem at a very early age. Van Unnik's summary is translated in W. E. Phipps, 'The Attitude of the Apostle Paul toward Scripture', unpublished Ph.D. dissertation, St Mary's College, University of St Andrews, 1954, pp. 32-6. Paul could have acquired even his Greek language and literature at Gamaliel's school; cf. Sotah 49 (*SBT*, pp. 265, 269f).

to explain any of his OT relationships not grounded in the practice of the early Church or originating in his own thought.[1] Klausner, in a considered opinion, goes even further: 'Intensive research over many years has brought the writer of the present book to a deep conviction that there is nothing in the teaching of Paul—not even the most mystical elements in it—that did not come from authentic Judaism.'[2]

Having recognised the place of Judaism in Paul's thought, a note of caution should be added. From that day on the Damascus road, the home of Paul's heart and of his mind never again lay in Judaism; if his name could ever have graced a rabbinic tractate as 'R. Saul', it is certain that 'St Paul's' writings are of a different genus altogether. Dom Gregory's words are pertinent and apt: 'St Paul has by now stood his trial on the charge of Hellenising Christianity to make it acceptable to the Greeks —and the verdict is decisively "Not Guilty". . . . It would not be altogether surprising if in a few years' time he had to stand another trial, on a charge of "Rabbinising" a Galilean Gospel and making it unintelligible to Greeks. However, St Paul had much experience of trials and usually managed to come off fairly well.'[3]

CONTEMPORARY JEWISH EXEGESIS[4]

To determine the character of first century Jewish exegesis there are three main sources apart from the NT to which one may appeal: rabbinic literature, writings of later Palestinian

---

[1] Alexandrian Judaism is also to be considered, but its importance is secondary and probably mediate. The significance of Hellenism, even for Paul's thought as a whole, has been revised sharply downward since the days of Adolph Deissmann. C. A. A. Scott (*Christianity According to St Paul*, Cambridge, 1939) regards it as negligible: 'So far as the content of his preaching was not due to the fact of Christ, its content and also its form were derived almost exclusively from Judaism' (p. vii). In his ministry 'he starts from Jewish postulates, assumes the validity of Jewish Scriptures, and operates with Jewish argument and illustration' (p. 9). The influence of Greek mystery religions in Pauline thought is critiqued in J. S. Stewart, *A Man in Christ*, London, 1935, pp. 66ff. Cf. Kennedy, *St Paul and the Mystery Religions*. Literary practices similar to the Stoic 'Diatribe' and the συνστοιχοί (*infra*, p. 52) appear in the Pauline epistles but relate to matters of style rather than content. Cf. R. Bultmann, *Der Stil der paulinischen Predigt und die kynisch-stoische Diatribe*, Göttingen, 1910; A. Bonhöffer, *Epiktet und das Neue Testament*, Giessen, 1911.

[2] J. Klausner, *From Jesus to Paul*, London, 1942, p. 466.

[3] G. Dix, *Jew and Greek*, London, 1953, p. 3.

[4] Cf. C. Guignebert, *The Jewish World in the Time of Jesus*, London, 1939; G. F. Moore, *Judaism*, 3 vols., Cambridge, 1927; E. Schürer, op. cit.

Judaism (i.e. 150 B.C.-A.D. 100), and works emanating from the Jewish community in Alexandria.

The rabbinic literature, as finally codified in the Targums, Talmud and Midrash, represents a development of almost a thousand years.[1] After the return from the Babylonian Exile in the fifth century B.C., oral teaching became a fixed and growing supplement to the Holy Scriptures.[2] The Targums, reduced to writing comparatively early,[3] were Aramaic paraphrases designed to render the OT text in the vernacular; in the very nature of the case, however, they assumed an interpretive character. Exegesis proper took the form of Midrash (דרש = investigate),[4] a running commentary on the text, and of the Mishnah, a topical commentary on related texts and traditions.[5] The latter (second-third century), with its own commentary—the Gemara, formed the Talmud (compiled *c.* fifth century) in which the Scriptures were ingeniously interpreted to accommodate the laws and traditions of the rabbis.[6]

Although the Peshat (פשט), or primary meaning, theoretically remained supreme, rabbinical exegesis almost exclusively applied the texts to contemporary situations by means of

---

[1] See J. W. Etheridge, *The Targums of Onkelos and Jonathan . . . with Fragments of the Jerusalem Targum*, London, 1865; I. Epstein, ed., *The Babylonian Talmud*, London, 1935, Seder Nezikin, pp. xiii–xxvii; H. Freedman, *The Midrash*, London, 1939, I, pp. ix–xxiii; J. Z. Lauterbach, *Mekilta*, Philadelphia, 1935, I, pp. xiiiff. For a good introductory survey see R. A. Stewart, *The Earlier Rabbinic Tradition*, London, 1949; cf. H. Danby, *The Mishnah*, Oxford, 1933, pp. xiiiff.

[2] According to Jewish tradition, revelation, which began with the Patriarchs, ceased with Malachi. Cf. F. Weber, *Jüdische Theologie*, Leipzig, 1897, pp. 8off; Josephus, *contra Apion*, I, 41, (Thackeray, I, p. 179). L. Zunz (op. cit., pp. xviii–xx), sought to narrow the gap between the written and oral law by showing that later portions of the OT were often liturgical interpretations of the older and that oral traditions exhibited something of the same character. This may explain why in the NT the major prophet—Isaiah, Jeremiah—is often named even though the secondary writing—Zechariah, Malachi—is more directly cited. Cf. Mark 1.2; Matt. 27.9.

[3] Gamaliel (first century) is said to have possessed a Targum of Job. Zunz contends that most OT books were in translation about that time. (Zunz, op. cit., pp. 61f, 64; cf. Shab. 115a; *SBT*, p. 565.)

[4] Cf. Ezra 7.10.

[5] This difference of form, and the tendency of the Mishnah-form to depart further and further from any scriptural reference, caused them to develop into separate and competing disciplines. Cf. Freedman, op. cit., I, p. xiv.

[6] e.g. the rabbinical custom of an early breakfast in summer is derived from Isa. 49.10: 'They shall not hunger nor thirst, neither shall the heat nor sun smite them'; cf. B. K. 92ab (*SBT*, p. 534). Rabbinical rulings came to have a value independent of Scripture, and often Scripture proofs were recognised as a mere formality if not superfluous. Cf. Weber, op. cit., p. 92; Z. H. Chajes, *The Student's Guide Through the Talmud*, London, 1952, pp. 29–32; B.K. 46b (*SBT*, p. 264).

Halacha (הלכה) and Haggada (הגדה).[1] The former, largely used in the Talmud,[2] related to the exposition of legal provisions; Haggada encompassed everything else.[3] Mielziner finds an example of both types in Lev. 19.3: halachic exposition notes that 'man' (איש) not only means male but also includes woman; the Haggada explains that 'mother' stands before 'father' to counterbalance the natural tendency of a child to fear his father.[4]

The oldest norms of rabbinic interpretation are the seven rules of Hillel (c. 30 B.C.):

1. *a fortiori* (קל וחומר),
2. analogy of expressions (גזירה שוה),
3 and 4. generalisation (בנין אב מכתוב אחד),
5. general and particular (כלל ופרט),
6. analogy of a similar passage (כיוצא בו ממקום אחר),
7. contextual explanation (דבר הלמד מעניגו).

For example, a bailee must pay if a rented animal is stolen, but not if it dies (Exod. 22.9ff); *a fortiori*, a gratuitous bailee, who is bound if the animal dies, must pay if it is stolen, though the Scripture does not specifically so teach (Exod. 22.14).[5] If 'sixty years' (Lev. 27.7) be interpreted as over sixty (i.e. sixty-one and over), *by analogy*, so should 'twenty years' in the preceding context, since the same word, שנה, is used.[6] A mill-stone shall not be taken as security because it is a man's 'life' (Deut. 24.6); the rule may be *generalised* to include anything used to prepare food.[7] Since the *particular* phrase, 'to do evil or ... good' (Lev. 5.4), implies the future, the *general* injunction, 'If a soul swear ...', applies only to oaths of the future, for the general is only as inclusive as the particular.[8] Exod. 16.29 is

---

[1] M. Mielziner, *Introduction to the Talmud*, New York, 1925, pp. 117ff; cf. W. Bacher, 'Bible Exegesis—Jewish', *SJE*, III, pp. 162-74; G. Aicher, *Das Alte Testament in der Mishna*, Freiburg 1906, pp. 107-40.

[2] Though considerable haggadic matter is also there. Cf. Shab. 30a-33b (*SBT*, pp. xxxiv, 131-58); Ber. 54a-64a (*SBT*, pp. 327-405); Mielziner, op. cit., p. 57.

[3] e.g. parables, legends, homiletical illustrations and ethical teaching; cf. Mielziner, op. cit., pp. 56ff; W. Bacher, 'The Origin of the Word Hagada', *JQR*, 4 (1892), pp. 406-9.

[4] Kid. 30b-31a (*SBT*, pp. 148f); cf. Mielziner, op. cit., pp. 148f; Gn. R., LXXXVII, 5; XCIV, 9 (*SMR*, II, pp. 808, 877).

[5] B. M. 95a (*SBT*, p. 549). [6] Ar. 18a (*SBT*, pp. 106f).

[7] B. M. 115b (*SBT*, p. 656). [8] Shebu. 26a (*SBT*, pp. 137f).

qualified by the *context*; otherwise it would forbid leaving one's house at all on the Sabbath.[1]

These rules are a type of reasonable inference which is as old as logic, and they find parallels in all literature; but the casuistical use to which the rabbis put them produced conclusions far beyond the 'reasonable inference' of most minds. For example, no Israelite could suffer in Gehenna: The gold plate on the altar resisted fire, how much more a transgressor in Israel.[2] Not bad in themselves, they were susceptible to abuse; and for this abuse the rabbis are well known.[3]

After the destruction of the temple in A.D. 70 a rival method of exegesis, popularised by Akiba, extended exegetical casuistry to unknown lengths.[4] Although opposed at first,[5] its ensuing dominance is responsible for many of the extravagances of rabbinic exegesis,[6] e.g. the emphasis on Gematria,[7] Notarikon[8] and Themoura.[9]

There are several objections to taking the rabbinics of the Talmud and Midrash as representative of first century Judaism. The literature is late and includes only the views of the Pharisaic element which became dominant after A.D. 70. The destruction of Jerusalem and the subsequent dispersion, as well as the rise of Christianity, doubtless affected the literature.[10] Nevertheless,

---

[1] Shab. 1 (*SBT*, p. 1).   [2] Hag. 27a (*SBT*, p. 171).

[3] Although not accounting for all their rabbinical fancies, some of their exposition was given with tongue in cheek: 'The greatest fault is to be found . . . is perhaps that they did not observe the wise rule of Johnson who said to Boswell on a certain occasion, "Let us get serious, for there comes a fool!" And the fools did come in the shape of certain Jewish commentators and Christian controversialists who took as serious things which were only the expression of momentary impulse . . . ' (S. Schechter, *Studies in Judaism*, London, 1896, p. 240).

[4] Cf. Gen. R., LIII, 15 (*SMR*, I, p. 474).

[5] Cf. Shebu. 26a (*SBT*, p. 138) for one controversy between Ishmael and Akiba.

[6] Cf. Mielziner, op. cit., pp. 124ff; Singer, op. cit., pp. 164ff; P. P. Levertoff, *Midrash Sifre on Numbers*, London, 1926, p. xiv.

[7] i.e. exegesis by letter-number equivalence; cf. Nu. R., XIII, 15f; XVIII (*SMR*, VI, pp. 535f, 734ff); F. Weber, op. cit., pp. 121f.

[8] i.e. constructing words from the letters of a word.

[9] i.e. commutation of Letters to fit a secret meaning; cf. F. W. Farrar, 'Rabbinic Exegesis', *The Expositor*, Second Series, 5 (1877), pp. 362-78.

[10] An attempt at approximate dating is made in C. G. Montefiore and H. Loewe, *A Rabbinic Anthology*, London, 1938, pp. 709-37. Some talmudic references are applied to Paul (e.g. Ab. III, 11f; *SBT*, pp. 34f; cf. Klausner, op. cit., pp. 600ff, and passages mentioning the Minim (מינים) or heretics are understood of Christians e.g. Shab. 116 (*SBT*, pp. 567ff); cf. R. T. Herford, *Christianity in the Talmud and Midrash*, London, 1903 In Sanh. 38b (*SBT*, p. 244) the Minim are definitely distinguished from Gentiles and identified with apostate Jewish (Christian?) elements. Because of the late character of the writing Schweitzer concluded that

in general one may accept as genuine the NT parallels in the Talmud; it is not likely that alterations were in the direction of Christianity to any extent.[1]

The apocalyptic writings of later Judaism have an entirely different spirit from the rabbinic tomes. Formerly regarded as popular and individualistic,[2] it is now realised that this literature also had its 'schools'[3] and in them—their messianic emphasis and their interpretive methods—is evidenced a truer line of succession from the prophets to Christ than the Judaism of the rabbinic order. Indeed, Fourth Ezra and the Apocalypse of Baruch, written shortly after Paul's day, 'in their wide survey of the ordering of the world, offer the largest field of illustration for the Pauline epistles.'[4]

The recently discovered manuscripts of the Qumran Sect shed considerable light on apocalyptic Judaism of the first century B.C.[5] Although the precise nature of the community is still undetermined, they were dissenters from orthodox Pharisaism with some affinities with, and differences from, the Essenes.[6] Their prophetic emphasis[7] (*contra* the rabbis and Philo) and the peculiar character of their exegesis make them especially interesting from the NT point of view.

The writings of this party, evidently including the well-known

we know practically nothing of first century Rabbinism. A. Schweitzer, op. cit., p. 48; cf. A. S. Peake, 'Quintessence of Paulinism', *Bulletin of the John Rylands Library*, IV (September 1917), pp. 9, 10.

[1] Cf. C. G. Montefiore, *Rabbinical Literature and Gospel Teachings*, London, 1930, p. xvii; Edersheim (*Jesus the Messiah*, II, p. 710) suspects that interpretations were altered in opposition to Christian teaching.

[2] Thackeray, *Paul and Jewish Thought*, pp. 13f; Schürer, op. cit., ii, II, pp. 48f.

[3] The Dead Sea Scrolls reveal not only a sectarian community but a school of thought with considerable affinity to the NT. The composite character of First Enoch also suggests something more than isolated individuals; *CAP*, II, pp. 193ff; cf. *infra*, pp. 139ff.

[4] Thackeray, *Paul and Jewish Thought*, p. 20; cf. Peake, 'Quintessence of Paulinism', pp 10f.

[5] The dating of the scrolls has been a matter of controversy, but the vast majority of opinion favours the first or second century B.C. Cf. A. Dupont-Sommer, *The Dead Sea Scrolls*, Oxford, 1952, p. 32.

[6] Cf. B. J. Roberts, *The Dead Sea Scrolls and the Old Testament Scriptures*, Manchester, 1953, p. 75; M. H. Gottstein, 'Anti-Essene Traits in the Dead Sea Scrolls', *VT*, VI (April 1954), pp. 141-7; Dupont-Sommer, op. cit., pp. 70, 85-96; *CAP*, II, pp. 788ff.

[7] Cf. OT quotations in the Zadokite Fragments: Law (ten times), Prophets (eleven times), Hagiographa (once). In Paul the emphasis is the Pentateuch, Psalms, Isaiah; in Zadokite Fragments, the Pentateuch, the Twelve, Isaiah.

Zadokite Work, contain much apocalyptic material.[1] Brownlee classified the hermeneutic of the Habakkuk Scroll and, apart from its eschatological character, found the form to be essentially rabbinic Midrash.[2] He detects various rabbinic devices used to obtain the desired interpretation. For example, the first word of Hab. 1.9 is read with the preceding verse.[3] The practice of Notarikon and Themoura as well as the influence of Hillel's rules are, according to Brownlee, also in evidence.[4] As in the rabbis, allegorical interpretation is a minor element; but, in contrast, DSH makes no appeal to other Scriptures.

While Brownlee minimises the relation of DSS exegesis with the NT,[5] other writers have noted their hermeneutical affinities: 'In this type of exegesis the prophetic oracles are specifically made to refer to the historical person who is the author of the interpretation and to the historical circumstances he brings about, including the final redemption of all who believe in him. One cannot but sense the fundamental difference between this interpretation and the casuistic pilpulism of the Mishnaic appeal to Scripture and the ingenious metaphorical expansions of Philo. Whereas the Rabbis seem to have had a genius for inductive reasoning and the Jewish Greeks made the Scripture merely an allegory, apocalyptic passionately expounds the interpretation of the Divine promise of the Saviour and the

---

[1] e.g. Habakkuk, portions of Micah, Ps. 68, 107. Cf. B. J. Roberts, 'The Qumran (Dead Sea) Scrolls: A Survey', *The Congregational Quarterly*, 32 (April 1954), pp. 114-24.

[2] Brownlee here defines Midrash not as is usually done—a style or form of writing—but as an exegetical method devoting itself to the derivation of hidden meanings (p. 76). W. H. Brownlee, 'Biblical interpretation among the Sectaries of the Dead Sea Scrolls', *BA*, 14 (September 1951), pp. 54-76.

[3] Cf. Gamaliel's proof of the resurrection: 'Behold thou shalt sleep with thy fathers and rise up' (Deut. 31.16); Sanh. 90b (*SBT*, p. 605).

[4] e.g. Hab. 1.12: צוּר ('O Rock') in the text and יָצוּר ('will be distressed') in the commentary; cf. Brownlee, op. cit., pp. 54ff, 73, 74ff. However, it is not at all certain that the commentary's interpretation rests merely on cabalism. The text (Hab. 1.8f) mentions a coming in violence with faces set toward the East; the commentary elaborates that they come in anger with nostrils dilated with wrath. Brownlee sees here an equation of Jewish and Aramaic synonyms (faces=nostrils= anger). Such practices may occur, but, on the other hand, Kahle discerns the literature's influence on the Karites (*c.* eighth century) whose renewed emphasis on the *Peshat* was in contrast to the cabalism of their day. P. Kahle, 'The Karites and the Manuscripts', *VT*, III (1953), p. 834; cf. Bacher, 'Bible Exegesis', p. 165; *CAP*, II, p. 794.

[5] Brownlee, op. cit., pp. 74f: '[The] Gospels never depart from the simple meaning of the words unless it be in the supposed verbal play which derives Nazarene from branch (*n s r*) (Matt. 2.23; Isa. 11.1). . . .'

Salvation which has been kept hidden in the Word of God until the time of its fulfilment. This seems to be basic to the story of Jesus at Nazareth, Luke 4.16ff, and equally basic to the Teacher of Righteousness in the Habakkuk scroll.'[1]

Roberts views their exegesis as 'growing out' of the original context with no violence to the essential OT teaching.[2] Stendahl compares the method with Matthew's use of the OT and concludes that exegesis in the latter is not principally halachic or haggadic but approaches 'the *midrash pesher* of the Qumran Sect, in which the OT texts were not primarily the source of rules, but the prophecy which was shown to be fulfilled'.[3]

Jewish exegesis outside Palestine centred in Alexandria with Philo as its major representative. As the rabbis sought to harmonise Jewish customs with the Scripture, Philonic exegesis interpreted the OT in terms of Hellenistic philosophy. Its principal characteristic was the extensive use of allegory through which the Pentateuch was shown to exemplify Greek philosophical ideas. Some apocalyptic writings also stem from Alexandria (e.g. Wisdom); but they do not differ essentially from their Palestinian counterpart.

PAULINE AND JEWISH LITERARY METHODS[4]

GENERAL

Much methodological procedure is common to all writers and is worthy of comment only if it does not occur. Döpke, asserting the rabbinic manner of NT citation, advanced such 'proofs' as free and exegetical paraphrase and composite quotations, which were about as rabbinic as the use of papyrus.[5] Employing a citation in a sense differing from its original context, noted by Thackeray and Lietzmann as rabbinical, is in the same category.[6] The commonly used fragmentary quo-

---

[1] Roberts, *Scrolls and Old Testament Scriptures*, p. 79.

[2] Ibid., pp. 79f; cf. Dodd, *According to the Scriptures*, pp. 126ff.

[3] K. Stendahl, op. cit., p. 35.

[4] *Midrash pesher* as a hermeneutical method in Paul is considered in Chapter IV, *infra*, pp. 139ff.

[5] Döpke, op. cit.; cf. F. Johnson (op. cit., pp. 382-7) for a detailed critique. Bonsirven (op. cit., pp. 335f) points out a difference from the rabbinical practice in Paul's free quotations: the rabbis normally stick to the letter; when they do depart, they indicate it by the formula *al tigre*.

[6] Lietzmann, op. cit., p. 34; Thackeray, *Paul and Jewish Thought*, p. 187; cf. F. Johnson, op. cit., pp. 167ff. Illustration from daily life is another universal

tation, with the continuance of the given portion sometimes implied,[1] the insertion of hortatory, ethical sections,[2] and other procedures more distinctively Jewish, were probably acquired by Paul in his training for the rabbinate. It is most natural, and not in the least derogatory, to find these methods in his epistles. As Prat well states, 'the interests of truth did not require him to unlearn all that he had been taught'.[3]

Some methods more peculiar to Jewish commentators are the use of Midrash, or running commentary[4]; the practice of quoting from the Law, the Prophets and the Hagiographa; and the employment of Hillel's rules and emphasis upon grammatical exegesis (although these too are found in general usage). In Rom. 9-11 and Gal. 3 Paul employs the ancient midrashic form of commentary;[5] but his incisive manner and compact, integrated treatment is quite at odds with the rabbinic system. Often to support an opinion the rabbis quote the Law, Prophets and Hagiographa in succession and Paul also adopts this custom on occasion.[6] It is not habitual with the apostle, however, and probably represents only an incidental reminiscence. Hillel's principles of *a fortiori* and analogy are implicit in many Pauline passages,[7] but here too the rabbinic affinities can be too greatly stressed. One instance of *a fortiori* which arises in connexion with an OT quotation is found in 1 Cor. 9.9.[8] Some have in-

procedure common to Paul and the rabbis. But, as Michel observes, for Paul it is merely an accessory, but in the rabbis the מָשָׁל is given the rôle of proof (*Bibel*, p. 10).

[1] e.g. 1 Cor. 2.9; cf. Dodd, *According to the Scriptures*, p. 47; F. Johnson, op. cit., pp. 62-73.

[2] Cf. D. G. Bradley, 'The *Topos* as a form in the Pauline Paraenesis', *JBL*, 72 (December 1953), pp. 238-46; F. Delitzsch, *Brief an die Römer*, Leipzig, 1870, p. 16.

[3] Prat, op. cit., I, p. 23.

[4] As well as Halacha and Haggada. Cf. C. W. Dugmore, *The Influence of the Synagogue upon the Divine Office*, London, 1944.

[5] Cf. Rom. 4; 1 Cor. 10; Gal. 4. On Paul's contrasting and reconciling of texts (Rom. 9) cf. Ber. 25a (*SBT*, p. 151). The reference to מִדְרָשׁ in 2 Chron. 24.27; 13.22 may point to the ancestry of this practice.

[6] Cf. Rom. 11.8-10; 15.9-12. See Appendix III; cf. Mak. 10b (*SBT*, p. 67): Num. 22.12, 20; Isa. 58.17; Prov. 3.34; B. K. 92b (*SBT*, p. 536): Gen. 28.9; Jud. 9.3; Sirach. 13.15; Sanh. 90b (*SBT*, p. 605): Deut. 31.16; Isa. 26.19; S.S. 7.9; cf. Surenhusio, op. cit., pp. 49f. The custom is evidenced in Christ as well; cf. Luke 24.44; Matt. 12.3-8; Luke 16.16, 29.

[7] e.g. Rom. 4-5. Paul's exposition in 1 Cor. 7 is an example of NT Halacha; the allegory in Gal. 4 is Haggada.

[8] This text (Deut. 25.4) was interpreted by the rabbis, in the light of the succeeding context, to allow a woman to object to a levirite marriage. Yeb. 4a (*SBT*, p. 10); cf. Bonsirven, op. cit., pp. 288f.

terpreted Paul as ruling out the literal meaning of the OT altogether here.[1] The question largely hangs on whether παντῶς (v. 10) is taken as 'entirely' or as 'undoubtedly'. In view of the other NT usage,[2] the character of Pauline typology,[3] and general Jewish interpretation, the latter meaning denoting an *a fortiori* argument is much to be preferred.[4] It is not a 'proof-text' but an appeal to the mind of the reader made under the general assumption that what 'was written beforehand' (Rom. 15.4) had significance for the Messianic Age. The rabbis were as conscious of grammatical minutiae as modern commentators, but perhaps with more dubious results. For example, in prayer one must bow one's head before mention of the Divine name because Mal. 2.5 says 'bowed before thy name' (not *at* thy name).[5] The differentiation between the singular and plural accounts for the assertion that the Torah was given with five voices.[6] The distinction which Paul makes between the singular and plural of σπέρμα (זֶרַע) in Gal. 3.16 has been pointed to as an example of rabbinical artifice in the apostle. As to method it is common both to the rabbis and modern commentators; whether the interpretation is the result of an arbitrary rabbinical twist is discussed below.[7]

---

[1] e.g. J. Moffatt, op. cit., p. 117; C. H. Dodd, *The Epistle of Paul to the Romans*, London, 1932, p. 180.

[2] It is found only in Luke and Paul. The former (cf. Luke 4.23; Acts 18.21 mg; 21.22; 28.4) uniformly has 'undoubtedly'; Paul, with the negative, has 'certainly not' (Rom. 3.9; 1 Cor. 5.10; 16.12), and the only other is 'by all means' (1 Cor. 9.22).

[3] *Infra*, pp. 88, 126ff. For Paul the whole relationship of OT to NT depends upon its being real history; to find the contrary here would be inconsistent with this pattern.

[4] So Thackeray, op. cit., pp. 193ff. Philo (*de somniis*, I, xvi; Colson, V, pp. 345ff), reasoning that God is not concerned about a debtor's cloak, allegorises Exod. 22.27. Cf. The Letter of Aristeas, 144-50 (*CAP*, II, p. 108): 'It was not for the sake of mice and weasels that Moses drew up his laws but for righteousness; the animals are brought in to teach moral lessons.' But even Philo does not view the symbolic interpretation of the law as always abrogating its literal significance: 'Why we shall be ignoring the sanctity of the temple and a thousand other things if we are going to pay heed to nothing except what is shown to us by the inner meaning of things. . . .' (*de mig. Abr.*, 92f; Colson, IV, p. 185). This text (Deut. 25.4) is given a very literal interpretation as an example of Moses' kindness to animals (*de virtu.*, 145; Colson, VIII, p. 253). The rabbis, for their part, forbade allegorical interpretation of passages regarding kindness to animals (Jerus. Berakoth 5; cf. Thackeray, *Paul and Jewish Thought*, p. 195).

[5] Ber. 12a (*SBT*, p. 69). Also, the resurrection of the dead is shown in Deut. 11.21 because the land was promised to 'them' (i.e. the Patriarchs) not to 'you'. Sanh. 90b (*SBT*, p. 605). Cf. Mark 12.26f.

[6] Ber. 6b (*SBT*, p. 29).

[7] *Infra*, pp. 70ff.

Besides the procedures mentioned above, certain other Pauline practices may be compared with Jewish usage: his introductory formulas (IF), his combined quotations, and his use of allegory.

INTRODUCTORY FORMULAS

The nature of Paul's IF has already been considered. For the most part they are formulas traditional to the Jews and find parallels even in the OT[1]; their congruity with IF in rabbinical literature has been noted from the time of Surenhusius.[2] The rabbis, in the great majority of cases, use some form of אמר; most frequently found is the Niphal שנאמר (Danby: 'as it is written').[3] Similarly, in the Zadokite Work and Habakkuk commentary this verb is most usual.[4] The following may be compared:

Zad. Frag.

9.1, 5, 6, 40—כאשר אמר	2 Cor. 6.16—καθὼς εἶπεν ὁ θεός
9.19—אשר אמר אל	
7.4; 10.3; 14.1—כתוב	Gal. 3.13—ὅτι γέγραπται
9.8—כאשר כתוב	Rom. 1.17—καθὼς γέγραπται
7.10—ומשה אמר	Rom. 10.19—Μωϋσῆς λέγει
8.8—אשר אמר ישעיה	Rom. 10.16—'Ησαίας λέγει
Pes. 81b (SBT, p. 426)— כתוב אומר	Rom. 4.3—ἡ γραφὴ λέγει
Yeb. 39a (SBT, p. 248)— כתוב אמר	
Aboth 3.7 (SBT, p. 31)[5]— ככתוב בדויד	Rom. 11.2[6]—ἐν' Ηλία τί λέγει ἡ γραφή

---

[1] Cf. 2 Ezra 20.34 (Neh. 10:34): ὡς γέγραπται; 4 Kings 14.6; Dan, 9.13: καθὼς γέγραπται; 2 Ezra 16.6 (Neh. 6:6): ἦν γεγραμμένον; Exod. 24.4: ἔγραψεν Μωϋσῆς. See Appendix IV. Cf. 2 Chron. 36.2; 3 Kings 2.27: πληρωθῆναι τὸ ῥῆμα κυρίου; 2 Chron. 20.37; ἐπροφήτευσεν 'Ελειαδὰ.

[2] Surenhusio, op. cit., pp. 25f; Döpke, op. cit., pp. 60-69. For parallels in Greek and Latin writers cf. J. Scott, op. cit., p. 88.

[3] See B. Metzger, 'The Formulas Introducing Quotations of Scripture in the New Testament and the Mishnah', JBL, 70 (December 1951), pp. 297-307; cf. Danby, op. cit.

[4] Cf. CAP, II, p. 789; M. Burrows, 'The Meaning of 'ŠR 'MR in DSH', VT, II, (July 1952), pp. 255-60.

[5] Referring to 1 Chron. 29.14.

[6] Referring to 1 Kings 19.14

Yoma 35b, 66a (*SBT*, pp. 165-308)—כלתוב בתורה משה

I Cor. 9.9—ἐν ... τῷ Μωϋσέως νόμῳ γέγραπται

Sanh. 2a (*SBT*, p. 2)—שנאמר··· ואומר

Rom. 15.9f—καθὼς γέγραπται ... καὶ πάλιν λέγει

Kid. 82a (*SBT*, p. 423)—מהו אומר

Rom. 10.8—ἀλλὰ τὶ λέγει

The above parallels indicate the extensive agreement between the IF in Paul and Jewish writings, even, as in the last two examples, in interrogativè and combined IF. Metzger finds, on the whole, a greater variety of IF in the NT; also the Mishnah shows a preference for verbs of saying in contrast to Paul's 'it is written'.[1] Both the NT and the Mishnah recognise the instrumentality of the human author; their IF indicates that both 'had the very highest view of the inspiration of the Scriptures which they quote'.[2] Warfield's words are apropos: 'There is probably not a single mode of alluding to or citing Scripture in all the NT which does not find its exact parallel among the Rabbis. The New Testament so far evinces itself a thoroughly Jewish book.'[3]

COMBINED QUOTATIONS

Two forms of combined quotations are found in the Pauline letters: merged or amalgamated quotations, and chain quotations or *haraz* (חרז). The latter method, according to Edersheim, had its origin in the preaching of the synagogues in which the preacher quoted from the Pentateuch and then strung on similar passages from the Prophets and Hagiographa.[4] In the Talmud this type of combination is not uncommon, but Paul seldom follows this order.[5] The apostle never introduces his

[1] Metzger, op. cit., pp. 305f. Cf. Edersheim, *Jesus the Messiah*, I, p. 187n. For frequent use of 'it is written' cf. Shab. 33a (*SBT*, pp. 151ff). The frequency of different formulas seems to vary with the particular tractate or section, with clusters of one or another type.

[2] Metzger, op. cit., p. 306. [3] Warfield, op. cit., pp. 118f.

[4] Edersheim, *Jesus the Messiah*, I, p. 449; cf. Swete, *Introduction*, p. 252. J. Scott (op. cit., p. 27) finds combined quotations in the OT (e.g. Jer. 30.8 from Isa. 10.27 and Nahum 1.13), but they only faintly resemble the NT type.

[5] *Supra*, pp. 3f. See Appendix III; cf. E. v. Dobschütz, 'Zum paulinischen Schriftbeweis', *ZNTW*, 24 (1925), pp. 306f.

haraz in the explicit rabbinical manner, i.e. The Law says . . . , the Prophets say . . . . , the Writings say. . . . However, the rationale behind the Jewish usage, 'not as though the word of the Law needed confirmation, but to show how the Scripture emphasises the lesson by iteration',[1] is evidently operative also in Paul's mind.

Neither do Paul's combinations rest merely on the basis of a 'key-word'. Although a number of Pauline citations appear to be united under a *Stichwort*,[2] the significance is far deeper than a verbal congruence.[3] The recurrence of the *Stichwort* is perhaps a designed mnemonic, but at times it is only a natural coincidence in the subject matter. Certainly it is the sense element that is basic for Paul. The verbal aspect is in the nature of effect rather than the underlying cause.[4]

Examples of the *haraz*, so frequent in Rom. 9-11, 15, are numerous in the Talmud. The conjunction is usually 'and'[5] or 'and then',[6] though sometimes a longer connective occurs.[7] In Mak. 24a (*SBT*, p. 173) successive verses (Amos 7.5, 6) have an IF inserted in similar fashion to Paul's citation in Rom. 10.20, 21. A *haraz* reminiscent of Rom. 9-11 is found in the same section of the tractate in which Moses, Jeremiah, Moses, Ezekiel, Moses and Isaiah are cited successively with the writer's name being adduced in the Pauline manner.

Merged quotations are a rarity in the rabbis. Especially noteworthy is the amalgamation of nine passages in Sanh. 38b (*SBT*, pp. 244f).[8] Two passages are also merged in Shab. 20a

---

[1] Moore, op. cit., I, pp. 239f. Cf. Meg. 31a (*SBT*, p. 188).

[2] e.g. λίθος: Rom. 9.33 (Isa. 8.14; 28.16); λαός: Rom. 9.25f (Hos. 2.23; 1.10); (unseeing) ὀφθαλμούς: Rom. 11.8, 19 (Isa. 29.10; Deut. 29.4; Ps. 68(69).23f); ἔθνη: Rom. 15.9-12 (Ps. 17(18).40; Deut. 32.43; Ps. 116(117).1); σόφοι: 1 Cor. 3.19 (Job 5.13; Ps.93(97):11, implied); θάνατος: 1 Cor. 15.54f (Isa, 25.8; Hos. 13-14) cf. 2 Cor. 6.16ff. See Vollmer, op. cit., p. 36.

[3] *Infra*, pp. 139ff.

[4] In a secondary sense the presence of the key-word may be the cause for the selection of a particular verse from the relevant passage; cf. *infra*, pp. 103ff. In any case they illustrate the unity of the quotation as a whole.

[5] e.g. Ber. 18a (*SBT*, p. 109): Prov. 19.17; 14.31; Mak. 13b (*SBT*, p. 95) cf. 1 Tim. 5.18; 2 Tim. 2.19 cf. Surenhusio, op. cit., pp. 45ff; *SBK*, III, p. 314 (on Rom. 15.10).

[6] e.g. Mak. 16a (*SBT*, p. 114); Deut. 24.10-13, 19-21 and Lev. 19.13; 5.23; cf. Rom. 15.11.

[7] e.g. 'and it says' cf. Ber. 6a (*SBT*, p. 25f); Pes. 7b, 8a (*SBT*, p. 31f); Rom. 15.10.

[8] Viz. Gen. 1.26, 27; 11.7, 5; 35.7, 3; Deut. 4.7; 2 Sam. 7.23; Dan. 7.9 (referring, against the Minim, the alternating singular and plural verbs to God and His

(*SBT*, p. 85), but, as edited, the first ends a paragraph and the second begins the succeeding one.[1] The scarcity of such combinations may be the result of the maxim: 'One Biblical verse may contain several teachings but a single teaching cannot be deduced from different Scriptural verses.'[2] At any rate, Bonsirven's conclusion appears to be borne out: 'Fréquemment, il est vrai, les rabbins utilisent plusieurs textes pour prouver une thèse, mais alors ils introduisent dans chaque texte une formule (ordinairement: "il dit"): il est rare de les voir amalgamer plusieurs sentences bibliques.'[3] In the *haraz*, then, Paul follows the practice of the rabbis, but for the source of his frequently used merged quotations one must look elsewhere.[4]

Allegory

The similarity of Pauline allegory to that of the Jewish world depends on the definition of the word. Taken merely as an extended metaphor (as contrasted with the parable or extended simile), the method is employed by the apostle in connexion with a divinely designed type[5] or with the illustrative use of an OT passage.[6]

In rabbinic literature several passages are classified as allegory[7]: The Midrash on Gen. 40.9 identifies the vine of Pharoah's dream with Israel, and its three branches with Moses, Aaron and Miriam.[8] The Song of Solomon was interpreted throughout as an allegorical description of God and Israel.[9] The Mashal (מָשָׁל) or parable is the more frequent form however[10]; and the few allegorical interpretations which do occur are rather seedy.[11]

The whole of Paul's typological exegesis has more in common,

---

heavenly court); also cf. Sanh. 39a (*SBT*, p. 246); Num. R. II, 15f (*SMR*, V, pp. 51ff): Jer. 2.2f and Hos. 2.4, 2; 1.9 and Isa. 1.18, 16.

[1] Ezek. 15.4; Jer. 36.22.
[2] Based on Ps. 62.12 and Jer. 23.9; cf. Sanh. 34a (*SBT*, p. 214).
[3] Bonsirven, op. cit., p. 336: 'Frequently, it is true, the rabbis utilise several texts to prove a point but then they introduce each text by a formula (ordinarily: "it says"); it is rare to see several biblical verses amalgamated.'
[4] See *infra*, pp. 86ff.   [5] e.g. 1 Cor. 10.4: 'That Rock was Christ.'
[6] Cf. Gal. 4.25: 'this Hagar is Mt. Sinai.' However, the text here is questionable. Cf. Lightfoot, *Galatians*, pp. 193ff.
[7] Cf. W. Bacher, *Die Agada der Tannaiten* Strassbourg, 1890, II, pp. 112, 515.
[8] Gen. R., LXXXVIII, 5 (*SMR*, II, pp. 815f).
[9] Cf. *SMR*, IX, p. vii.   [10] Cf. Sanh. 39a (*SBT*, pp. 246f).
[11] Bonsirven, op. cit., pp. 207-51, esp. pp. 246f; W. O. E. Oesterley, 'The Exegesis of the Old Testament'. *Record and Revelation*, ed. H. W. Robinson, Oxford,

as a method, with the Alexandrian school than with the rabbis.[1]
The same passages which form the backbone of Pauline typology
—the Creation, Patriarchal and Exodus narratives—also serve
as the subject of much of Philo's exegesis. However, the similarity is more formal than real. For Paul these things are actual
history—moulded by the Lord of history—whose significance
is only revealed in Christ; for Philo, who is one with the Greeks
in this, there is no historical perspective. The literal sense is
only the 'body' of appearance whose 'soul' lies in the allegorical
meaning.[2]

The allegory of the two covenants in Gal. 4.21-31 is the
Pauline text most often compared with Philonic exegesis. Apart
from its allegorical aspect, the alleged use of Gematria (i.e. the
numerical valuation of letters) and onomatology raise further
questions concerning Paul's methodology. In so far as onomatology may enter into the passage, there is nothing particularly
Alexandrian or rabbinic in it. The significance of names is a
frequent phenomenon in the OT itself, both as mere word-play
and as illustrative of significant relationships.[3] Its presence in
this text (viz. the equation of Hagar and Sinai, v. 25) is conjectural, however; probably the Hagar-Sinai parallelism is of
no more etymological significance than the other συνστοιχοί.[4]

1938, p. 404. The condemnations in Aboth III, 11; IV, 2 have been interpreted
as directed against the Alexandrian allegorists who depreciated the literal sense of
the Torah; cf. SBT, p. 35.

[1] Beside the allegories of Philo cf. The Letter of Aristeas, pp. 143-67 (CAP, II,
pp. 108-10): Clovenfooted animals are to the initiated the symbol of memory.
D. Windfuhr ('Der Apostel Paulus als Haggadist', ZATW (1926), pp. 327-30), in
comparing some Pauline typology (e.g. 2 Cor. 6.16ff) with Jewish Haggada, overlooks the more significant element in the apostle's exegesis. However, it is true that
the rabbis have the nucleus of an Exodus typology although they do not formulate
it as such. Cf. infra, p. 132.

[2] Cf. de migr. Abr., 199f. (Colson, IV, p.248); de Abr., 200 (Colson, VI, p. 99).

[3] Cf. Gen. 17.5; 21.3-6; 32.28; Ber. 7b (SBT, p. 36); Sanh. 19b (SBT, pp. 102f);
Gen. R. XXV, 2 (SMR, I, p, 205); Philo, leg. alleg., III, 244 (Colson, I, p. 467).

[4] Cf. E. de W. Burton, The Epistle to the Galatians, Edinburgh, 1921, pp. 259-62;
Lightfoot, Galatians, pp. 192-8. The use of συνστοιχεῖν (v. 25) possibly alludes to
a columnar arrangement of the elements in the narrative which, according to
Dodd, was an accepted practice. Cf. C. H. Dodd, 'A Problem of Interpretation',
Studiorum Novi Testamenti Societas, II (1951), p. 11; J. H. Moulton and G. Milligan,
The Vocabulary of the Greek Testament, London, 1914-29, p. 612. The parallel
arrangement in the Galatians passage follows this order:

1	2	3	4
Hagar	Ishmael (flesh)	Sarah	Isaac (Promise)
Sinai Covenant		New Covenant	
Present Jerusalem	Children of the Present Jerusalem	New Jerusalem above	Children of the New Jerusalem above

More speculative is the suggestion that Paul's parallelism employs or is based upon a fanciful Gematria. Aside from being entirely superfluous to any sane interpretation of Paul, the system also fails to work textually.[1]

Even in this passage which Paul designates as ἅτινά ἐστιν ἀλληγορούμενα (Gal. 4.24), one finds an interpretation more in accord with Pauline typology than with Alexandrian allegory. The illustration of the 'law versus promise' theme from the Hagar story and the recognition of its historicity are in marked contrast to the symbolics of Philo which often ignore anything apart from the purely allegorical.[2] Michel concludes his discussion of the passage with a pertinent remark concerning its essential typological character: 'Auch an dieser Stelle handelt es sich doch mehr um eine typologische Beziehung als um eine Allegorie selbst (Hagar ist Typus der mosaischen Gesetzgebung am Sinai und entspricht dem jetzigen Jerusalem). So zeigt sich auch hier die Besonderheit des paulinischen Schriftverständnisses: Paulus denkt mehr typologisch als allegorisch im eigentlichen Sinne.'[3]

In conclusion, Paul's treatment of the OT often finds much in common with the methods of his day as reflected in Jewish literature; his IF and *haraz* are especially to be noted in this regard. In other respects Pauline methods find few parallels in contemporary Jewish writings. The use of merged quotations is little found in the rabbis. In contrast to Philo, Paul's use of

---

[1] Cf. A. F. Puukko, 'Paulus und das Judentum', *Studia Orientalia*, II (1925), p. 75. Lietzmann (op. cit., p. 31) does not consider Paul incapable of it but finds it unworkable. Cf. Lightfoot, *Galatians*, p. 370. In the rabbis see *supra*, p. 42. In the Greek world cf. Deissmann, *Light from the Ancient East*, pp. 275ff. In Rev. 13.18 some system of numerics is employed, not to exegete Scripture but to spell out a name or symbol. Contrast Gen. R., XLIII, 2 (*SMR*, I, p. 353): Abraham's servants were named Eliezer because it says 318 (Gen. 14.14), and the letter value of 318 is Eliezer: א (1) + ל (30) + י (10) + ע (70) + ז (7) + ר (200) = 318. Only a rabbi could get this from the OT, and only a rabbi would find it in Paul.

[2] Cf. H. A. A. Kennedy, *Philo's Contribution to Religion*, London, 1919, pp. 40f. Philo allegorises the same story (*de congress. erud. grat.*, 11-24, Colson, IV, pp. 463f; Quaes. in Gen. III, 21, R. Marcus, *Philo Supplement*, London: 1953, I, pp. 206f) along a different line: Abraham is a learner; Hagar represents his preliminary instruction, and Sarah follows as the chief goal of learning—true virtue.

[3] Michel, *Bibel*, p. 110: 'This passage also is treated more as a typological relationship than as allegory proper. (Hagar is a type of the Mosaic legislation at Sinai and corresponds with the present Jerusalem.) Thus the special character of the Pauline understanding of Scripture is also shown here: Paul thinks more typologically than in a specifically allegorical sense.'

allegory is very minor and its character altogether different from that of Alexandrian writers; and his typological view of OT history is a rare, if not unknown, element in contemporary Jewish exegesis. In all things but allegorical interpretation, Paul's Jewish methodology reflects a Palestinian milieu, and even in that the Alexandrian contact does not appear to be close or direct.[1] The apostle is not averse to using methods from his Jewish training as they suit his purpose; on the other hand, some of his methods seem to arise from a Christian hermeneutic and from the practices of the apostolic community and cannot be explained by his Jewish background.

PAULINE AND JEWISH EXEGESIS

The influence of Paul's general cultural milieu, and in some particulars his rabbinic training, on his style and dialectical methods is quite apparent. There remains, however, a second question as to the extent to which contemporary Jewish *interpretations* find parallels or echoes in the Pauline literature. Furthermore, do such parallels represent merely a legitimate interpretation common to the whole or part of Judaism, or do they evidence the adoption of rabbinical speculations quite extraneous to any reasonable view of the OT text? The relation of Pauline theology to Judaism is a large subject; the ensuing section, therefore, confines itself to passages quoting from or bearing upon the OT.[2]

GENERAL

A number of apocryphal and rabbinic parallels are in the nature of a common phraseology or literary custom with little or no interpretive significance.[3] For example, the words of Deut. 30.11-14 are employed in Baruch to describe the in-

---

[1] G. H. Box, 'The Value and Significance of the Old Testament in Relation to the New', *The People and the Book*, ed. A. S. Peake, Oxford, 1925, p. 464, concludes that 'the apostle derived his knowledge of the method not directly from Alexandria, but from his general rabbinic training'.

[2] Paul's general hermeneutic is determined by the fact of Jesus as Messiah and is, of course, at variance with anything in Judaism. Its affinities, as a method, with the Qumran community are discussed in a later chapter (*infra*, pp. 139ff).

[3] e.g. 'they that sleep', 'the last trump'. In his introduction to the various apocryphal books Charles (op. cit.) lists such NT parallels. See also Ryle, *Philo*, pp. xxxiiiff; Nägeli, op. cit., pp. 68-75.

accessibility of Wisdom[1]; Paul (Rom. 10.6-8) uses the language of the same passage to represent the accessibility of salvation in Christ. The wording of 1 Cor. 2.9 also seems to have been traditional in Judaism to depict the glory of the future age.[2] The mention of Jannes and Jambres in 2 Tim. 3.8 is probably no more than a convenient labelling from Jewish oral tradition.[3]

In other passages a common interpretive element appears more pronounced. Paul probably shares a common view of צחק in Exod. 32.6 as implying idolatry (1 Cor. 10.7)[4]; and in Eph. 4.8 he evidently agrees (against the LXX) with a targumic interpretation of לקח in Ps. 67(68).19.[5] The reference in Gal. 4.29 to the persecution (ἐδίωκεν) of Isaac by Ishmael is sometimes adduced as a rabbinic interpretation of מצחק in Gen. 21.9f[6]; however, Paul probably has in mind more the

[1] Who hath gone up into heaven and taken her
　　and brought her down from the clouds
　Who hath gone over the sea and found her
　　and will bring her for choice gold.
　　　　　　　(Baruch 3.29f; *CAP*, I, p. 590).
Cf. 4 Ezra 4.8; Targ. Jer. II: 'O, that we had one like Jonah who could descend into the depths of the sea and bring it to us.' (Quoted in Thackeray, *Paul and Jewish Thought*, pp. 153f).

[2] W. D. Davies, *St Paul and Rabbinic Judaism*, London, 1948, p. 307. Thackeray (*Paul and Jewish Thought*, pp. 185f) ascribes it to a Jewish anthology or a paraphrase of Isa. 64.4. The latter passage is interpreted of the world to come, as contrasted with the Messianic Age in Ber. 34b (*SBT*, p. 215) and applied variously, e.g., the reward of scholars, wine to feast the righteous; cf. Sanh, 99a (*SBT*, p. 670).

[3] Whether Paul regarded the names as genuine is impossible to say, but there is no reason to refer his use to an apocryphal book; the appellation, with slight variation, was widespread, and Paul's ascriptions are entirely within the Biblical narrative. Cf. Pliny, *Historia Naturalis*, xxxi, 11; Eusebius, *Praep. Evangelica*, ix, 8; Zad. Frag. 7.19; Men. 85a (*SBT*, p. 513); K. Kohler, 'Jannes and Jambres', *S.J.E.*, VII, pp. 71f.

[4] Cf. Exod. R., I, 1 (*SMR*, III, p. 1). On the other hand Paul does not employ the passage with reference to immorality (1 Cor. 10.8) in contrast with the rabbinic idea that the words 'sat down' are always connected with moral degradation; cf. Levertoff, op. cit., pp. 133f.

[5] i.e. in taking the meaning 'to fetch' or 'to receive in order to give'; *supra*, p. 16n. Abbot (op. cit., p. 112) regards it as an ancient Jewish interpretation. Cf. A. Edersheim, *Prophecy and History in Relation to the Messiah*, London, 1885, pp. 116f: 'For popular use the Scriptures were no longer quoted in the Hebrew, which was not spoken, or from the LXX, which was under the Rabbinic ban, but *targumed*, rendered into the vernacular; the principle being very strongly expressed that in so doing, it was not the letter but the meaning of the passage which was to be given.'

[6] The LXX has παίζοντα and adds μετὰ Ἰσαὰκ . . ., perhaps indicating a lacuna in the MT. מצחק may mean either playing or mocking; Sarah's anger implies the latter. In this context, as in Exod. 32.6, the Midrash applies the word to idolatry not persecution; but the same narrative goes on to say that, while pretending to play, Ishmael shot arrows at Isaac. That Paul's analogy for the persecution of Christians by Jews rests on this tradition is rather doubtful, but there may be a common interpretive tradition through which the two are related.

hostility of their descendants, though the other may be present as well. The chronology (430 years) of Gal. 3.17 is possibly another instance of a mutual exegesis of an OT text (Exod. 12.40).[1]

As to more general themes, the classic quotations from Gen. 15.6 (Rom. 4.3) and Hab. 2.4 (Rom. 1.17) occur in rabbinic literature, occasionally together, but with a different import.[2] In *DSH* the interpretation of Hab. 2.4 is much closer to the NT concept, viz. deliverance from judgment through faith in the Teacher of Righteousness.[3] Philo's words also show a remarkable similarity to Pauline thought: 'For the soul, clinging in utter dependence on a good hope, and deeming that things not present are beyond question already present by reason of the sure stedfastness of Him that promised them, has won as its meed faith, a perfect good; for we read a little later "Abraham believed God" (Gen. 15.6).'[4]

MESSIANIC CONSCIOUSNESS

The messianism of pre-Christian Judaism is quite germane to Paul's use of the OT even though it stands only as a shadow to the reality. The whole secret of the Christology of the NT, writes Gunkel, lies in the fact that it was the Christology of pre-Christian Judaism.[5] In the rabbis it was a standing principle to refer the predictions of the prophets to the 'days of the

[1] Paul's chronology is in accord with the LXX, Samaritan Pentateuch, and Jubilees. Actually, as Kahle (*Cairo Geniza*, pp. 337ff) points out, this is probably a textual rather than hermeneutical tradition. Cf. Burton, op. cit., pp. 183f.

[2] e.g. Exod. R. XXXIII, 5 (*SMR*, III, p. 284): Abraham believed God (Gen. 15.6) and Israel inherited this faith (Hab. 2.4); therefore through Abraham's merit Israel sings in the Messianic Age. Mak. 24a (*SBT*, p. 173): The myriad of Torah injunctions are reduced by the prophets; e.g. Isaiah reduced them to two principles, to do justice and righteousness (Isa. 56.1), and Habakkuk to one, the righteous shall live in his faith (Hab. 2.4). However, as Strack points out, these are not contrary to justification by works; faith itself is viewed as a work; cf. *SBK*, III, p. 186; cf. O. Michel, *Römerbrief*, Göttingen, 1955, pp. 48f.

[3] Cf. Dupont-Sommer, op. cit., p. 44. It is true that *DSH* refers this 'to all those who practise the law', but this need not involve a syncretism any more than the NT's usage, e.g. John 5.29; Rom. 7.16; 8.7, 13; 1 John 3.7. Dupont-Sommer (op. cit., pp. 63f) identifies the Master of Justice with the Messiah in the Zadokite Fragments, but that work evidently distinguishes them (Zad. Frag. 9.29; *CAP*, II, p. 820).

[4] Philo, *de. migr. Abr.*, 43f (Colson, IV, p. 157).

[5] H. Gunkel, *Zur religionsgeschichtlichen Verstandnis des Neuen Testament*, p. 93, quoted in B. B. Warfield, 'The Divine Messiah in the OT', *Princeton Theological Review*, XIV (July 1916), p. 377.

Messiah',[1] and this principle is almost always in evidence in Paul's interpretations. In apocalyptic writings, besides *DSS*, the Testament of Levi 18.1ff (*CAP*, II, pp. 314f) gives important information for messianic doctrine in late Judaism.[2]

Coming to specific Pauline quotations, one finds that Ps. 17.49ff (Rom. 15.9) is explained messianically in the Midrash,[3] as evidently is Isa. 52.12 (2 Cor. 6.17).[4] The frequently used Ps. 110 (cf. Rom. 8.34; 1 Cor. 15.25; Eph. 1.20; Col. 3.1) is also referred to the Messiah,[5] but the most usual rabbinic application is to Abraham.[6] The Talmud applies Isa. 59.19f (Rom. 11.26) and Isa. 11.2 (cf. Rom. 15.12 on Isa. 11.10) to messianic times[7]; the Targum also interprets the latter chapter of the Messiah, and this is probably its meaning in the significant passage, Isa. 28.16 (Rom. 10.11).[8]

Taken as a whole, however, such parallels are not frequent, and where they do occur, are only partial. Almost a century ago Westcott examined the question and found that of ninety-four passages quoted messianically in the NT only forty-four were interpreted in the same manner in Jewish writings; there are few revisions of that estimate to be made today.[9] Whether there were changes for controversial purposes[10] or whether the extant rabbinic literature just does not stand in the main stream of messianic Judaism, one cannot be certain. In the light of

---

[1] Cf. C. H. Dodd, *The Apostolic Preaching and its Developments*, London, 1936, p. 37; Ber. 34b (*SBT*, p. 215).

[2] Cf. M. Black, 'The Messiah in the Testament of Levi, XVIII', *ET*, 60 (1948-49), pp. 321f. The presence of fragments of the 'Testaments' in *DSS* evidently points to their pre-Christian origin (cf. Vincent Taylor's comment in *ET*, 66 (December 1954), p. 76). For further NT parallels cf. Edersheim, *Jesus the Messiah*, II, pp. 710-37.

[3] Lam. R. I, 16, 51 (*SMR*, VII, p. 138).

[4] Exod. R. XV, 18 (*SMR*, VII, p. 183).

[5] Gen. R. LXXX, 9 (*SMR*, II, p. 795). Edersheim (*Jesus the Messiah*, II, p. 720) finds other messianic applications of the Psalm, but he overstates the case in saying that it is 'throughout applied to the Messiah'.

[6] Lev. R. XXV, 6 (*SMR*, IV, p. 320); Gen. R. XXXIX, 8 (*SMR*, I, p. 316); Ned. 32b (*SBT*, p. 99); Sanh, 108b (*SBT*, p. 747).

[7] Sanh. 98a, 93b (*SBT*, pp. 626, 663).

[8] J. F. Stenning, *The Targum of Isaiah*, Oxford, 1949, pp. 40, 88: Isa. 28. 16 'concerns a strong king in Zion under whom the believing righteous are not to be dismayed'. Rashi takes it to mean the Messiah; cf. Edersheim, *Jesus the Messiah*, II, p. 725.

[9] B. F. Westcott, *An Introduction to the Study of the Gospels*, Cambridge, 1860, p. 144. A. Vis (*Messianic Psalm Quotations in the New Testament*, Amsterdam, 1939) finds virtually no trace of parallel rabbinic interpretations.

[10] Edersheim, *Jesus the Messiah*, II, p. 710.

Jewish apocalyptic, one suspects that both reasons are true.
There are general parallels of messianic interpretation between
Jewish writings and the NT, and undoubtedly these provided a
bridge for many Jews to accept Jesus as the Messiah.[1] But the
main sources for Paul's messianic interpretations of the OT are
the principles and emphases received from the apostolic tradition and his own exegesis of the OT as a Christian. One would
find it hard to root this element of his thought immediately in
Judaism.

THE DOCTRINE OF THE FALL

The Pauline interpretation of the early passages of Genesis
has been compared with Jewish thought in several respects:
(1) Adam's sin as affecting his posterity; (2) the occasion of the
Fall as involving Eve's chastity; (3) the male alone as the δόξα
of God; (4) the Adam-Christ typology as a Gnostic or Philonic
doctrine of the Heavenly Man.

The *locus classicus* of Paul's doctrine of the Fall is Rom. 5.12ff.[2]
Although the passage is celebrated as having enunciated the
principle of original sin, this was not Paul's primary purpose at
all. The immediate question asked how one could be made
righteous by the merit or act of Christ. To answer this Paul
drew the classic analogy of Adam and Christ; as all ἐν τῷ ᾿Αδάμ
had been involved in the sin and death of Adam, so all ἐν τῷ
Χριστῷ were involved in the righteousness and life of Christ.
The analogy is based upon an extension of the OT doctrine of
temporal solidarity to a matter of eternal significance.[3] The
logical progression is as follows[4]:

1. Death is the penalty of sin.
2. Sin is not counted if there is no law.
3. Yet death came upon people before the law of Moses was
   given.

[1] The cases of Simeon and Anna (Luke 2.25ff, 36ff) are not in point since theirs
was a supernatural revelation. Charles (*CAP*, II, p. 794) suggests that the beliefs
and emphases of the Zadokites (=Qumranites?) makes it not improbable that they
were among the 'great company of the priests' (Acts 6.7) who became Christians.
[2] It is implicit in 1 Cor. 15.21f as well.
[3] Cf. E. E. Ellis, 'The Biblical Concept of the Solidarity of the Human Race as
Seen in Blessing and Punishment', unpublished B.D. Thesis, Wheaton College
Graduate School, 1953, pp. 58-76.
[4] Rom. 5.12ff; cf. Gen. 2.17; 3.17, 19.

4. Death even came upon people who did not sin in the way Adam did, that is, upon infants who had not sinned against the law of conscience or of natural or special revelation.[1]

5. Hence, their death is the result of Adam's sin.

In the rabbinic doctrine of the *yetzer hara* (יצר הרע) or evil impulse and in the apocalyptic writings the effect of Adam's sin on his posterity is, as in Paul, clearly present.[2]

'For though it was thou [Adam] who sinned, the fall was not thine alone, but ours also who are thy descendants' (4 Ezra 7.118; *CAP*, II, p. 591).

'God created man for incorruption . . . , but by the envy of the Devil death entered into the world, and they that belong to this realm experience it' (Wisdom 2.23; *CAP*, I, p. 538).

'When [Adam] saw that through him death was ordained as a punishment, he spent 130 years in fasting . . . ' (Er. 18b; *SBT*, p. 127).

'When Adam sinned and death was decreed against those who should be born, then the multitude of those who should be born was numbered' (2 Baruch 23.4; *CAP*, II, p. 495).

'From a woman did sin originate, and because of her we all must die' (Sirach 25.24; *CAP*, I, p. 402).

'For though Adam first sinned and brought untimely death upon all, yet of those who were born from him each one has prepared for his own soul torment to come, and again each one of them has chosen for himself glories to come . . . Adam is therefore not the cause, save only of his own soul, but each of us has been the Adam of his own soul' (2 Baruch 54.15, 19; *CAP*, II, pp. 511f).[3]

As is evident in the above selections, the doctrine received much more emphasis in the apocalyptic writings than in the rabbis. Thackeray, holding that Rom. 5.12ff teaches only an

---

[1] Cf. Gen. 6.5. This is not explicitly so stated but seems to be reasonably inferred.

[2] See Thackeray, *Paul and Jewish Thought*, pp. 30-40; F. R. Tennant, *The Sources of the Doctrine of the Fall and Original Sin*, Cambridge, 1903, pp. 145-234; Weber, op. cit., pp. 218ff. Tennant (pp. 169-76), *contra* Weber, finds very little evidence for associating the doctrine of the *yetzer hara* specifically with the effects of Adam's sin.   [3] Cf. 4 Ezra 3.21, 26f.

inherited moral corruption and *liability* to sin, finds this passage in general agreement with current Jewish thought.[1] Tennant also concludes that Paul connects sinfulness with the Fall in an undefined way.[2] In any case, the *yetzer hara* of the rabbis in no way inhibits man's free will or his capacity to control his evil inclinations; 'herein lies the main difference between the teaching of the synagogues and that of the church'.[3]

Some rabbis may have regarded death as something more than a natural consequence arising from Adam's sin, but there is little support for an involvement in Adam's sin or guilt. Paul, on the other hand, definitely places the condemnation ($\kappa\alpha\tau\acute{\alpha}$-$\kappa\rho\iota\mu\alpha$) for Adam's sin upon all and concludes that through his disobedience 'many were constituted ($\kappa\alpha\theta\acute{\iota}\sigma\tau\eta\mu\iota$) sinners'.[5] Granting the importance of man's responsibility in Paul's theology, it is difficult to agree with Thackeray's view of Rom. 5.12ff.[6] The very ground of the analogy depends upon some sort of involvement in Adam's sin and guilt; whatever the deficiencies of the Federal and Augustinian theories, this much they recognise. The passage seems better understood on the basis of a solidarity relationship grounded in the nature of man and the world order. But any explanation which views man's guilt as Adam's disobedience *plus* his own sin must either ignore the very point of the analogy or regard righteousness as accruing from Christ's obedience *plus* man's own good works. This surely is not what Paul had in mind.

In conclusion, Paul is in general agreement with his contemporaries in attributing the presence of death to the consequence of Adam's sin. But in explaining this as a punishment accruing through a solidarity relationship and gathering from it the rationale under which God makes men righteous, the apostle goes far beyond anything in Jewish literature.

---

[1] Thackeray, *Paul and Jewish Thought*, p. 37. Contrast *CAP*, I, p. 402.

[2] Tennant, op. cit., p. 267. Contrast N. P. Williams, *The Ideas of the Fall and of Original Sin*, London, 1927, pp. 123ff.

[3] Tennant, op. cit., pp. 175f. The *yetzer hara* evidently does not enter into the constitutive nature or will of man but acts as an external force upon a weakened or susceptible nature. Sometimes it is equated with Satan. e.g. B. B. 16a (*SBT*, p. 79); cf. Yoma 69b (*SBT*, pp. 327f.).

[4] e.g. Er. 18b.

[5] Rom. 5.16, 18f.

[6] The words $\dot{\epsilon}\phi'$ $\ddot{\omega}$, whatever their precise connotation, are not the decisive element in the passage.

The Nature of Eve's Sin

In Jewish writings there are several instances in which lust for Eve is viewed as Satan's motive in tempting man.[1] Compare, for example, Yeb. 103b (*SBT*, p. 711): 'When the serpent copulated with Eve, he infused her with lust.' A similar thought is found in Sotah 9b (*SBT*, p. 40): '[The serpent] said, I will kill Adam and marry Eve.'[2] However, in other cases the motive is malice,[3] or when lust is cited, it is viewed as an effect on the race resulting from the eating of the fruit rather than the occasion of the Fall[4]; with few, if any, exceptions the Genesis account of the 'fruit' is accepted in literal fashion.[5]

The writings cited above are quite late; and when one attempts to trace the roots of the legend into the first century its character becomes very tenuous. The fullest account of the temptation in the earlier writings is in the Apocalypse of Moses, xv-xxii (*CAP*, II, pp. 145ff), where Eve recounts the events: The serpent climbed the tree and, coating the fruit with the poison of lust, he bent the branch for Eve to eat. She, in accordance with her oath, gave the fruit to Adam. The story (with some Christian theologians) identifies lust—in the general, not necessarily sexual sense—as the root of all sin; and perhaps it is the source of the rabbinical idea of lust being injected into Eve. But only with the most forced and unrealistic symbolics can Eve's chastity be brought into question. Nor do the phrases elsewhere that Satan deceived or seduced Eve or that Eve hearkened to the serpent ordinarily involve more than the Genesis account.[6] The only first century (?) document even

---

[1] *SBK*, III, p. 525; Weber, op. cit., p. 219.

[2] Cf. Gen. R. XVIII, 6 (*SMR*, I, p. 147). The story that Adam and Eve cohabited with demons after the Fall is irrelevant. Cf. Gen. R. XXXIV, 6 (*SMR*, I, p. 203); Gen. 5.3.

[3] Shab. 63a (*SBT*, p. 299); cf. Wisdom 2.24 (*CAP*, I, p. 538).

[4] Apoc. Mosis xv-xxii (*CAP*, II, pp. 145ff); cf. Shab. 146a (*SBT*, p. 738); A. Z. 22b (*SBT*, p. 114).

[5] e.g. Sanh. 29a (*SBT*, p. 178); A. Z. 5b (*SBT*, p. 22).

[6] 2 Enoch 31.6, 2 Baruch 48.42 (*CAP*, II, pp. 451, 507). Cf. G. Friedlander, *Perke de Rabbi Eliezer*, London, 1916, pp. 97ff. Protevangelium 13.1 (second century) is an exception: On learning of Mary's pregnancy Joseph reflects the legend in expressing his fears: 'Is not the story of Adam repeated in me? For as at the hour of his giving thanks the serpent came and found Eve alone and deceived her, so has it befallen me also.' (M. R. James, *The Apocryphal New Testament*, Oxford, 1953, p. 44.)

slightly resembling the later talmudic tractate[1] is 4 Macc. 18.6 (*CAP*, II, p. 684), and it is not at all certain that the allusion is to the Fall. There, speaking of her chastity, a woman says that 'no beguiling serpent sullied the purity of my maidenhood'.

The rabbinic fable has been suggested as lying behind Paul's thought in 2 Cor. 11.2f, 11.[2] Paul declares that he has espoused the Church as a chaste virgin to Christ; but he fears that 'as the serpent beguiled (ἐξηπάτησεν)[3] Eve by his subtility (πανουργία)'[4] so also the Church might be led away from Christ. The analogy, false apostles : Church :: serpent : Eve, is made in a context in which conjugal loyalty forms the setting, at least for one side of the equation. That this figure of conjugal loyalty should find its realisation in the sin of Eve would not only be in keeping with the analogy but would also heighten and amplify its effect considerably.[5] Satan's recognised power to tempt to incontinency[6] and the admonition for women to veil themselves 'because of the angels'[7] are noted as generally supporting the idea in 2 Cor. 11, but for establishing the specific nature of Eve's temptation they are gratuitous.

If the legend had had general currency in the first century, and if Paul's analogy of Eve and the Church were confined to this instance, the case for their connexion would be virtually absolute.[8] However, it is probable that the lust-laden apple of

---

[1] i.e. Yeb. 103b (*SBT*, p. 711). This is the only talmudic reference which actually states that Eve had intercourse with Satan. Thackeray (*Paul and Jewish Thought*, p. 50) gives one other which says that Cain is the offspring of Eve and Satan (Jalk. Schim. Beresch. 42). Other passages only cite Satan's lust for Eve as the motive for his desire to secure Adam's death through sin.

[2] Thackeray, *Paul and Jewish Thought*, pp. 50ff. 1 Tim. 2.13f is also cited but is not in point; that the woman was the one deceived is no more than a reasonable deduction from the Genesis account.

[3] Cf. Philo, *leg. alleg.*, III, 59 (Colson, I, p. 341).   [4] Not ἐπιθυμία; cf. 1 Cor. 3.19.
[5] Viz. unfaithful Church : Christ :: unfaithful Eve : Adam.   [6] 1 Cor. 7.5.
[7] 1 Cor. 11.10. The reference is to good, possibly guardian angels (cf. Matt. 18.10; Acts 12.15), not evil angelic powers (cf. 2 Pet. 2.4; Jude 6, 14), whose influence over Christians was forever abolished by Christ's victory (cf. G. H. C. MacGregor, 'Principalities and Powers: The Cosmic Background of Paul's Thought', *New Testament Studies*, I, 1 : September 1954, pp. 22f). Gen. 6.2 (LXX-A: οἱ ἄγγελοι τοῦ θεοῦ) is not in point; the meaning is, rather, that the flouting of this mark of subjection is offensive not only to their fellow Christians but also to the angels present. Cf. Ps. 137(138).1 LXX; Luke 12.8, 9; 15.7, 10; A. Robertson and A. Plummer. *First Epistle of St Paul to the Corinthians*, Edinburgh, 1911, pp. 233f; *SBK*, III, pp. 437f.

[8] It is only used in illustration in any case, but it implies a credulity and fancy that elsewhere sets Paul apart from the rabbis. Also, Paul often couches important teaching in just such analogous form, e.g. Rom. 5.12ff.

the Apocalypse of Moses only later emerged as the unchaste Eve. Stories of sexual intercourse with angelic beings in the pre-Flood age were not unusual, but there is little if any first century material ascribing to this the occasion of Eve's temptation.

Assuming the limited use of the fable in the first century, it does not follow that it is involved in Paul's analogy. The Church as Christ's bride or virgin is a figure found elsewhere in Paul's letters[1]; this, plus the Pauline concept of Christ as the second Adam, gives an adequate basis for the comparison without any recourse to the legend. The emphasis Paul makes is not that as Eve committed a certain sin so the Church is in danger of the same offence, but, passively, as Eve was deceived by Satan speaking through the serpent so the Church is in danger of being deceived by Satan working through false apostles.[2] If the legend was in mind it would, of course, extend the force of the analogy, but there is not sufficient evidence, either in Jewish literature or in Paul, to warrant finding it in this passage.

THE PRIORITY OF THE MALE IN CREATION

Paul might agree with the little boy's maxim that 'girls are all right as long as they stay in their place', for the apostle had definite opinions on the place of women in the life of his Churches. Ordinarily his instructions are in application of a principle involved in the order of creation and in Eve's susceptivity in the first sin.[3] In 1 Cor. 11.7ff Paul comes into contact with a rabbinic tradition in declaring that man 'is the image ($\epsilon i \kappa \dot{\omega} \nu = $ צלם) and glory ($\delta \dot{o} \xi a = $ כבוד) of God, but the woman is the glory of the man'. The rabbis also make the point that 'the glory of the Holy One' is derived from the males[4] and woman is the man's glory.[5] It is worth noting that Paul, like the rabbis, contrasts the sexes as to $\delta \dot{o} \xi a$ not as to $\epsilon i \kappa \dot{\omega} \nu$, which Gen. 1.27 ascribes to both. The view is not contrary to the

---

[1] Eph. 5.30ff; cf. Matt. 25.1ff; Rev. 19.7.
[2] 2 Cor. 11.13ff.   [3] 1 Cor. 11.8; 1 Tim. 2.13f.
[4] Num. R. III, 8. (SMR, V, p. 81) on Num. 3.15. Perhaps Paul would not go along with the included attitude of resignation that sons are a heritage from the Lord (Ps. 126(127).3), 'and if females come, they also are a reward'.
[5] Rashi on Isa. 44.13; cf. SBK, III, pp. 424, 435; Moore, op. cit., I, p. 449.

general tenor of the Genesis narrative (the probable ultimate source), but it finds no explicit formulation there. It is probable, therefore, that Paul and the later rabbinical writings share a common exegetical tradition at this point.

THE DOCTRINE OF THE SECOND ADAM

In 1 Cor. 15.45 Paul, continuing the earlier (v. 22) Adam-Christ typology, distinguishes between the natural man ($\psi\upsilon\chi\grave{\eta}\nu$ $\zeta\tilde{\omega}\sigma\alpha\nu$) and the immortalising spirit ($\pi\nu\epsilon\tilde{\upsilon}\mu\alpha$ $\zeta\omega o\pi o\iota o\tilde{\upsilon}\nu$). His quotation (Gen. 2.7) is quite free and the latter half is entirely missing from the OT text.[1] The former is named $\acute{o}$ $\pi\rho\tilde{\omega}\tau o\varsigma$ $\check{\alpha}\nu\theta\rho\omega\pi o\varsigma$ $'A\delta\grave{\alpha}\mu$ and the latter $\acute{o}$ $\check{\epsilon}\sigma\chi\alpha\tau o\varsigma$ $'A\delta\grave{\alpha}\mu$. Paul goes on to identify the last Adam as the 'Lord from heaven' and 'the heavenly one' ($\acute{o}$ $\epsilon\pi o\upsilon\rho\acute{\alpha}\nu\iota o\varsigma$, v. 48). The argument concludes: 'Mortality is the form or likeness of the first Adam . . .; Adam's descendants are involved in Adam's fate (v. 48). But we shall likewise participate in the destiny of the "heavenly one"; we shall bear his likeness by ourselves becoming immortal or heavenly beings (v. 49).'[2]

Philo (on Gen. 2.7) contrasts two types of men, a heavenly man ($o\upsilon\rho\acute{\alpha}\nu\iota o\varsigma$ $\check{\alpha}\nu\theta\rho\omega\pi o\varsigma$) and an earthly one ($\acute{o}$ $\gamma\acute{\eta}\ddot{\iota}\nu o\varsigma$).[3] The distinction is essentially Platonic[4] and based upon the repetitive Genesis account (Gen. 1.27; 2.7).[5] The first is a 'miniature heaven',[6] 'altogether without part or lot in corruptible and terrestrial substance'[7]; the earthly man is made of clay. Both are placed in the garden, but it is to $\acute{o}$ $\gamma\acute{\eta}\ddot{\iota}\nu o\varsigma$ that Eve is given and the present creation belongs.[8]

Paul's argument in 1 Cor. 15 has been interpreted as pointing to a Gnostic or Philonic view of the early Genesis narrative, but there are a number of objections to such an explanation. Paul never uses the term 'heavenly man' ($o\upsilon\rho\acute{\alpha}\nu\iota o\varsigma$ $\check{\alpha}\nu\theta\rho\omega\pi o\varsigma$), and his expression 'earthly one' ($\acute{o}$ $\chi o\ddot{\iota}\kappa\acute{o}\varsigma$) differs from Philo's. The use of Gen. 1.27 (1 Cor. 11.7) in connexion with 'earthly' men

---

[1] Supra, pp. 14f, 36f; infra, pp. 139ff.
[2] Black, 'Doctrine of the Second Adam', p. 171.
[3] Philo, leg. alleg., I, 31ff, 53ff, 88f (Colson, I, pp. 167ff, 181f, 205).
[4] Philo treats them as two distinct men, but at times it seems only to be a way of distinguishing the 'soul' and 'body' of man. Cf. Moore, op. cit., I, p. 452.
[5] Cf. Philo, de opific. mun., 69, 82 (Colson, I, pp. 55, 67).   [6] Ibid.
[7] Philo, leg. alleg., I, 31 (Colson, I, p. 167).
[8] Ibid., I, 53f; II, 4f (Colson, I, pp. 181, 227).

thwarts any suggestion that the apostle shares a Philonic view of double creation. Furthermore, the sequence which Paul gives (earthly—heavenly) is antithetical to Philo's picture (heavenly—earthly); Christ, for Paul, is the last Adam, the head of a new race. Black evaluates the relation of Paul and Philo at this point: 'If the Apostle was familiar with Philonic or pre-Philonic teaching, he is interpreting it in terms of his own mystical experience of the risen Christ. Or rather, he is making restrained and cautious use of current *theologumena* to give expression to his own Christology.'[1]

It is a baseless conjecture to equate Paul's second Adam in I Cor. 15 with the Gnostic figure of *Ur-mensch*.[2] As Manson well points out, if Paul knew of a tradition identifying Messiah and *Ur-mensch*, he does not take over the idea but rather opposes it (v. 46f).[3] It is not *Ur-mensch* but 'the second man' or ὁ μέλλων Ἀδάμ (Rom. 5.14) who is the Lord from heaven. In Stewart's strongly worded indictment, 'Paul's great thought of the eternal Christ owes nothing whatsoever to the picture of the "Heavenly Man" in the Book of Enoch or elsewhere; it is sheer blindness and banality to suggest, as has not been infrequently done, that a mechanical equating of Jesus with the ready made concepts of a pre-Christian Messianism was the origin of Paul's glowing and inspired Christology'.[4] The Gnostic conception of a Heavenly Man, Black concludes, ' . . . so far as it can be regarded as "pre-Christian", proves on closer examination to be largely a reconstruction from sources some as late as Islamic times, others even later. . . . there is no unequivocal evidence pointing to the existence of such a conception in pre-Christian sources, particularly within Judaism.'[5]

THE ANGELS AT SINAI

Apart from the early chapters of Genesis there are several other similarities in Pauline and Jewish exegesis which merit consideration in some detail. The rôle of angels in the giving of

---

[1] Black, 'Doctrine of the Second Adam', p. 171. Cf. Vollmer, op. cit., pp. 54f.
[2] Cf. J. Weiss, *Der Erste Korintherbrief*, Göttingen, 1925, p. 375; R. Reitzenstein, *Die Hellenistischen Mysterienreligionen*, Leipzig, 1927, pp. 346ff. For a criticism of Reitzenstein cf. W. Manson, *Jesus the Messiah*, London, 1943, pp. 174ff and his bibliography.
[3] Ibid., pp. 188f.   [4] J. S. Stewart, op. cit., p. 48.
[5] Black, 'Doctrine of the Second Adam', p. 177.

the law, the legend of the following rock, and the interpretation of 'seed' in Gal. 3.16 are three cases in point.

In the first instance Paul states in Gal. 3.19 that the law was enacted (διαταγείς) 'through the agency of angels in the hands of a mediator', i.e. Moses[1]; the promise, in contrast, was given directly to Abraham by God. The presence of angels at Sinai is mentioned occasionally in Jewish writings and in the NT,[2] and is evidently based upon Ps. 67(68).18(17).[3] The LXX text in Deut. 33.2, which has the reading ἄγγελοι μετ' αὐτοῦ, discloses the same picture. The Hebrew text is unclear; if the LXX reading is not correct, it may well give an ancient exegetical gloss on the Hebrew קדש.[4] In any event its place in the LXX and the Psalms points to a very ancient interpretation of the passage and obviates any reference on Paul's part to Jewish writings. Both got it from a common source, the OT, and the rabbinical accretions find no place in Paul's text.

THE FOLLOWING ROCK

In the Exodus typology of 1 Cor. 10.1ff Paul speaks of a spiritual rock which followed (πνευματικῆς ἀκολουθούσης πέτρας) the Israelites in the wilderness and identifies this rock with Christ. There is a cumulative legend in rabbinic literature to which the Pauline phrase has been related in one degree or another.[5] Thackeray, who is certain that Paul has this legend in mind, traces the source of the tradition to a targumic interpretation of Num. 21.17.[6] It does appear that, throughout, the rabbinic references to the legend have to do almost exclusively with this text.[7]

[1] Cf. Burton, op. cit., pp. 189f.
[2] e.g. Acts 7.38, 53; Heb. 2.2; cf. Col. 2.14f; Shab. 88 (SBT, pp. 417f, 421f); Josephus, Antiquities, XV, 5, 3, trans. W. Whiston, London,1906, p. 454; Exod. R. XXIX, 2 (SMR, III, pp. 337f); Num. R. XI, 3, 7 (SMR, V, pp. 419, 443); cf. SBK, III, pp. 554ff. According to Sanh. 38b (SBT, p. 245) God consults his angels on all things; cf. Jub. 2.1 (CAP, II, p. 13). In Exod. R. XXVIII, 1 (SMR, III, p. 31) the angels are depicted as opposing the giving of the Law; cf. Shab. 88b (SBT, pp. 421f).   [3] Cf. F. Delitzsch, The Psalms, London, 1888, II, p. 296.
[4] Cf. Puukko, op. cit., p. 80.
[5] Envelopment in the cloud (1 Cor. 10.1f) is also mentioned in Jewish sources; however, Paul's reference probably stems directly from an interpretation of Exod. 40.34, 38 or Ps. 104(105).39. Cf. Wisdom 10.17; Josephus, Antiquities, III, §79 (Thackeray, IV, p. 355); Ta. 9a (SBT, p. 38).
[6] Thackeray, Paul and Jewish Thought, pp. 205ff; cf. Targ. Onkelos on Num. 21 (Etheridge, p. 300).
[7] Lev. R. X, 9 (SMR, IV, 134) on Num. 20.10 most probably does not refer to the well.

In full flower the legend went somewhat as follows[1]: A movable well, rock-shaped and resembling a sieve, was given to the Israelites in the desert. As to origin, it was one of the ten things created on the evening of the Sixth Day. About the size of an oven or beehive, it rolled along after the wanderers through hills and valleys, and when they camped it settled at the tent of meeting. When the princes called, 'Rise up, O well' (Num. 21.17), water flowed from its many openings as from a flask.[2] The well performed many services. Occasionally it gave everyone a drink at the door of his tent.[3] Sending forth a river of water to the sea, it brought back all the delights of the world.[4] The fertile ground along its banks grew grass which served as an effective deodorant[5]; fruits, vegetables and trees which produced a perfume for the women also grew along its course.[6] The water, too, had healing properties for all who used it.[7] Though no larger than a beehive, this devoted servant of Israel once swelled up and filled a whole valley; thus it killed and collected the bones of Israel's enemies in a victory not equalled since the Red Sea swallowed Pharaoh.[8] At the death of Miriam the well dried up and disappeared, for it was given for her merit.[9] But for the sake of the Patriarchs it was restored, and continued with the Israelites until they reached the Sea of Tiberias; there it found its final resting place. And if one has clear eyes, he can stand on a summit and see its reflection in the depths to this day.[10]

Such is the story of the 'well'. There seem to be two distinct strands of tradition—the following beehive or rock and the

---

[1] This synthetic reconstruction naturally has no facsimile in the rabbinic material.

[2] Tosephta Sukka 3, 11ff (*SBK*, III, pp. 406f); Num. R. I, 2 (*SMR*, V, pp. 4f); Shab. 35a (*SBT*, p. 164); Num. R. XIX, 26 (*SMR*, VI, p. 777); Aboth V, 6 (*SBT*, p. 63); Pes. 54a (*SBT*, pp. 264, 267).

[3] Targ. Jerus. on Num. 21 (Etheridge, p. 412).

[4] Tosephta Sukka 3, 11ff (*SBK*, III, p. 406).

[5] Deut. R. VI, 11 (*SMR*, VII, p. 145).

[6] S. S. R. 12.3; 14.1 (*SMR*, IX, pp. 223, 225).

[7] Num. R. XVIII, 22 (*SMR*, VI, p. 742); Eccl. R. V., 8, 5 (*SMR*, VIII, pp. 143f).

[8] Num. R. XIX, 25 (*SMR*, VI, pp. 773ff).

[9] Ta. 9a (*SBT*, p. 38); Lev. R. XXVII, 6 (*SMR*, IV p. 351); Num. R. I, 2 (*SMR*, V, pp. 4f); S. S. R. 5.2; 12.3 (*SMR*, IX, pp. 200, 223); cf, Num. 20.1f: 'And Miriam died . . . and there was no water.'

[10] Shab. 35a (*SBT*, p. 164); Lev. R. XXII, 4 (*SMR*, IV, p. 282); Num. R. XVIII, 22; XIX, 26 (*SMR*, VI, pp. 742, 777). ·

following stream; the latter is probably the earlier of them. The
Targum of Onkelos is not clear in this regard[1]; Midrash Sifre
(c. A.D. 125?) on Num. 11.21 is certainly in the 'stream' tradition: 'Did not a brook follow them in the wilderness and
provide them with fat fish more than they needed?'[2] Pseudo-
Philo (c. A.D. 100?) strikes a similar note.[3] It is quite difficult
to determine the precise character of the fable in the first
century; apart from the above-mentioned sources there is little
evidence.[4] Certainly the rabbinical references are not lacking
(as in the case of Eve's temptation), and their abundance points
to the early existence of the legend in some form. The story
grew erratically with each writer so as to preclude any definite
classification at a given date, but it is probable that the first
century version spoke only of a following stream of water.
While the well is mentioned in two late accounts[5] as being in
the shape of a rock or crag (סלע), it is nowhere called a rock;
also, 'it is to be noticed that the legend is based entirely upon
the well of Num. 21.17f and is unrelated either with the rock
(צור) of Exod. 17.5f or with the crag (סלע) of Num. 20.7-11
(though it is brought into connexion with the latter by some
later writers, e.g. Rashi)'.[6]

Between 1 Cor. 10.1ff and the Well Legend there are one or
two points of comparison. Both refer to water from which
Israel drank, Paul from one passage (Exod. 17.6; cf. Num.
20.7ff) and the legend from another (Num. 21.16ff; cf. Exod.
15.23ff). Paul speaks of a 'spiritual following rock' in the
wilderness; the legend concerns a following stream or, later, a
rock-shaped well. The correspondence is not especially close,

[1] Etheridge, op. cit., p. 300: ' . . . and from [the time] that it was given to them
it descended with them to the rivers, and from the rivers it went up with them to
the height.'

[2] Levertoff, op. cit., p. 77. On its ancient origin see pp. viiif.

[3] M. R. James, *The Biblical Antiquities of Philo*, London, 1917, pp. 7, 105ff:
' . . . well of water following them, brought He forth for them' (X, 7); ' . . . The
water of Marah was made sweet and followed them in the desert forty years, and
went up into the hills and came down into the plains . . .' (XI, 15 on Exod. 15.23).

[4] The supposed connexion of the Targum on Isa. 16.1 with the legend is quite
improbable: 'They shall bring tribute to the anointed one of Israel, who has pre-
vailed over him who was as a wilderness . . .' (J. F. Stenning, *The Targum of
Isaiah*, Oxford, 1949, p. 52).

[5] Num. R. I, 2 (*SMR*, V, pp. 4f); Tosephta Sukka 3,11f (*SBK*, III, pp. 406f).
The Midrash Rabbah is very late, probably twelfth century (*SMR*, I, p. vii).

[6] S. R. Driver, 'Notes on Three Passages in St Paul's Epistles', *The Expositor*,
Third Series, IX (1889), p. 17.

but the phraseology, 'spiritual following rock', is peculiar enough to be suggestive. When the story of a following stream exists in a closely parallel context, some relationship is not altogether improbable. Certainly the adoption of such a puerile fable would be 'totally out of harmony' with the character of Paul's mind.[1] But Driver's suggestion of a merely verbal relationship is a possible explanation: 'St Paul views the water which the Israelites drank in the wilderness as provided for them by Christ in his pre-existent Divine nature, who attended and watched over his people, whom he represents under the figure of a rock, accompanying them through their journeyings. The particular expression chosen by the apostle may have been *suggested* to him by his acquaintance with the legend current among the Jews; but it is evident that he gives it an entirely different application, and that he uses it not in a literal sense, but figuratively.'[2]

However the relationship may not be so direct as Driver supposed. The word-play of the Targum of Onkelos on Num. 21.16ff accounts for a part of the legend's inception, but it is not the ultimate or most important factor in the origin of the 'following stream' tradition. In Isaiah and the Psalms there are several references to the water from the rock:

' . . . the waters gushed out ($\epsilon\rho\rho\acute{u}\eta\sigma\alpha\nu$), and the streams overflowed' ($\kappa\alpha\tau\epsilon\kappa\lambda\acute{u}\sigma\theta\eta\sigma\alpha\nu$) (Ps. 77(78).20).

' . . . the waters gushed out and ran ($\epsilon\pi o\rho\epsilon\acute{u}\theta\eta\sigma\alpha\nu$) in the dry places like a river' (Ps. 104(105).41; cf. Ps. 113(114). 8).

' . . . and if they thirsted, through ($\delta\iota\acute{a}$) the desert he will bring ($\acute{a}\xi\epsilon\iota$) water to them . . . from the rock he will bring forth ($\acute{\epsilon}\xi\acute{a}\xi\epsilon\iota$) water to them . . . and the waters will gush out' (Isa. 48.21 LXX).

Each of these passages bears upon the same OT text that Paul alludes to in 1 Cor. 10. The $\epsilon\pi o\rho\epsilon\acute{u}\theta\eta\sigma\alpha\nu$ and $\delta\iota$ ' $\epsilon\rho\acute{\eta}\mu o\upsilon$ $\acute{a}\xi\epsilon\iota$ may well provide the origin for the 'following stream' tradition. 'Following rock' and 'following stream from the rock', are not an impossible equation; and taking into account the priority of the stream tradition in rabbinic material, this is a likely key

---

[1] Driver, op. cit., p. 18.
[2] Ibid. Cf. Deut. 32.4, 10ff, 15, 18, 30ff.

to the apostle's thought.[1] Such an interpretation could also
have provided the inspiration for the Targum's word-play on
another passage (Num. 21.16ff); if so, Paul and the Targum
are related more directly to a particular interpretation of the
passages by the prophets than to each other. The Targum,
applying it to Num. 21.16ff, either sets the legend in motion or
applies an inchoate form of it to this particular passage. Paul,
on the other hand, takes the prophetic description and employs
it for his own typological purpose.[2]

THE SEED OF ABRAHAM

No discussion of rabbinical affinities in the Pauline letters
would be complete without some reference to Gal. 3.16. Paul
has been arguing that the true children of Abraham are those
who share Abraham's faith and that any dependence upon the
law for righteousness is diametrically opposed to such a status
(Gal. 3.6f, 9ff). Furthermore, this Abrahamic righteousness is
available alike to Gentiles and Jews through Jesus Christ. The
apostle notes in verse 16 that the promises, upon which Israel's
hope of a future kingdom rested, were given to Abraham and
to his seed ($\tau\hat{\omega}$ $\sigma\pi\acute{\epsilon}\rho\mu\alpha\tau\iota$).[3] In halachic fashion, Paul points out
that God did not say 'to seeds' ($\tauο\hat{\iota}\varsigma$ $\sigma\pi\acute{\epsilon}\rho\mu\alpha\sigma\iota\nu$) as of many, but
'to his seed'; this seed is Christ, whom God has made the heir
of all things. The conclusion, then, is that all who belong to
Christ are Abraham's seed ($\sigma\pi\acute{\epsilon}\rho\mu\alpha$) and heirs according to the
promise (v. 29).

The distinction between the singular and the plural in Gal.
3.16 is paralleled in the Talmud; there can be little doubt that
the apostle agrees with rabbinic methods in this respect.[4] The

[1] Cf. P. Fairbairn, *The Typology of Scripture*, London, 1953, pp. 53ff.

[2] Beside Philo's equation of the rock with the wisdom or Word of God (Philo,
leg. alleg., II, 86; *quod. deter.*, 115ff; Colson, I, p. 279; II, pp. 279f) a further
parallel with 1 Cor. 10.4 has been observed in the figure of Metatron. The following presence of Metatron is compared to Paul's following presence of Christ; cf.
Sanh. 38b, (*SBT*, p. 246 on Exod. 33.15). A. Murtonen ('The Figure of Metatron',
VT, III (1953), pp. 409-11) concludes that the talmudic Metatron in origin and
evolution is a sort of Jewish counterpart to Jesus.

[3] See Burton's discussion (op. cit., pp. 505-10).

[4] e.g. Shab. 84b (*SBT*, p. 403) on Isa. 61.11: seed (of one kind) and seeds (of
diverse kinds); but in B. B. 19a (*SBT*, p. 98) the plural used is of the same kind of
seed. Sanh. 37a (*SBT*, pp. 233f) and Gen. R. XXII, 9 (*SMR*, I, p. 189) on
Gen. 4.10: blood of Abel and bloods of his descendants (=seeds: זֶרְעִיּוֹת).
Philo (and modern commentators for that matter) also argues from the use of a
singular; e.g. τέκνον in Gen. 17.16 (*de. mut. nom.*, 145ff; Colson, V, p. 217).

important question, however, is whether Paul in employing this grammatical exegesis indulges in an 'extremely fanciful and sophistical' argument.[1] The argument has been reconstructed thus: If Abraham's descendants were in view, a plural (e.g. זרעים) would be required; but God used the singular זרע. Therefore it *must* refer to one person, i.e. Christ. If this is Paul's argument, then it must be confessed that its baseless caprice out-rabbis the rabbis; only Akiba could applaud it and even he would substitute something more intricate. This view of the passage assumes that Paul the Hebrew was entirely ignorant of the fact that the singular זרע was used continually in the Hebrew (and Greek) OT as a collective denoting one's descendants,[2] and that the singular number, therefore, could not be determinative for his usage. Or it puts the apostle in the rôle of a charlatan fooling his audience with a bit of chicanery. But Paul was neither naïve nor deceitful; if anything is known of his character, certainly that is.

However, to dismiss an improbable exegesis does not determine the true meaning of the passage. Its problematic character is precisely the reason that the 'rabbinic artifice' explanation continues to serve as a simple alternative. Burton at length despairs of a solution and concludes that the text has been corrupted.[3]

The true significance of Paul's usage lies in the argument running throughout the chapter.[4] It is whether the 'faith' descendants or the 'law' descendants are the true seed; Paul argues that it is only to the former class of posterity that the promises belong. The Jews employ the same restricted use of 'seed' with regard to Isaac and Ishmael; Paul takes the collective character of the word to imply a class restriction of a different kind. 'A plural substantive would be inconsistent with the interpretation given; the singular collective if it admits of

---

[1] Thackeray, *Paul and Jewish Thought*, p. 70.

[2] Cf. Burton, op. cit., pp. 505f. The singular is sometimes used of an individual descendant or of a particular class or line of descendants (e.g. Gen. 4.25; 21.13; 1 Sam. 1.11; 2 Sam. 7.12; 1 Chron. 17.11). Among the later writings the plural 'seeds' is occasionally used to denote descendants. See Targ. Onkelos and Sanh. 37a (*SBT*, p. 233) on Gen. 4.10. The significance of the collective nature of זרע and σπέρμα for Paul's interpretation is no modern discovery; in 1650 Drusius (op. cit., p. 1316) noted the fact in his exegesis.

[3] Ibid., p. 509.

[4] The Sarah-Hagar allegory (Gal. 4.21ff) follows the same line of thought.

plurality (as it is interpreted by Paul himself, Rom. 4.18; 9.7),[1] at the same time it involves the idea of unity.'[2]

Although the seed of Abraham meant the Jewish people, this concept had a peculiar significance for Pauline and NT thought. Israel was embodied in Messiah, and the Christian community formed the remnant of true Israel. Not all were Jews who called themselves Jews (Rom. 2.28f; Rev. 2.9); the faith-less majority were as separate from the true posterity as were the descendants of Ishmael (Gal. 3.7; Rom. 9-11).[3] It was to the faith-seed that the promises belonged, and this class was determined not by physical descent but by faith-union with Messiah. Rom. 4.13 forms a fitting commentary on the Galatians passage: 'For the promise that he should be heir of the world was not to Abraham, *or to his seed*, through the law, but through the righteousness of faith.'[4] Even Abraham's heirship rested in this faith-union although its many messianic implications were as yet unrevealed. And so the conclusion, 'if ye be Christ's, then are ye Abraham's seed and heirs according to the promise'.

Burton rightly objects that to take the mere Χριστός in a corporate sense (of the body of Christ) or to take σπέρμα in an individual sense is contrary to Paul's usage elsewhere. However, it is probable that the use of Χριστός here is exceptional. To view Messiah in a corporate sense is not contrary to Paul or the OT.[5] The ἐν Χριστῷ relationship and the Adam-Christ typology involve a solidarity concept that may well be present in this passage also.

Paul was not unaware of the grammar; his point was that the grammar was aptly suited to contain his exegesis. The grammar

---

[1] And, in the course of the present argument, Gal. 3.29. Cf. Acts 3.25.

[2] Lightfoot, *Galatians*, p. 142.

[3] Paul makes some reservations in Rom. 11. The physical seed are beloved 'for the fathers' sake', and God will incorporate them once more, as a group, into the true Israel of faith. However, this is not in contrast to Paul's view elsewhere; the physical-seed has no separate inheritance but rather is made a part of the faith-seed. See *infra*, pp. 136ff.

[4] Cf. Rom. 9.6.

[5] Note especially the 'Servant of the Lord' passages in Isaiah. Israel was viewed in a corporate sense, and this 'corporate body' was—as Abraham's true 'seed'—finally embodied in the One, Jesus Christ; it is now in Him that the true Israel—Christ's 'body'—inheres. Cf. F. Delitzsch, *Isaiah*, Edinburgh, 1890, II, p. 236; O. Cullmann, *Christ and Time*, London, 1951, p. 116; T. W. Manson, *The Teaching of Jesus*, Cambridge, 1931, pp. 227ff; C. R. North, *The Suffering Servant in Deutero-Isaiah*, Oxford, 1948, pp. 44f, 215ff.

alone could never do more than circumscribe the meaning; while most often it was a collective denoting one's posterity in general, זֶרַע also represented a restricted class of posterity and sometimes even an individual. Paul found the true meaning of the promise by interpreting it of Christ. In the end, then, the passage does not involve a question of grammatical accuracy but of theological interpretation, and Paul's interpretation involves no rabbinical sophistry. He notes that it is a collective and not a simple plural, and within the limits of the grammar interprets it of Christ, or better, of that particular type of seed which is identified with and headed up in Christ.

In concluding the consideration of Pauline affinities with Judaism a few other similarities of interpretation should be noted. Paul takes Hos. 2.23; 1.10 (Rom. 9.25f) of judgment on Israel because of their rejection of Messiah, and sees in the remnant (the Messianic Community) the true sons of God. Similarly Zad. Frag. 9.40ff (*CAP*, II, p. 821) applies Hos. 3.4 to God's judgment of Israel for their rejection of the New Covenant; the Covenant Community, however, is to be blessed of God. Behind the thought of Luke 2.34a probably lies the texts of Isa. 8.14; 28.16 (Rom. 9.33)[1]; it may be that this points to a messianic use of the texts in pre-Christian Judaism. On the whole, however, agreements in thought are not frequent. Only about half a dozen of Paul's quotations are used with any frequency in the Talmud,[2] and about twenty are not found at all.

THE BEGGARLY ELEMENTS

When Paul warned Timothy and Titus to beware of Jewish fables and commandments of men (1 Tim. 1.4; Tit. 1.14; 3.9), no doubt he had in mind many of the things exemplified in the rabbinic literature. Although some of their exegesis is praiseworthy and sometimes ingenious in justifying good traditions or judicial rights, nevertheless its essential character is indeed 'weak and beggarly'.[3] Prat has well summarised it: 'In the slough of Apocryphal and rabbinical writings a few particles of gold can sometimes be met with, but with how much dross they

---

[1] M. Black, *An Aramaic Approach to the Gospels and Acts*, 2nd ed., Oxford, 1954, p. 114.
[2] Gen. 2.7 (1 Cor. 15.45); 2.24 (1 Cor. 6.16); Exod. 20.12-17 (Rom. 13.9; Eph. 6.2-3); Lev. 19.18 (Rom. 10.5); Deut. 19.15 (2 Cor. 13.1); 25.4 (1 Cor. 9.9).
[3] Gal. 4.9.

are combined.'[1] To realise the great gulf which separates Paul's use of the OT from that of the rabbis, one need only observe a few examples from talmudic literature:

1. 'The dust of the first man was gathered from all over the earth because Ps. 139.16 says God saw the unformed substance, and Zech. 4.10 says the eyes of the Lord run to and fro through the whole earth' (Sanh. 38b; *SBT*, p. 241).

2. 'That God says his prayers is proved when Isa. 56.7 says *my* (i.e. God's) house of prayer' (Ber. 7a; *SBT*, p. 30).

3. 'The laws of the Torah are suspended when life is endangered for Lev. 18.5 says "he shall live (not die) in them"' (Yom. 85b, *SBT*, pp. 421f; A. Z. 27b, *SBT*, p. 137; Chajes, op. cit., p. 198). Contrast Rom. 10.5; Gal. 3.12.

4. 'Why did Obadiah hide fifty prophets in the cave' (1 Kings 18.4)? 'Because the cave would only hold fifty' (Sanh. 39b; *SBT*, p. 253).

5. 'The first man had two faces because Ps. 139.5 says, "Thou hast formed me behind and before"' (Ber. 61a; *SBT*, p. 381).

6. 'The first man reached from earth to heaven because it says (Deut. 4.32), "since the day God created man upon the earth and from one end of the heaven"' (Sanh. 38b; *SBT*, p. 243).

7. 'As for prayer instructions, R. Shesheth bowed like a reed (i.e. abruptly) and came up like a serpent' (i.e. showily) (Ber. 12b; *SBT*, p. 69).

8. 'Whoever places his bed north and south will have male children because Ps. 17.14 says, "Whose belly thou fillest with treasure, who have sons in plenty".' Treasure, צפונד, also means north (Ber. 5b; *SBT*, p. 22).

9. 'Michael is greater than Gabriel because he reached his goal in one flight (Dan. 10.13) while Gabriel took two' (Dan. 9.21; 'fly' occurs twice) (Ber. 4b; *SBT*, p. 15).

10. 'Hos. 1.10 shows that the Holy One, blessed be He, having given vent to harsh utterances against Israel, could not stand it and relented in the same context' (Num. R. II, 16; *SMR*, V, 53). Contrast Rom. 9.26.

[1] Prat, op. cit., II, p. 357.

Although there are exceptions[1] and the above examples are particularly graphic, they are by no means untypical or extreme and can be adduced *ad infinitum et ad nauseam* from almost any section of the Talmud. The ruling principle of rabbinic exposition of Scripture is well expressed in Sanh. 34a (*SBT*, p. 214): 'A verse is capable of as many interpretations as splinters of a rock crushed by a hammer, for Jer. 23.29 says, "Like a hammer that breaketh a rock in pieces. . . ."'

Their splinterised, purposeless, speculative musings which 'suspend dogmatic mountains on textual hairs'[2] have not the remotest kinship with Paul's theology or hermeneutical principles. While some peripheral methodological procedures are held in common with the rabbis, it is no less than superficial and inept to write, as Johannes Weiss has done, that 'one must recognise a fixed, stereotyped rabbinical method as forming the basis of all the apostle's theological thinking. . . .'[3] The contrast which Bonsirven draws shows a much saner appreciation of the facts: The rabbis worshipped the letter and sought to justify their traditions by arbitrary exegesis; Paul's usage, on the other hand, is not arbitrary or against the literal sense if the typological usage be granted.[4] Toy sums up the rabbinic exegesis in the principle 'that every sentence and every word of the Scripture was credited with any meaning that it could possibly be made to bear. . . .'[5]

Concerning Paul's relation to Jewish thought Kennedy has given a better evaluation than most: 'It is indeed a current fashion to minimise his relation to the ancient Scriptures of his people, as compared with his indebtedness to the teachings of post-canonical Judaistic literature, in its various branches. . . . His writings reveal every here and there affinities with his

---

[1] Rabbinic juristic rulings are sometimes quite adroit; e.g. the *onus probandi* in a lawsuit falls on the plaintiff because Exod. 24.14 says, 'If any man have any matters to do, let him come to them.' Other rabbis object that this is only common sense; the real purpose of the verse is to show judges that they should give prior consideration to the petition of the plaintiff. Exception is then made if the defendant's property is in serious danger of depreciation (B. K. 46b; *SBT*, p. 264).

[2] F. W. Farrar, *The Life and Work of St Paul*, London, 1879, I, p. 49.

[3] Weiss, *Primitive Christianity*, p. 440. Toy (op. cit., p. xxiii) goes almost as far in equating NT exegesis with 'that of the Talmud only far more cautious and reserved . . .'.

[4] Bonsirven, op. cit., pp. 337f.

[5] Toy, op. cit., xxiii; For a more sympathetic appraisal of the rabbinic method cf. M. Kadushin, *The Rabbinic Mind*, New York, 1952, pp. 70ff.

native environment. But the remarkable fact remains that these affinities are largely superficial, that they disclose themselves at the circumference rather than at the centre of his thought.'[1]

PAUL'S USE OF NON-CANONICAL LITERATURE
GENERAL

The question of Paul's knowledge and use of Jewish Apocrypha has been debated since Eichhorn's introduction to apocryphal literature in 1795,[2] and it continues to be a matter of dispute. His knowledge of Palestinian writings in general circulation may be presumed; as for the literature of the *diaspora* the problem becomes more complex. In either case the question is quite theoretical if divorced from the question of Paul's use of this material in his writings. What writings were in general circulation? Which ones would be seen and used by a student for the rabbinate? To what extent does the extant literature represent the really 'important' literature of Paul's day, and for his party?

Paul's only non-canonical citations are from Greek literature; the use of Greek literary forms such as $\sigma\nu\nu\sigma\tauοιχεῖν$ (Gal. 4.25) and the Stoic diatribe evidence a probable acquaintance with Hellenistic writings.[3] Charles cites Pauline parallels with a number of apocrypha and pseudepigrapha,[4] but for the most part they are only in the nature of a similar phraseology. The agreements with Sirach are altogether of this type, displaying at best only such phrases as 'pass the flower of her age' (Sir. 42.9; 1 Cor. 7.36), or 'treasures of wisdom' (Sir. 1.25; Col. 2.3).[5]

In the apocalyptic books, Enoch (62.4), describing the judgment, speaks of 'pain . . . as on a woman in travail'; Paul (1 Thess. 5.3) similarly writes, 'destruction . . . as travail upon

[1] H. A. A. Kennedy, *St Paul's Conceptions of the Last Things*, London, 1904, pp. 43ff.
[2] J. G. Eichhorn, *Einleitung in die apokryphischen Schriften des Alten Testaments*, Leipzig, 1795.
[3] Cf. Puukko, op. cit., p. 35. These practices may, of course, have been common stock.
[4] Viz. Tobit, Wisdom, Enoch, Letter of Aristeas, Testaments of the Twelve Patriarchs, 4th Ezra (*CAP*, I, pp. 199, 526f; II, pp. 92, 163ff, 292, 559). Cf. M. R. James, op. cit., pp. 59f.
[5] Cf. Sir. 5.3 (1 Thess. 4.6); 7.34 (Rom. 12.15); 37.28 (1 Cor. 6.12). The affinities claimed by P. C. Spicq (*Les Epitres Pastorales*, Paris, 1947, pp. cxxxiff) are not very convincing. The least unlikely is a common sentiment on not trusting worldly riches (Sir. 5.2, 8; 1 Tim. 6.17).

a woman with child'. But the use of this figure elsewhere[1] suggests that it is only an idiom in common use. This is also true of other phrases such as 'according to his good pleasure' (Eph. 1.9; Enoch 49.4) and 'God blessed forever' (Rom. 9.5; cf. Enoch 77.1). Some parallels are more striking (e.g. 'the wrath of the Lord came upon them to the uttermost'; Test. Levi. 6.11; cf. 1 Thess. 2.16), but none warrant affirming a direct acquaintance.[2] Jowett is probably correct in regarding all Pauline similarities to apocalyptic writings as explainable on the supposition of a common source.[3]

In the light of the above observations Paul's use of non-canonical Jewish literature is very doubtful at best. There are, however, some Jewish writings whose correspondence with Paul extends beyond terminological resemblance. Of these, 4th Ezra, the Wisdom of Solomon, and Philo show the greatest number of similarities. The first is somewhat later than Paul, but the relation of the last two to the apostle has been a matter of some debate.

THE WISDOM OF SOLOMON

A short article by Eduard Grafe in 1892 was most influential in convincing the theological world of Paul's dependence upon Wisdom.[4] His conclusions were accepted in the English world and, to a considerable extent, by Continental theology. At the turn of the century Thackeray regarded Paul's use of Apocrypha to be established 'only in the case of one work—the Wisdom of Solomon'.[5] Holmes argues at length for Grafe's position.[6] On the Continent the development after Grafe was rather different.

---

[1] e.g. Ps. 47(48).6; Jer. 13.21; Mic. 4.9.

[2] Certainly Charles' supposition that the Testaments were a *vade mecum* for Paul is a shot in the dark (*CAP*, II, p. 292).

[3] Jowett, op. cit., p. 200. However, F. C. Porter is probably mistaken (and has defined 'apocalyptic' too narrowly) in contending that Paul's disinterest in the whole idea is the reason for his disuse of Jewish apocalyptic ('The Place of Apocalyptical Conceptions in the Thought of Paul', *JBL*, 41 (1922), pp. 183-204.

[4] E. Grafe, 'Das Verhältnis der paulinischen Schriften zur Sapientia Salominis', *Theologische Abhandlung* für C. von Weizsäcker, Freiburg, 1892, pp. 251-86. Grafe's was the significant work though others had previously noted a relationship. Farrar (*Life and Work of Paul*, II, p. 643) marked such passages as Wis. 2.24 (Rom. 5.12); 3.8 (1 Cor. 6.2); 9.15 (2 Cor. 5.2); 11.23ff (Rom. 11.32).

[5] Thackeray, *Paul and Jewish Thought*, p. 223. So, with reservations, Sanday and Headlam (op. cit., p. 269): 'If St Paul learnt from the Book of Wisdom illustrations of the Divine Power, and a general aspect of the question, he obtained nothing further. His broad views and deep insight are his own.'   [6] *CAP*, I, pp. 526f.

Though he was not without support,[1] many were not impressed
with his conclusions. Gunkel, in his second edition of *Wirkungen
des Heiligen Geistes* in 1899, continued of the opinion that 'die
Ähnlichkeit der Gedankenreichen ist rein formal, ein Einfluss
auf Paulus sehr unwahrscheinlich'.[2] Focke's 'Introduction' also
opposed Grafe's conclusions.[3] Several fundamental parallels
between Paul and Wisdom are adduced by Grafe: (1) the
power of God versus the nothingness of man; (2) God's patience
towards His enemies, though He knows it profits them nothing;
(3) the contrast between the fate of God's enemies and His
children.[4] In addition, similarities are found in the description
of heathen idolatry[5] and of the body-soul relationship.[6] Grafe
concludes that although the borrowing is more a formal adoption of concepts than an essential dependence, nevertheless Paul
has been substantially influenced by this Alexandrian writing.[7]

In a convincing criticism Focke questioned whether the
above similarities were to be explained on the basis of a Pauline
dependence, or whether each writing merely stemmed from the
same soil. Grafe had observed only the formal side of the
question, and in this lay the weakness of his position; their
essential difference of viewpoint, even where formal agreement
occurred, was fatal to Grafe's hypothesis.[8]

Michel, agreeing with Focke's analysis, found in Rom. 1.18ff
and Wis. 12-14 the most significant congruities between the
two writers.[9] The similarity here is not merely common opposition to idolatry; both aver that through the Creation the
Creator can be known, and both distinguish a definite judgment
upon men for the sin of idolatry. Nevertheless, a number of
differences appear: (1) according to Rom. 1.20f the heathen

---

[1] e.g. Schürer, op. cit., ii, III, p. 234.

[2] H. Gunkel, *Wirkungen des Heiligen Geistes*, Göttingen, 1899, pp. 79f: 'The
similarity of their train of thought is purely formal, an influence on Paul very
improbable.'

[3] F. Focke, *Die Entstehung der Weisheit Salomos*, Göttingen, 1913, pp. 113-26.

[4] Cf. Rom. 9.19-23 and Wis. 11.22; 12.8-20.

[5] Rom. 1.18ff, 24-32; Gal. 2.8-10 and Wis. 12-14.

[6] 2 Cor. 5.1ff and Wis. 9.15.

[7] The provenance of the book is almost certainly Egypt. Cf. Oesterley, *An
Introduction to the Apocrypha*, pp. 209f; *CAP*, I, pp. 524f.

[8] Focke, op. cit.

[9] Michel, pp. 16ff; after a close study of the related texts Bonsirven concludes,
with Focke and Michel, that it is very doubtful that Paul made use of Wisdom
(op. cit., p. 291).

recognised the *Uroffenbarung* of God in nature but rejected it and turned to idols; Wisdom, contrariwise, views the heathen idolatry as a childish ignorance persisted in, but which is done in a genuine attempt to find God.[1] The fundamental concept in Romans that idolatry resulted from a deliberate disaffection of the will from God is entirely lacking in the apocryphal book.[2] (2) The judgment of idolatry also differs. Paul notes the declining state of the pagan world from image worship (Rom. 1.23) to creature (κτίσις) worship (v. 25) to utter spiritual indifference (v. 28); and the progression is not merely rhetorical. In contrast, Wisdom distinguishes a better and worse type paganism. Worship of the creation draws only a mild rebuke (Wis. 13.1-9, n.b. vv. 6, 8) while the worship of images or animals is judged more sharply (Wis. 12.24; 13.10f).

In spite of the similar material and formal agreements[3] the picture given by the two writers is quite distinct. For the author of Wisdom the basic fault is in the intellect, for Paul it is in the will. Over against the progressive spiritual deterioration in Romans stand two relatively guilty types of idolatry in Wisdom. For Paul the result is their abandonment by God to increasing licentiousness culminating in a judgment of death; Wisdom views God's judgment as first a child's corrective (Wis. 12.25f), which if unheeded brings greater evils and God's punishment (Wis. 14.22ff). In the overall picture, Paul sees guilty men under God's judgment, while Wisdom thinks of foolish men deceived by child's play. There is very little unity in the essential character of the two passages.[4]

In the correspondence of other passages as well the evidence points more to a mutual tradition, often originating immediately in the OT,[5] than to a Pauline dependence on the apocryphal work.

[1] Wis. 13.2, 6ff; 14.1f, 11 (*CAP*, I, pp. 556ff).
[2] Weber (op. cit., pp. 65ff) and Michel (*Bibel*, p. 17) are probably mistaken in finding in Paul's text an allusion to the rabbinical notion that the Torah was first offered to the heathen but rejected. Cf. Exod. R. XVII, 2 (*SMR*, III, p. 212). However, references to Gentile rejection of earlier revelations are pertinent (e.g. Yalkut, I, p. 765; Weber, pp. 66f).
[3] Grafe, op. cit., pp. 272f: ἐπίγνωσις (Rom. 1.28) and ἐπιγιγνώσκειν (Wis. 13.1); νοεῖν (Rom. 1.20; Wis. 13.4); ἀσύνετος (Rom. 1.21; Wis. 11.15).
[4] Cf. Puukko, op. cit., p. 43.
[5] e.g. on the power of God and nothingness of man cf. Job 9.19; Jer. 27.44; Nah. 1.6; Ps. 75(76).8; on Rom. 1.23 cf. Ps. 105(106).20f. Paul's illustration of the potter and the clay (Rom. 9.21ff) is also in contrast to its use in Wisdom (15.7) and points to the OT. Cf. Isa. 29.16; 45.9; Jer. 18.6.

God's purpose in deferring judgment is depicted quite differently by Paul and Wisdom.[1] If Oesterley's dating of Wisdom as '40 A.D. or a few years later' is correct, it is very doubtful indeed that the work could have exerted the influence on Paul that is asserted for it.[2] Michel has properly concluded that both Paul and Wisdom 'sind von einer bestimmten apologetischen Tradition abhängig', and any further profitable research will lie in this direction.[3]

PHILO

The only other influence from the Alexandrian school discerned in Paul's OT usage is that of Philo. The use of allegory (Gal. 4.21ff) and the identification of Christ with the rock in the wilderness are the two instances most often adduced.[4] If there were Philonic or other Alexandrian influences on the apostle, they were probably not direct. Vollmer, after studying the question of Paul's relation to Philo, considered the results inconclusive; the agreements which did occur only made Paul's acquaintance with the Alexandrian writer less improbable than before.[5] Puukko, also rejecting any direct relationship, suggests that Apollos may have introduced Paul to current Alexandrian thought.[6] Paul's relation to Philo is best explained, as in the case of Wisdom, as mutual dependence upon a common tradition.[7] The affinities between the two are not sufficient to

[1] Cf. Rom. 9.22-24; Wis. 12.1-11. In Wisdom it is to give the wicked time to repent; Paul views God as enduring evil in order to shape and use it for his own good purposes.

[2] Oesterley, *An Introduction to the Apocrypha*, p. 209. Many writers see a direct influence of Wisdom on Paul and date the book considerably earlier; cf. *CAP*, I, pp. 520f, 526f. Sanday and Headlam (op. cit., pp. 51ff, 267ff) give such an estimate: '[It is clear] that at some time in his life St Paul must have bestowed upon the Book of Wisdom a considerable amount of study. . . . [His indebtedness] did not extend to any of the leading ideas of Christianity, and affected the form rather than the matter of the arguments to which it did extend' (p. 52). In viewing Wisdom as a source for Paul, however, these writers may have underestimated the possibility of a common tradition as the bond between them.

[3] Michel, *Bibel*, p. 18: '[Both] are dependent upon a fixed apologetic tradition.' Cf. Focke, op. cit., pp. 120ff.

[4] *Supra*, pp. 52f, 70n. The faith of Abraham, the exegesis in 1 Cor. 9.9, and the 'heavenly man' are other instances of real or alleged similarity (see *supra*, pp. 46f, 56, 64f).

[5] Vollmer, op. cit., p. 98.

[6] Puukko, op. cit., pp. 39f, 70.

[7] So Michel (*Bibel*, p. 111), who cites the synagogue worship as the means by which such exegetical traditions spread. Philo's relation to the Apocrypha is similarly explained by Ryle (*Philo and Scripture*, p. xxxiii).

establish any closer connexion, although Puukko's conjecture is not an improbable one.

A number of concepts in Philo which have considerable affinity to Pauline thought have been noted by Kennedy: '[Although] along a very diverse line of development, Philo arrives at a position regarding the law which approximates to that of St Paul. . . . Each in his own manner has come to realise the accomplishment of Jeremiah's epoch-making utterances: "I will put my law in their inward parts, and write it in their hearts" (Jer. 31.33).'[1]

Philo also resembles Paul in making salvation totally dependent upon the word of God[2] and approaches Paul's idea of 'adoption' as sons of God. Speaking of Abraham as God's friend (Gen. 18.17) Philo says, 'But he who has reached this portion . . . alone is nobly born, for he has registered God as his father and become by adoption His only son. . . .'[3] Philo's concept of the Spirit of God is also regarded by Kennedy as resembling the NT. But in Philo 'it is one special description of a fluctuating and elusive category like the Logos, while St Paul indissolubly associates it with . . . the person and activity of the living Lord'.[4]

Kennedy recognises that 'a large amount of the material embodied in Philo's voluminous writings is quite obviously inherited tradition'.[5] Furthermore, it is doubtful whether attempts to relate Philo directly to NT writers have 'led to important results'.[6] His study serves to strengthen the hypothesis of a common tradition underlying certain Philonic concepts which appear in clearer light in the NT, but there are no grounds for assuming a direct connexion. Jowett's essay on 'St Paul and Philo'[7] sums up the relation of Christianity to Alexandrian Judaism: '[Alexandrianism] was mystical and dialectical, not moral and spiritual . . .; it was a literature not a life. . . . It spoke of a Holy Ghost; of a Word; of a divine man; of a first and second Adam; of the faith of Abraham; of bread which came down from heaven; but knew nothing of the God who had made of one blood all nations of the earth; of the victory

---

[1] Kennedy, *Philo*, p. 56; cf. H. Windisch, *Die Frömmigkeit Philos*, Leipzig, 1909.
[2] Ibid., pp. 149ff.   [3] Philo, *de sobr.*, 56 (Colson, III, p. 473).
[4] Kennedy, *Philo*, pp. 191f.   [5] Ibid., p. 9.   [6] Ibid., p. 23.
[7] Jowett, op. cit., pp. 382-434.

over sin and death; of the cross of Christ. It was a picture, a
shadow, a surface, a cloud above, catching the rising light ere
He appeared. It was the reflection of a former world, not the
birth of a new one. It lifted up the veil of the temple, to see in
a glass only dreams of its own creation' (p. 454).

COMMON TRADITION

Because of its emphasis on placing Scripture in its historical
environment modern biblical scholarship has often tended to
convert parallels into influences and influences into sources.[1]
Further, the limited number of extant contemporary documents
has sometimes resulted in an exaggeration of their importance
and in an underestimation of the general currency of a particular phrase or concept. Too often, also, the investigator has
uncritically assumed that the Biblical writer must have a
'source' but that the apocryphal literature can be taken as pure
spring water. In comparing Pauline correspondence with the
apocryphal literature it has been the writer's impression throughout that they pointed not so much to a direct source of influence
as to current *theologumena* and traditional concepts or interpretations. This seems to be the most probable explanation of Paul's
relation to the Alexandrian writings discussed above. Knox's
observation is appropriate: 'Consequently, it is never possible
to be certain how far a similarity of ideas and even language
may not be due to the fact that two writers are borrowing from
a common source. Further, since all Jewish writers appeal in
the last resort to the OT and use it in accordance with a more
or less conventional system of interpretation, it is manifest that
there are always wide possibilities of the occurrence of striking
similarities which have no further relation to one another than
a common use of the same passage of the OT.'[2]

CONCLUSION

The importance of Paul's Jewish heritage cannot be ignored
if his writings are to be fully understood. The influence of

[1] Selwyn (op. cit., pp. 8f) gives a pertinent illustration from one of Chamber-
lain's speeches. Certain phraseology was attributed to Channing. After Chamber-
lain denied it, both were found to have been unconsciously dependent upon a
traditional idiom of expression.
[2] W. L. Knox, *St Paul and the Church of Jerusalem*, Cambridge, 1925, p. 126.

Jewish literary methods particularly and of scriptural interpretations to a lesser degree is frequently apparent. And, where distinguishable, with few exceptions they point to a Palestinian rather than a Hellenistic Judaism; in no case has a direct use of writings of the *diaspora* been established. As might be expected, a greater correspondence is evidenced in procedures[1] such as IF and combined quotations than in hermeneutical principles or interpretations. However, Christianity appealed to an existing state of expectancy which was the outcome of a previous development; it would be very strange, therefore, if some continuity between Pauline and Jewish exegesis were not found. The important consideration is not that Paul borrowed a Jewish interpretation but that Christ's apostle, led by the Holy Spirit, used it as a true interpretation. Often, too, rabbinic parallels are important in giving illustrations for a scriptural usage rather than revealing its origin.[2]

The significant conclusion, however, is the great chasm separating the writings of Paul from the rabbis. The apostle's OT exegesis was not just an adoption of current traditions but reveals a vitality and understanding totally foreign to rabbinical literature. If Paul used Jewish interpretations, he culled and moulded them to a Christological understanding of the OT; if he was a 'child of his times', they were for Paul the times of Messiah, His Cross and resurrection, and His revelation of the true meaning of Scripture. Paul was a disciple of Christ not of Gamaliel.

Paul's use of Jewish legends has been exaggerated. The accusation that he 'naïvely treats the haggadic embellishments of OT stories on the same footing with the Scripture itself'[3] is an all too common cliché. But when all the facts are assembled, such assertions are manifestly unjustified.

The Pauline use of the OT cannot really be understood in terms of his Jewish contemporaries. This is especially true where principles of interpretation are involved.[4] The affinities

---

[1] Even these are sometimes only general literary methods without any rabbinic peculiarity.

[2] Cf. I. Abrahams, 'Rabbinic Aids to Exegesis', *Cambridge Biblical Essays*, London, 1909, pp. 159-92.   [3] Schweitzer, op. cit., p. 46.

[4] Exegesis is chiefly in mind here; as for hermeneutical methods, Paul's use of *midrash pesher* does have affinities with elements in apocalyptic Judaism. See *infra*, pp. 139ff.

which occur are in peripheral areas and never reach to the heart of his thought. After his conversion the OT became a new book for Paul; all that went before now stood only as a prelude—a prelude set quite apart from all that was to follow. Although echoes of the prelude remain, the real meaning which the OT has for him lies at a different source. And to find it one must go to Christ and to the apostles.

CHAPTER III

PAUL AND THE APOSTOLIC CHURCH

INTRODUCTION

IN emphasising his direct revelation from Jesus Christ Paul asserts the independence of his message from any earthly authority: 'For I would have you know, brethren, that the gospel which was preached by me is not man's gospel. For I did not receive it from man, nor was I taught it, but it came through a revelation of Jesus Christ.'[1]

Nevertheless, after his conversion the apostle did not remain forever in isolation; and the form of his *kerygma* evidences a common stock of early Christian teaching emanating both from Christ's ministry and from apostolic emphases and interpretations of His ministry.[2] One element of this common material relates to the use and interpretation of the OT by the apostles and by the Lord as reported by them.[3] The present chapter is an examination of this element.

Paul's knowledge of Christ's teaching via the apostolic tradition is evident in various places, and it is probable that some parallels with the apostles find their ultimate source in Christ.[4]

---

[1] Gal. 1.11f RSV.

[2] P. Carrington (*The Primitive Christian Catechism*, Cambridge, 1940) develops this very suggestively along the lines of a prevalent catechetical pattern. Cf. G. E. Phillips, *The Transmission of the Faith*, London, 1946, p. 58. Selwyn, op. cit., p. 459: 'That common catechetical and liturgical sources underlie most of the Epistles of the NT seems to be proven beyond a doubt.'

[3] No attempt has been made to debate the authenticity of the Gospel sources used. The extreme position of R.Bultmann(cf. *Die Geschichte der synoptischen Tradition*, 2nd ed., Göttingen, 1931) has been justly characterised by V. Taylor (*Gospel Tradition*, p. 107) as one of 'violent exaggeration'. W. Manson (*Jesus the Messiah*, pp. 20-32) points out the weakness of the form-critics' conclusions: In typing 'true' and 'false' elements their judgment is upon the substance rather than the form of the tradition and is, for the method, gratuitous; further, their assumption that the records are the Church's invention and not historical reminiscence ignores basic elements of the tradition and of its milieu. To be borne in mind also is the importance of the 'witness' in the Jewish mind (cf. A. Barr, 'The Factor of Testimony in the Gospels', *ET*, 49 (1937-8), p. 401) and the concern which is present in the early Church to give, and to receive, an accurate account (Luke 1.1-4).

[4] See *supra*, pp. 28f. Cf. 1 Cor. 9.24 (1 Tim. 5.18); 1 Thess. 4.15; Gal. 3.1; Rom.

The correspondence in the use and interpretation of the OT is an especially significant aspect of the unified message of the early Church; it affected not only their interpretations of Scripture but the biblical textual tradition as well.[1] There are only about a dozen OT passages quoted both by Paul and by other NT writers,[2] but this does not fully reveal the extent of intercurrence. There is a significant correspondence in the use of typology, the emphasis placed upon certain sections of the OT, and the interpretations and application of quotations in common.[3] Certain methods, such as merged quotations and typological exegesis, associate Paul closely with other NT writings in contrast to contemporary Jewish literature. Selwyn has noted the 'interdependence of the various Epistles on a common stock of teaching and hymnody current in the Church'[4]; there are some grounds for including the oracles and OT paraphrases of early Christian prophets in this classification.[5]

PAULINE AND NEW TESTAMENT PARALLELS WITH CHRIST'S TEACHINGS

A continuity of OT interpretation from Christ through the apostolic tradition to Paul appears in a number of instances. The whole concept of Christianity being the true Israel lies embryonic in the earliest stages of the Christian movement. The figure of the bridegroom and bride, applied to God and Israel in the OT,[6] is used in the NT of Christ and His people. The figure is found in John the Baptist's preaching (John 3.29), the parables of Christ (e.g. Matt. 25.1ff), and the Pauline epistles (2 Cor. 11.2f; Eph. 5.31f). Similarly, the spiritual nature of true Abrahamic sonship, so emphasised by Paul (Rom. 4; Gal. 3-4), is intimated much earlier in John the

12.14 (Matt. 5.44); 1 Thess. 4.8 (Matt. 10.40); 1 Cor. 13.2 (Matt. 17.20); οὐκ οἴδατε in 1 Cor. 6.2, 9, 15, 19 (Matt. 19.28; 13.42f; John 15.5; 2.21f). After examining such passages, A. W. Argyle ('Parallels between the Pauline Epistles and Q', *ET*, 60 (1948-9), pp. 318-20) concludes that such similarities 'imply that Paul's mind was steeped in the tradition of our Lord's ethical sayings . . .' (p. 320).

[1] Manson ('The Cairo Geniza: A Review', p. 184) rates the doctrinal and liturgical influences as most important in shaping first century textual traditions.
[2] See Appendix IV.
[3] For their common hermeneutical method, see *infra*, pp. 139ff.
[4] Selwyn, op. cit., p. 19; cf. p. 459.   [5] *Infra*, pp. 107ff.
[6] Cf. Hos. 1-2; Ezek. 16.20. The Jewish interpretation of the Song of Solomon also follows this theme.

Baptist's message: 'Bring forth, therefore, fruits worthy of repentence, and begin not to say within yourselves, "We have Abraham for our father." For I say unto you that God is able from these stones to raise up children unto Abraham.'[1]

In John 8.33-43 Christ rejects the claim of the Pharisees to be Abraham's seed ($\sigma\pi\acute{\epsilon}\rho\mu\alpha$, v. 33) with this observation: 'If you were Abraham's children ($\tau\acute{\epsilon}\kappa\nu\alpha$, v. 39), you would do the works of Abraham.' In the epistles this involves 'works' resting in and proceeding from Abraham's faith.[2] The Jews' rejection of Messiah is interpreted both in John (12.38) and in Romans (10.16) as the fulfilment of Isa. 53.1 and is in accordance with the veiled parabolic predictions of the Lord Himself.[3] Again, Paul (Rom. 11.8) and the Fourth Gospel (John 12.40) both attribute the rejection to a judicial blinding, although different OT Scriptures are cited.[4] The 'rejected stone' imagery (Matt. 21.42; Mark 12.10f; Acts 4.11; Rom. 9.33; 1 Pet. 2.6ff) in which Israel's rejection is implied also has its origin in the words of Christ.[5] From these parallels one may reasonably assume that the identification of the followers of Christ with the 'true Israel' or the remnant, though finding clearest expression in the apostles, is implicit in the teaching of John the Baptist and Christ. And some of the same OT passages which Paul employs in this regard are used with similar import by Christ and the Gospel writers.

In other subjects, too, Paul finds close affinity with the teachings of the Lord Jesus. The apostle's insistence that righteousness through the law requires the keeping of the law ('for he who does these things shall live in them', Rom. 10.5; Gal. 3.12) echoes the sentiment voiced by Christ in his answer to the lawyer's query concerning eternal life. After the lawyer cited the commandments, Christ answered, 'Do this and you will live' (Luke 10.28).[6] With regard to the sanctity and significance of the marital bond both Christ (against divorce) and

---

[1] Luke 3.8f; cf. Matt. 3.9f; John 6.29.
[2] Cf. Gal. 3.7; Jas. 2.23.   [3] e.g. Matt. 22.1ff.
[4] Isa. 29.10 (Deut. 29.4) and Isa. 6.9. The Pauline citation may be a 'testimony' summary of several passages; cf. Dodd, *According to the Scriptures*, p. 38. Cf. Mark 3.5; 6.52; 8.17. For Christ's own usage cf. Matt. 13.14ff; John 9.39.
[5] The primary element in the combination is Ps. 117(118).22f, a *verbum Christi*, although Paul omits it as irrelevant to his purpose; cf. Selwyn, op. cit., p. 268; *infra*, pp. 89ff.   [6] Cf. Jas. 1.22; 2.10.

Paul (against fornication) appeal to the same Scripture.[1] Paul's statement that the whole law is fulfilled in one word, 'Thou shalt love thy neighbour as thyself' (Gal. 5.14), is a maxim for the whole of the NT: According to the Lord the Golden Rule *is* the Law and the Prophets (Matt. 7.12); and on the two commands, loving God and loving one's neighbour, hang all the Law and Prophets.[2] Similarly, the philosophy of turning the other cheek, enunciated in the Sermon on the Mount (Matt. 5.38-48) is also found in Romans; and in the context is a λέγει κύριος quotation which appears to have been common to the early Church.[3]

Paul's typological use of the OT also reflects in large degree —and in a complex interlocking pattern—the teachings of Christ. The 'rock' or 'stone' (mentioned above) as a messianic title was, according to Selwyn, probably 'first made by the Lord Himself'.[4] Although this probably needs some qualification, there can be little doubt that Christ is the source of the NT usage (cf. Matt. 21.42). Paul also identifies Christ with the 'rock' in the wilderness in 1 Cor. 10.1ff; this may be closely related to the 'rejected stone' tradition in the early Church. In any case, other elements in the Exodus typology appear to be rooted in applications made by the Lord.[5] In John 6 Christ, taking the setting of the Exodus, depicts Himself as the true Manna: 'I am that bread of life. Your fathers did eat manna in the wilderness and are dead. . . . I am the living bread which

---

[1] Matt. 19.5; 1 Cor. 6.16; cf. Mark 10.8; Eph. 5.31f. The οἱ δύο is not in the Hebrew; the LXX wording enhances the δύο-μία transition.

[2] In Luke 10.25 the questioning lawyer sums up the law in the same way, thereby giving the occasion for the parable of the Good Samaritan. James (2.8) cites Lev. 19.18 as the 'royal law' (νόμον βασιλικὸν).

[3] Rom. 12.14-21; cf. v. 19; Heb. 10.30. The quotation (Deut. 32.35), identical in Romans and Hebrews (λέγει κύριος is textually uncertain in Hebrews), varies considerably from the OT; closer to the NT is the Targum: 'Vengeance lies before me . . .' (Etheridge, op. cit., p. 668). Romans, in the same context (v. 14), has a further affinity to the Matthean account. Cf. Rom. 2.1ff; 14.4 (Matt. 7.1ff); Rom. 2.13; 10.5 (Matt. 7.21ff).

[4] Selwyn, op. cit., p. 158; cf. Davies, op. cit., pp. 152f. The Targum on Isa. 28.16 has a strong messianic flavour: 'Therefore, thus saith the Lord, Elohim, I will appoint in Zion a king, a strong king, powerful and terrible. I will make him strong and powerful, saith the prophet; but the righteous who have believed in these things shall not be dismayed when distress cometh' (Stenning, op. cit., p. 88). It would be strange, too, if the Jews never took the 'stone' in Dan. 2.34 messianically.

[5] Some figures, of course, are drawn directly from prophetic (e.g. Ps. 105-107; Isa. 48.16) and midrashic descriptions of the significance of the Exodus. e.g. baptism in the sea; cf. *SBK*, I, pp. 1054f. See *supra*, pp. 66n; *infra*, pp. 132ff.

came down from heaven. . . . Whoever eats my flesh and drinks my blood has eternal life, and I will raise him up at the last day.'[1] Paul refers to the Lord's Supper, the symbolic eating of Christ's flesh and drinking of His blood, in the same Exodus context[2]; and granting Paul's knowledge of Christ's typological application there is no reason to doubt that it—or a common apostolic typology derived from it—lies behind the apostle's usage.

The 'rejected stone' typology, based upon Isa. 28.16; 8.14; Ps. 117(118).22ff, has been clearly demonstrated by Dodd to be a pre-Pauline *testimonium* current in the early Church[3]:

1. Both Rom. 9.33 and 1 Pet. 2.6ff quote the two Isaiah passages in agreement with each other but at variance from the LXX.
2. Paul did not borrow from Peter, even assuming the earliest possible date for the latter.
3. That Peter borrowed from Romans is possible 'only on the unlikely assumption that he first disentangled the conflated passages, and then supplemented them with parts of Isa. 28.16 which Paul had omitted . . . [and yet] not from the LXX, since his version does not entirely agree with the LXX even where there is no Pauline parallel'.[4]
4. 'The simpler, and surely the more probable, hypothesis is that both Paul and the author of First Peter made use of a two-fold *testimonium* already current in the pre-canonical tradition. . . .'[5]

In Rom. 9.33 Paul does not employ the other OT text in First Peter, a *verbum Christi* from Ps. 117(118).22ff. But in Eph. 2.19ff he does allude to this text in a combination of the 'stone' and 'temple' imagery. With 1 Pet. 2.6 (cf. Matt. 21.42; Mark 12.10f) Paul refers to Christ as the chief cornerstone (ἀκρογωνιαῖον), and both speak of Christians as the house of God. Although he does not, as Peter (v. 5), explicitly call Christians 'living stones'

---

[1] John 6.31-59, viz., 48f, 51, 54.

[2] 1 Cor. 10.1ff. Paul's comparison of the Communion elements with the OT types is a warning that Christ's words are not to be taken with any idea of *ex opere operato*. Cf. Rev. 15.3f; C. F. Burney, *The Gospel in the Old Testament*, Edinburgh, 1921, p. 44. For a further discussion of the Exodus typology cf. *infra*, pp. 126ff.

[3] Dodd, *According to the Scriptures*, pp. 35f, 41f. See Appendix II for the texts.

[4] Ibid., p. 43.   [5] Ibid., p. 43.

(λίθοι ζῶντες) of the building, this is clearly implied. It is probable, then, that the 'building of God' is as much a part of the *testimonium* as the 'cornerstone'.

Paul goes on to denominate Christians as the temple of God (ναὸς θεοῦ) and householders or members of God (οἰκεῖοι τοῦ θεοῦ).[1] The designation ναὸς θεοῦ is fairly common in Paul. The Corinthians are reminded of it as if it were basic to their Christian knowledge: 'Know ye not (οὐκ οἴδατε) that ye are the temple of God?' (1 Cor. 3.16; cf. 6.19). In 2 Cor. 6.16ff the apostle supports this concept with a *catena* of OT texts.[2] In the light of this temple typology the connexion of Stephen's quotation in Acts 7.48f with Pauline thought becomes apparent. Paul's statement on Mars Hill that God does not dwell in temples made with hands (ἐν χειροποιήτοις ναοῖς κατοικεῖ, Acts 17.24) is almost verbatim with Stephen's words (ἐν χειροποιήτοις κατοικεῖ).[3] In Eph. 2.21 Christians are the κατοικητήριον τοῦ θεοῦ, and quite apparently this is the unrecorded goal of Stephen's argument: The 'tabernacles' built by the Jews—and Solomon's temple was no different—could never be God's permanent abode; and the prophecy in Isa. 66.1 makes this very clear.[4] The quotation is a 'pointer' and it is in Isa. 66.2 that the significant point is made. A concise summation was given by Alexander a century ago: 'First, the temples made by men are contrasted with the great material temple of the universe; then this is itself disparaged by Jehovah as his own handiwork, and still more in comparison with the nobler temple of a spiritual nature, the renewed and contrite heart.'[5] The combined quotation in 2 Cor. 6.16ff does not include this passage; but Stephen's words are of the same typological struc-

---

[1] Eph. 2.19ff. Ναὸς θεοῦ (as σῶμα Χριστοῦ) usually has reference to Christians in a corporate sense. But there is apparently an oscillation between the part and the whole in Paul's thought which permits the figure to be used of the individual as well (cf. 1 Cor. 6.19). Cf. τὴν ἐκκλησίαν τοῦ θεοῦ in Acts 20.28; Gal. 1.13; etc.

[2] Lev. 26.11f; Ezek. 37.27; Isa. 52.11; 2 Kings (Sam.) 7.14.

[3] In Acts 7.48 ναοῖς is omitted but is definitely implied. In fact, Stephen's entire speech is largely a defence against the charge of destroying the temple (Acts 6.14) and, as Moule shows, hearkens back to the sayings of the Lord. Cf. C. F. D. Moule, 'Sanctuary and Sacrifice in the Church of the New Testament', *JTS*, Second Series, I (April 1950), pp. 29-41.

[4] The 'place of my rest' (מקום מנוחתי) is applied to the temple in contrast to the movable sanctuary in 2 Kings (Sam.) 7.5ff; 2 Chron. 6.41; Ps. 131(132).8.

[5] J. A. Alexander, *Prophecies of Isaiah*, Edinburgh, 1865, II, p. 459. Cf. Isa. 57.15; 2 Cor. 6.16.

ture; and his quotation should be considered a part of the 'temple-stone' *testimonium* which finds its fullest expression in 1 Pet. 2.5ff.[1]

In the Gospels it is primarily Christ's body that is the temple; and the repeated reference to the Lord's claim to build the temple in three days evidences the significance of the idea for the Gospel writers.[2] Paul's concept of the Church as the bride of Christ and the body of Christ (cf. Eph. 5.25-32; 2 Cor. 11.2f) is a part of the same pattern; and it is a pattern which is pre-Pauline and which points back, as does the 'stone' imagery, to pregnant sayings of the Lord.[3]

A. Cole examines the 'temple' concept as a catechetical 'form' of the Church in the NT and finds that 'the two issues, abolition of the old material temple and inclusion of the Gentiles, are closely linked both in the sayings of Jesus and in the later catechesis of the Church, so that the two problems are fundamentally one and the same'.[4] Cole's argument, viewed *in toto*, is quite appealing: In the Fourth Gospel (John 12.20ff) the 'Coming of the Greeks' is set forth as a sign to Jesus of his approaching death and resurrection (i.e. the destruction and rebuilding of the 'temple'); the cleansing of the temple takes place in this same context if the synoptic chronology is followed (cf. Matt. 21.9ff). In Acts, James (Acts 15.16ff) explicitly connects the rebuilt 'tabernacle' with the inclusion of the Gentiles, and the charge of violating the temple later brought against Paul (Acts 21.28) reveals the existing state of tension on this question.[5] 'It is no accident that the attack on Stephen, forced by the Jewish authorities, leads directly, by clarifying

---

[1] Both Acts 7.49 and 2 Cor. 6.16 are λέγει κύριος quotations. See *infra*, pp. 107ff. The apologetic of Hebrews is also based upon the concept that Christians have a high priest, an altar, a sacrifice—a temple. Moule (op. cit., p. 41) finds the key-words of the whole temple typology in the substratum of NT theology.

[2] In John 2.19, 21; Matt. 26.61; 27.40; Mark 14.58; 15.29; cf. Rev. 21.22. Actually, the Messianic Community as God's true temple is also implicit in the teachings of Jesus. Cf. Mt. 12.6; Mk. 12.10; 14.58 (ἀχειροποίητον); O. Michel, 'ναος,' *KTW*, IV, 887f.

[3] Cf. Moule, op. cit., p. 34; R. N. Flew, *Jesus and His Church*, London, 1938, pp. 55.8. See further C. K. Barrett, 'Pillar Apostles,' *Studia Paulina, Festschrift* for J. de Zwaan, Haarlem, 1953; M. Black, 'Theological Conceptions in DSS.' *Svensk Exeg. Årsbok*, Lund, 1954; J. Jeremias, *Jesus als Weltvollender*, Gutersloh, 1930, pp. 37ff, 273.

[4] A. Cole, *The New Temple*, London, 1950, p. 31.

[5] Ibid., pp. 31-50.

the issue, to a Christian attack on the Jewish concept of a strictly "visible church", with its ordered worship and hierarchy. Again it is no accident that this realisation by the Christians leads to the opening of the door to the "peoples".[1]

The most important Pauline passage on this subject is Eph. 2.11, 19-3.6, where the temple typology is connected with the inclusion of the Gentiles within 'the commonwealth of Israel'. The identification of David's 'seed' (2 Sam. 7.14) lies in the same framework of common tradition; both Stephen (Acts 7.46ff) and Paul (2 Cor. 6.16; cf. Gal. 3.16, 29) refer it to Christ and His 'body'.[2] There is, then, an interrelated 'complex' of ideas covering such important Pauline themes as the 'seed' of David, the true Israel, the temple of God, the body of Christ, and the calling of the Gentiles. It is a pattern which lies in the substructure of NT theology, and, in its nucleus, it has its origin in the sayings of the Lord.

There are no definite NT parallels with Paul's Wisdom typology in which Christ and His Cross are declared to be the true wisdom.[3] But the apostle's several quotations (1 Cor. 1.19; 2.9, 16; 3.19f) describing the vanity of the 'wisdom of this world' and its barren and foolish goal reflects somewhat the attitude of Christ: 'I thank thee, O Father, Lord of Heaven and earth, because thou hast hid these things from the wise and prudent and hast revealed them unto babes.'[4] The thought in each is that God reveals Himself not to the 'wise' but to the humble and simple; Paul, of course, carries the theme much further.

[1] Ibid., p. 32.

[2] It is possible that Acts 7 may refer only to Christ and that the Church as the 'body of Christ' and the 'new temple' is the later contribution of Paul (cf. G. Johnston, The Doctrine of the Church in the New Testament, Cambridge, 1943, p. 75). However, Stephen's Isaiah citation argues otherwise; and the presence of the Semitic concept of 'corporate personality' makes it very likely that the messianic community already viewed itself in this fashion, if not with this precise terminology. Cf. Cole, op. cit., pp. 52f. Dodd (Gospel and Law, pp. 33f) observes that the Stoics also spoke of the community under the figure of the body and its members; regarding the 'body of Christ', 'the actual expression was apparently coined by Paul, but the idea is in no way peculiar to him'. Cf. E. Best, One Body in Christ, London, 1955, pp. 195, 203ff.

[3] Cf. 1 Cor. 1-3. It does bring to mind, however, the Lord's comparison of Himself with Solomon (Matt. 12.42; Luke 11.31; cf. John 8.32; 14.6); the contrast between earthly wisdom and wisdom from above in Jas. 3.13-17 is also similar. For a discussion of Paul's Wisdom Christology cf. Davies, op. cit., pp. 147-76.

[4] Matt. 11.25 (Luke 10.21).

Parallels with other New Testament Writers

Several Pauline citations which have no reference to the sayings of Jesus are common to other NT writers.[1] These deuterograph citations are significant in revealing topical emphases drawn from the OT by the early Church and in illustrating the way in which these passages were employed. Apart from the ethical emphasis marked by the recurrence of the commandments (often in connexion with Lev. 19.18),[2] the subject matter chiefly includes justification by faith, the nature of the true Israel, and Christ as the second Adam or representative man.

Hab. 2.4 is cited by Paul (Rom. 1.17; Gal. 3.11) to show that righteousness is not achieved through obedience to the law but through faith; the author of Hebrews uses the same passage to describe the proper attitude of the Christian toward the trials of life. In each case the life of the true believer rests on faith, but the application of the passage varies.[3] 'That Paul borrowed from Hebrews is out of the question. That the author of Hebrews borrowed from Paul is entirely unlikely because (a) he gives the words differently; (b) he cites much more of the passage, and (c) he evidently understands the words differently; he quotes the whole passage for the sake of its warning against ὑποστολή, and treats πίστις as the opposite of the weakness of character which leads to ὑποστολή. . . . It is much more likely that he drew upon a tradition which already recognised the passage from Habakkuk as a *testimonium* to the coming of Christ.'[4]

The same theme is present in the citation of Gen. 15.6 (Rom. 4.3; Jas. 2.23): 'Abraham believed God, and it was counted to him for righteousness.' Paul uses the passage to work out his proposition of righteousness apart from works. James, faced with an antinomian attitude towards faith, quotes the verse to point out the character of Abraham's faith: It was in the 'work'

---

[1] See Appendix IV.
[2] Rom. 13.9; Gal. 5.14; Eph. 6.2f and parallels.
[3] Cf. Westcott, *Hebrews*, p. 337.
[4] Dodd, *According to the Scripture*, p. 51. The applications of the passage in Paul and Hebrews are not contrary; πίστις can be set over against ὑποστολή in Hebrews and ἔργον in Paul because, in their respective contexts, ὑποστολή and ἔργον stand in the same category of unfaith. A common unity of thought underlies the particular interpretation.

of offering up Isaac that 'the Scripture was fulfilled which says, "Abraham believed God. . . ." ' Here it is not a case of one writer borrowing from the other; their applications of the verse are quite distinct. The mutual use of the particular Genesis passage is hardly adventitious and probably arises from its importance in the general apostolic tradition. However, in this case it is almost certainly Paul himself who makes the contribution to the common tradition; to refer one of Paul's fundamental propositions, which he analyses so carefully, to a mere adaption not only fails to account for the detailed consideration he gives the problem (cf. Rom. 4) but seriously underrates the originality of the apostle. James used the verse probably because of its importance to his readers, but it was very likely Paul who originally gave it that importance.

The nature of the true Israel is a second theme of importance. The relation of Paul's citations to the teaching of the Lord in this matter has already been considered. In the epistles other instances occur. (1) On the day of Pentecost Peter quoted (Acts 2.17ff) a rather lengthy passage from the prophecy of Joel (2.28-32) and declared that the events then transpiring were its fulfilment. The last verse quoted is found again in Rom. 10.13: 'Everyone who shall call on the name of the Lord shall be saved.' Paul's purpose is to show that in the Messianic Age both Jew and Gentile can come to God on equal terms. Peter gathers from the passage a description of the Messianic Era and the events inaugurating it; the verse in question is evidently an invitation to those Jews who crucified Messiah to 'call upon the name of the Lord'. (2) Texts from the first two chapters of Hosea are referred to in Rom. 9.25f and 1 Pet. 2.10. Paul's is a combined quotation (Hos. 2.23; 1.10); the other is a definite allusion to Hos. 2.23. Both refer the 'Israel' prophecy to Gentile Christians,[1] yet 'the independence of the two authors seems certain'.[2] (3) The verse, 'In Isaac shall your seed be

---

[1] Paul specifically does, and this seems to be the implication of οἱ ποτέ οὐ λαός in 1 Pet. 2.10.

[2] Dodd (*According to the Scriptures*, p. 75) gives good reasons for this conclusion: ' . . . in Romans the key-words are λαός and ἀγαπᾶσθαι (after the LXX of 2.23), in First Peter the key-words are λαός and ἐλεεῖσθαι (after the LXX of 1.6-8; 2.1).' Peter's reference appears to be *ad hoc* from Hos. 2.23 (the Hebrew has רֻחָמָה throughout); but, as Dodd suggests, it may reflect, as Paul, the LXX variations in other verses.

called', occurs in Romans and Hebrews.[1] Paul is concerned
to show the restricted character of Abraham's seed, that is, the
seed arising through the 'promise' and not through the 'flesh'.
In Hebrews the promise element is applied differently: It was
this pledge of God on which Abraham's faith rested when he
was called upon to offer up Isaac.[2] The use of this verse, as of
Gen. 15.6 mentioned above, most likely has its origin in Paul,
who treats this OT section so thoroughly. However, after the
initial concept entered the stream of apostolic tradition its field
of application continually expanded.[3] The extent to which the
sacrifice of Isaac entered into Pauline thought at this point is
uncertain, but it is notable that the 'resurrection' faith ascribed
to Abraham in Hebrews is the kind of faith Paul requires for
salvation in Rom. 10.9f.[4] (4) One other reference is of note: In
2 Kings 7.14 (LXX) God promises David that his seed shall
be established forever and continues, 'I shall be to him a father
and he shall be to me a son.' The immediate recipient in view
is Solomon, not merely Solomon the individual but Solomon
the king in whom Israel is personified.[5] Hebrews (1.5) applies
this promise to Christ the 'seed' in whom Israel is eternally
personified; and Paul (2 Cor. 6.18) cites it of Christians, the
true remnant of Israel and the 'body' of Christ.[6]

The Adam-Christ typology of 1 Cor. 15.22-28, 45-49 is yet
another motif with correspondence to other NT exegesis.[7] The

---

[1] Gen. 21.12; Rom. 9.7; Heb. 11.18; cf. Gal. 3.16.

[2] It is probably here that James' (2.23) reference to the offering of Isaac, as the
'work' demonstrating or fulfilling his faith, fits into the framework of the early
Church's exegesis.

[3] This type of expansion is quite evident in the patristic writings. Cf. Grafe,
Das Urchristentum und das Alte Testament, pp. 23ff.

[4] For possible allusions to the sacrifice of Isaac in Rom. 3.25 (cf. יִרְאֶה in
Gen. 22.8) and Rom. 8.32 (cf. Gen. 22.16 LXX) see H. J. Schoeps, 'The Sacrifice
of Isaac in Paul's Theology', *JBL*, 65 (December 1946), pp. 385-92.

[5] On this solidarity concept in Hebrew thought see A. R. Johnson, *The One and
the Many in the Israelite Conception of God*, Cardiff, 1942.

[6] Paul's citation, one in a *catena*, departs considerably from the OT text; but
this is doubtless its source. It is together with texts identifying Christians as λαός
θεοῦ (and ναός θεοῦ) and as the delivered remnant (Isa. 52.11; Ezek. 20.34). Cf.
Gal. 3.16. Christ's identification of Himself with His people must have been
indelibly impressed upon Paul at his conversion; cf. Acts. 9.5; Matt. 25.40, 45.

[7] The ἐν Χριστῷ (cf. 2 Cor. 5.17; Gal. 2.20) and the 'body of Christ' (cf. Eph.
5.22-32, Col. 1.24) concepts in Paul are related both to the Adam-Christ typology
and to the 'stone-temple' imagery. Which type is more basic is a moot point.
Their inter-relation probably points to their development as one comprehensive
idea, although the Lord's use of the 'stone' passage perhaps favours its priority.
But cf. *infra*, p. 97, on Christ's use of 'son of man'.

application of the titles, 'last Adam' and 'second man', to
Christ is found only in 1 Cor. 15, but it is within this context
(v. 27; cf. Eph. 1.22) that the quotation occurs, 'For he has
put all things under his feet' (Ps. 8.7).[1] The same verse appears
in Heb. 2.8 as a part of a longer citation. The Psalm itself
reflects upon the creation account and the place of man
(בֶן־אָדָם ... אֱנוֹשׁ, v. 5) in the created order; even 'the
words "put under his feet" sound like a paraphrase of the רדה
of Gen. 1.26, 28'.[2] Although 'son of man' (v. 5) may be taken
in a generic sense, the first man as the ideal type or representative is clearly in mind. Hebrews, after quoting the Psalm of
'man', concludes: 'But we do not yet see all things in subjection
to him (i.e. man). But we see Jesus. . . .' The transition is here
made from Adam, the Psalmist's type, to Christ, the last Adam,
in whom man's destiny is realised; and who 'was made a little
lower than the angels (Ps. 8.8 LXX) . . . that he might taste
death for everyone' (Heb. 2.9). The essential unity of Hebrews
with Paul's exegesis becomes even more apparent in the further
development of the Adam-Christ typology in 1 Cor. 15.[3] The
guarantee of man's resurrection, and through it the fulfilment
of his destiny, is the fact that the Lord Christ does taste death
and does become victor for every man:

> Death is swallowed up in victory.
> Where, O Death, is thy victory?
> Where, O Death, is thy sting?
> —Thanks be to God who gives *us* the victory
>   through our Lord Jesus Christ.[4]

Also pertinent is the citation in verse 45: 'The first man Adam
became a living soul; the last Adam became a life-giving spirit.'

---

[1] Cf. Matt. 21.16, where Christ quotes another verse of the Psalm.

[2] Delitzsch, *Psalms*, I, p. 198.

[3] The same typology, taken either from the Psalm or directly from Genesis,
seems to be involved in Phil. 2.5ff, classified by Lohmeyer as a Christological
hymn. Cf. Lohmeyer, *Kyrios Jesus*, pp. 25f. Cf. also Col. 1.18.

[4] 1 Cor. 15.55, 57; Hos. 13.14; Isa. 25.8. ' . . . When Paul used the magnificent
apostrophe, "Death where is thy sting? . . ." he was not employing a casual
literary reminiscence, but referring to a passage already recognised as a classical
description of God's deliverance of His people out of utter destruction.' Dodd,
According to the Scriptures, p. 76. Cf. Heb. 2.14; Rev. 20.14; 1 Cor. 15.1-5. Dodd
also (p. 77) takes 'the third day' in 1 Cor. 15.4 to refer to one of the Hosea (6.3)
testimonia; 'for the resurrection of Christ *is* the resurrection of Israel of which the
prophet spoke' (p. 103).

Neither of these citations follows the OT text very closely, and the latter half of verse 45 is not from the OT at all. Burney supposes that it is derived from early Christian *testimonia*: 'Prior to St Paul's conversion the earliest circle of Christian believers at Jerusalem was drawn not merely from the peasant class, but embraced (according to Acts 6.7) "a great company of priests" who scarcely would have been unversed in Rabbinic teaching but may be supposed to have applied such learning as they had acquired to the service of the new Faith. It is by no means improbable, therefore, that the passage as a whole may have been drawn from a collection of OT *testimonia*. . . . If then this interpretation of 1 Cor. 15.45 as wholly a quotation be correct, the implication is that sometime before St. Paul wrote his epistle in A.D. 55-6 the antithesis between the first Adam and Christ as the second Adam had been worked out in Christian Rabbinic circles and was used in argument.'[1] It is just possible that the Adam-Christ antithesis reaches back even further than Burney suspects. Delitzsch contends that Christ's use of the title 'son of man' has Ps. 8, as well as other Scriptures, in mind[2]; if this is so, it is not at all improbable that this (as the 'stone-temple') typology finds its ultimate source in the Lord's own teaching.[3]

In all the OT parallels between Paul and other NT writers[4] the striking observation is the underlying unity in the midst of an exegetical particularity. The pattern fits very remarkably when all the pieces are assembled; but 'piece by piece' the

---

[1] C. F. Burney, *The Aramaic Origin of the Fourth Gospel*, Oxford, 1922, pp. 46f; cf. Black, 'The Pauline Doctrine of the Second Adam', pp. 170f; *supra*, pp. 36, 58ff. Burney (pp. 43-7) finds allusions to the analogy in Luke's genealogy (' . . . Adam, who was the son of God', Luke 3.38) and in rabbinic literature. Cf. Gen. R. XII, 6 (*SMR*, I, p. 92) on Gen. 2.24: Six things lost through Adam's fall are to be restored through Messiah. Midrash Haggadol (fourteenth century, quoted in Burney, p. 46) on Gen. 16.11: Messiah is called *Yinnon* (יִנּוֹן=propagate, produce life: Ps. 72.17) 'because he is destined to quicken those who sleep in the dust'. Cf. Sanh. 98b (*SBT*, p. 667). For objections to Burney cf. Davies, op. cit., pp. 43f. Davies thinks that Paul himself originated the Adam-Christ typology and that other references stem ultimately from him.   [2] Delitzsch, *Psalms*, I, p. 156.

[3] It is interesting that Paul's quotation of Gen. 2.24 (Eph. 5.31) is paralleled in Matt. 19.5. But the diverse application does not suggest any typological connexion.

[4] One other near-parallel may be mentioned—Rom. 15.3 (Ps. 68(69).10b) and John 2.17 (Ps. 68(69).10a). Both apply the Scripture to Christ. It is very unlikely that the writers would choose parts of the same verse purely coincidentally; it may be supposed, therefore, that this Psalm was generally accepted and used messianically when these citations were made.

interpretation and application are too varied, for the most part, to support a theory of borrowing or direct dependence.[1] The most likely explanation is that these ideas, and these ideas associated with these particular OT texts, were—more or less—the common property of the apostolic Church.[2] The problems involved in this common use of OT texts in the NT have been the occasion for the hypothesis of the 'Testimony Book' and the various modifications made upon it.

THE 'TESTIMONY BOOK' HYPOTHESIS

'It may naturally be supposed that [the Jewish] race which laid stress on moral progress, . . . and which was carrying on an active propaganda, would have, among other books, manuals of morals, of devotion, and of controversy. It may also be supposed if we take into consideration the contemporary habit of making collections of *excerpta* and the special authority which the Jews attached to their sacred books, that some of these manuals would consist of extracts from the OT. . . . The existence of composite quotations in the NT, and in some of the early fathers, suggests the hypothesis that we have in them relics of such manuals.'[3]

With this suggestion by Hatch there began in 1889 a theory which gained wide acceptance by the turn of the century and by 1920 was virtually unanimously approved. Behind the theory, in its NT aspect, lay the same reasoning which was used in advancing Böhl's *Volksbibel* hypothesis, and indeed, which is basic to any attempt to answer the problem of NT quotations[4]:

[1] As noted above, the thought behind some of the parallels (particularly those in Hebrews) probably has Paul's mind as its source. But even here the diverse application of the texts suggests that the dependence is not directly upon Paul's epistles. A more probable hypothesis is that in the apostle's earlier teaching particular texts were incorporated under some exegetical principle or topic in his 'curriculum' (e.g. the seed of Abraham, the true Israel); the text could then be variously adapted, within the general principle, according to the particular desire of the user.

[2] Of course, certain prophecies and themes were more important for some than for others, and some interpretations were original to a particular writer or group and were only gradually disseminated. The Pauline OT references find most frequent and significant correspondence with 'Q' (material common to Matthew and Luke), the Fourth Gospel, Hebrews and First Peter; James and the speeches in Acts also contain marked affinities.

[3] E. Hatch, *Essays in Biblical Greek*, Oxford, 1889, p. 203. The idea was not novel, but Hatch's remarks were the catalyst for the ensuing research. Cf. Harnack, *A History of Dogma*, London, 1894, I, p. 175.

[4] The later theories of Kahle (*supra*, pp. 17ff) and Stendahl (*infra*, pp. 139ff) are other answers to the same problems.

(1) The NT contains quotations which vary from the LXX and MT but which agree with parallel NT and patristic citations. (2) The interdependence of the latter documents is improbable, either for historical reasons or because of the divergent manner in which the texts are cited and applied. (3) Consequently, the source should be viewed as a third document lying behind the parallels. This third document should not be viewed as a *Volksbibel* or a variant text or Targum but as a 'Testimony Book'; for 'following the contemporary habit, the early Christian propaganda would produce or adopt for its own purpose, short collections of extracts Messianic and otherwise, for the use of those who had to argue from the OT'.[1]

Vollmer, although pointing out the purely hypothetical character of Hatch's suggestion, viewed it as the probable answer to some variant and composite citations in the NT (e.g. 1 Cor. 2.9).[2] In Britain the idea was quite widely accepted,[3] and in 1906 Burkitt proposed that the *Logia* of Papias should be understood as a collection of OT proof-texts.[4] It remained, however, for the versatile mind of Rendel Harris to bring the testimony hypothesis into its own. To show that a 'Testimony Book', composed of OT texts used in Anti-Jewish polemic, was the earliest Christian document, he engaged in a thorough study of the data in NT and patristic writings.[5]

The earliest evidence for the use of testimonies is that of Melito (*c.* 165), which is referred to by Eusebius: At the request of one Onesimus Melito compiled six books of 'Extracts (ἐκλογὰς) from the Law and the Prophets concerning the Saviour and concerning all our faith....'[6] To Cyprian (probably as a reviser) and to Gregory of Nyssa (the authorship is doubtful)

---

[1] J. Moffatt, *An Introduction to the Literature of the New Testament*, 3rd ed., Edinburgh, 1920, p. 24. Actually, Hatch and Vollmer have Jewish collections in mind; viewed as a Christian literary effort, the theory is developed by Burkitt and Harris.

[2] Vollmer, op. cit., pp. 38-48. So Lietzmann, op. cit., p. 133. However, Jacobus (op. cit., pp. 9-29) dismissed the idea as 'purely speculative'.

[3] Cf. Swete, *Introduction*, pp. 252f; Thackeray, *Paul and Jewish Thought*, pp. 184f: 'The existence of such an anthology is by no means improbable, but it must be said that no very convincing proofs have yet been brought forward.'

[4] F. C. Burkitt, *The Gospel History and its Transmission*, Edinburgh, 1906, pp. 127ff. Burkitt's suggestion was not novel, but it was significant in the development of the 'testimony' hypothesis.

[5] J. R. Harris, *Testimonies*, 2 vols, Cambridge, 1916, 1920.

[6] Eusebius, *Ecclesiastical History*, IV, xxvi; trans. K. Lake, London, 1926, I, pp. 391f.

were ascribed similar collections.[1] These are taken to be not isolated efforts but instances of a general practice which dates back to the earliest days of Christianity. The dialogues used in post-apostolic apologetics, with their frequent reference to the OT, show, according to this hypothesis, a popular adaption of such testimony collections: 'It cannot be accidental that all the Greek and Latin Dialogues (except Justin's "Trypho", which is in a slightly different class) should put forward the same arguments in the same fashion, supported by the same proof texts.'[2]

Harris argued for the use of testimonies in the NT itself on the basis of several peculiarities in NT quotation[3]:

1. Recurrent quotations in the NT often agree with each other and with patristic writings in contrast to any known OT text.[4]

2. Some of these are combined quotations suggesting a common source in which the combination already existed.[5]

3. The same OT passages tend to be used in supporting a particular argument, and these arguments often appear under a specific concept or key-word as, for example, 'stone'.

Harris' concern is to show the early date and anti-Judaic character of the 'Testimony Book'.[6] Its presence in the Pauline literature is evident in the anti-Jewish arguments in Romans and Galatians. Justin's and Cyprian's *Testimonia* repeat some of these arguments. One prominent parallel is the quotation of Isa. 54.1 in Gal. 4.27, Justin's First Apology 53, and Cyprian's *Testimonia* 1.20. Justin's argument is closely aligned with

---

[1] Harris, op. cit., I, pp. 5f; Hunt, op. cit., pp. 226ff.

[2] Hunt, op. cit., p. 281. F. C. Conybeare (*The Dialogues of Athanasius and Zacchaeus and of Timothy and Aquila*, Oxford, 1898, pp. livff) attributes the similarities to a possible prototype dialogue such as 'Jason and Papiscus'.

[3] Harris, op. cit., I, pp. 8f; cf. Dodd, *According to the Scriptures*, pp. 24f.

[4] Sometimes the variants do appear in the texts of Aquila and Theodotion.

[5] This is given special force in the IF in Matt. 27.9 and Mark 1.2. There combined citations from Zechariah-Jeremiah and Malachi-Isaiah are ascribed simply to Jeremiah and Isaiah; this would be unlikely if the NT writers were working directly from the OT books.

[6] Harris, op. cit., I, p. 2. Hunt (op. cit., p. viii) follows much the same argument but endeavours by it to establish the influence of testimonies in the composition of the Gospels.

Cyprian, but it varies somewhat from Galatians[1]: 'He is not quoting St Paul directly. We must then either say that he is quoting St Paul indirectly in which case the *Testimony Book* becomes a pendant to the Epistles, or else we must say that the anti-Judaic parts of Romans and Galatians agree with Justin Martyr in a common dependence upon a primitive collection of Testimonies, and it is evident that the latter is the true explanation. . . .'[2] Harris finds much confirmation of this view from other parallel quotations in Paul, the patristic writers (especially Justin), and later 'Testimony' collections.[3] Perhaps the most noteworthy examples are the combinations in Rom. 9.25f[4] and Rom. 9.32f which recur in 1 Pet. 2.6-10. In the latter case the combination appears to be made under the key-word 'stone', in its messianic application to Christ. Cyprian's *Testimonia* have a section of 'Christ as stone' in which some of these OT passages (e.g. Isa. 28. 16; Ps. 117(118).22) are quoted; the same combination is found as well in some patristic writings (e.g. Barnabas VI).[5] Harris concluded that all these parallels found their proper explanation in a common dependence on the 'Testimony Book'; this document, therefore, was earlier than the NT canonical books and was probably to be identified (as Burkitt suggested) with Papias' *Logia*.

Harris' hypothesis was accepted as established by most writers and, with slight modifications, was applied to various problems of NT research.[6] However, there developed during this same period a broader interest in pre-canonical Christian

[1] According to Justin the passage shows that Gentile Christians would be 'more numerous and more true' than Jewish and Samaritan Christians. Paul's contrast is between the true Israel (Jew and Gentile Christians alike) and the unbelieving Jewish nation.

[2] Harris, op. cit., I, p. 24.

[3] Cf. Harris, op. cit., II, pp. 12-42; 'St Paul's use of Testimonies in the Epistle to the Romans', *The Expositor*, Eighth Series, 17 (June 1919), pp. 401-14; 'St Paul and Aristophanes', *ET*, 34 (January 1923), pp. 151-6; 'Josephus and His Testimony', *Evergreen Essay No.* 2, Cambridge, 1931, pp. 18-21.

[4] *Supra*, pp. 89ff. The combination also occurs in Cyprian's *Testimonia*, 1.19.

[5] Harris, *Testimonies*, I, pp. 26-32. Among other examples given by Harris (ibid., pp. 12-42) are Rom. 10.16 (John 12.37f; Justin, Dial. 42) and Eph. 4.8 (Justin, Dial. 39). In the latter case Justin is similar to Ephesians but enumerates the gifts differently.

[6] Cf. Moffatt, op. cit., p. 24; Box, op. cit., p. 445. J. A. Findlay, 'The First Gospel and the Book of Testimonies', *Amicitiae Corolla*, ed. H. G. Wood, London, 1933, pp. 57-71; D. Plooij, 'Studies in the Testimony Book', *Verhandlingen der Koninglijke Akademie van Wetenshappen*, Amsterdam, 1933. A. M. Hunter, *Paul and His Predecessors*, London, 1940, p. 70.

writings which served to modify and eventually undermine the 'Testimony Book' theory. Writing in 1929, Michel granted the probability of a 'testimony' collection for missionary and polemic purposes in the sub-apostolic Church and possibly even in Paul's day; nevertheless, Harris' theory underrated Paul's originality and his importance for later writers, who may well have used Paul and varied their texts to suit their own purpose. Also, the possibility of a key-word (*Stichwort*)[1] rather than 'testimonies' as the occasion for text combinations in Paul had not been sufficiently considered.[2]

Form criticism also played a part in detracting from the 'Testimony Book' hypothesis; for example, Papias' *Logia* and Paul's reference to 'the third day' in 1 Cor. 15.3f were taken to refer not to testimony collections but to sayings of Jesus and to an early Passion narrative.[3] But the field of study probably most significant in indirectly modifying the Harris hypothesis was that of early Christian liturgics. The influence of the synagogue on the form of early Christian worship was probably considerable[4]; however, some of the liturgy apparently reflects an anti-rabbinic attitude which Harris finds in his 'Testimony Book'. The importance of the Decalogue in the Church service,[5]

---

[1] e.g. Rom. 9.33 ($\lambda i\theta os$); 15.10-12 ($\xi\theta\nu\eta$). Cf. *supra*, pp. 50n. A difficulty for this theory is that the key-word is not always present. e.g. the absence of $\xi\theta\nu\eta$ in passages grouped under 'Gentiles' such as Rom. 9.25f, 29; Gal. 4.27 (Justin, First Apology 53).

[2] Michel, *Bibel*, pp. 52ff, 88ff. Michel's line of reasoning is similar in some respects to that later followed by Dodd. N. J. Hommes (*Het Testimoniaboek*, Amsterdam, 1935, pp. 304-23, 365) argues that most of the things Harris and Plooij attributed to a 'Testimony Book' are better explained by *Stichwort* combinations. He considers at length the quotations in Rom. 3.10-18; 11.8-10; 2 Cor. 6.16ff.

[3] J. V. Bartlett, 'Papias' Exposition: Its Date and Contents', *Amicitiae Corolla*, pp. 15-44; V. Taylor, op. cit., p. 48; cf. T. W. Manson, 'The Life of Jesus', *BJRL*, 27-30 (1943-7), 299, p. 39. Manson refers the Logia to Christian oracles—sayings analogous to the old prophetic writings, giving the commands and promises of God to the New Israel. These are largely sayings of Jesus and are to be equated not with Matthew but with 'Q'.

[4] W. O. E. Oesterley, *The Jewish Background of the Christian Liturgy*, Oxford, 1925. Oesterley's estimate is revised downward by C. W. Dugmore (op. cit., pp. 75ff, 106, 108, 113) and O. S. Rankin ('The Extent of the Influence of the Synagogue Service upon Christian Worship', *Journal of Jewish Studies*, 1 (1948), pp. 27-32); but they recognise its importance for the type and order of service. Cf. G. Dix, *The Shape of the Liturgy*, London, 1944, pp. 12, 39.

[5] Cf. Pliny, *Letters*, X, xcvi, trans. W. Melmoth, London, 1915, II, p. 403: '. . . they sang in alternate verses a hymn to Christ, as to a god, and bound themselves to a solemn oath, not to any wicked deeds, but never to commit any fraud, theft or adultery, never to falsify their word, nor deny a trust. . . .' This apparently indicates a use of the Decalogue in some form during the worship service.

which may have influenced its form of citation in the NT,
evidently 'had from the beginning an anti-synagogical tendency,
stressing the validity of the Decalogue in contrast to the Cere-
monial Law'.[1] Cullmann also, in agreement with Harris,
accepts the use of OT anthologies in the Church for polemic
purposes, but he does not view this as their only or primary
content. The anthologies were often liturgical or catechetical
in design and included apostolic, as well as OT, writings.[2] Rom.
9.32f and 1 Pet. 2.4-8 were regarded by Harris as basic points
of evidence for Paul's use of the 'Testimony Book'; but Selwyn
took the common document behind the passages not as *testimonia* but as an early Christian hymn or rhythmical prayer.[3]
In general, these writers concerned with liturgical development
continued to recognise or assume the early date of the 'Testimony Book',[4] but the character of the 'testimonies' was viewed
in much broader fashion than the anti-Jewish polemic stressed
by Harris.[5]

T. W. Manson goes a step further in modification of the
hypothesis. He takes the similarities in NT exegesis as indicative
of a 'Testimony Book' but not necessarily one in written form:
'We should think of the "Testimony Book" not as something
that was turned out in written form in the earliest days of the
Church, but rather as a collection of proof-texts assembled in
the course of preaching, and forming a part of the primitive
kerygma. . . . It would be natural that the texts that should be
cited in support of any particular article of the *kerygma* should
fall into groups in the collection of testimonies. But, again, it
is not necessary that they should be written down. . . . In other
words the early form of the "Testimony Book" was determined

---

[1] Rankin, op. cit., p. 31.

[2] O. Cullmann, *The Earliest Christian Confessions*, London, 1949; *Early Christian
Worship*, p. 24: 'It is probable, too, that already in the earliest period, not only
Christian writings but also OT writings were read.' The first witness is Justin,
First Apology 67: '. . . the memoirs of the Apostles (Gospels?) or writings of the
prophets were read aloud as long as time allowed.'

[3] Selwyn, op. cit., pp. 268, 267 (On Eph. 5.14). Cf. Prat, op. cit., I, p. 417;
supra, pp. 88ff.

[4] Stendahl (op. cit., p. 217), however, rejects the theory outright: 'The methods
of the synagogue in dealing with the texts of the OT, both in liturgical reading and
in teaching, account for most of the features Harris wanted to explain by his Book
of Testimonies.'

[5] In Acts 26.23 are possible 'titles' of a fuller catalogue of testimony *catena*. Cf.
Dodd, *According to the Scripture*, pp. 16ff.

by the form of the primitive teaching and the book itself was written on the "fleshly tablets" of the preacher's heart.'[1]

In the light of the developments considered above, Dodd's significant contribution in this field may be better appreciated. Dodd recognises the importance of the elaborate investigations of Harris but concludes that the theory of a pre-canonical Christian 'Testimony Book' 'outruns the evidence, which is not sufficient to prove so formidable a literary enterprise at so early a date'.[2] He makes the following specific objections[3]:

1. Instances where citations of two or more NT writers agree against the LXX are not numerous, 'certainly not more numerous than cases where one agrees with the LXX and the other differs, or where both differ from the LXX and from one another'.
2. Identical combinations of OT passages in parallel NT texts are few and perhaps special and exceptional; they are insufficient to establish a general theory.
3. The recurrence of a group of passages in which 'stone' stands as a symbol is striking in correspondence to a later known testimony grouping; but it is almost unique.
4. If there was a work of such importance that NT and patristic writers used it as a *vade mecum*, it is inexplicable that there should be no reference to it (except possibly Papias') and no extant derivative from it until Cyprian's edition in the third century.

Dodd thinks that the NT evidence points not to a 'Testimony Book' as such but to a method of Bible study which found literary expression only sporadically and which only later resulted in the composition of 'Testimony Books'. This method involved the selection and use of blocks or sections of OT Scriptures. These sections were viewed as 'wholes', and verses were quoted from them not merely for their own significance

---

[1] T. W. Manson, 'The Argument from Prophecy', *JTS*, XLVI (1945), p. 132. Some mention of Bonsirven's objections to Harris' theory should also be made. Agreeing with Michel's assessment, he argues that Paul's rabbinic memory obviates any recourse to Jewish or Christian *florilegia* if they existed (op. cit., pp. 292, 337). Cf. also Puukko, op. cit., pp. 53f.

[2] Dodd, *According to the Scriptures*, p. 26. Formerly Dodd was in general agreement with Harris' hypothesis. Cf. Dodd, *Romans*, pp. 32, 221.

[3] Ibid., pp. 26f.

but as pointers to the total context; and it is the total context, not just the particular verse quoted, which forms the basis for argument in the NT.[1] The selections did not form a book but 'something belonging to the body of instructions imparted, orally in the main, . . . to those whose duties in the Church led them to OT research; a sort of guide to the study of the Bible for Christian teachers'.[2] The pertinent passages 'were understood and interpreted upon intelligible and consistent principles' which viewed the Gospel facts as the fulfilment of the Scriptures.[3] 'The whole body of material—the passages of the OT Scriptures with their application to the gospel facts—is common to all the main portions of the New Testament, and in particular it provided the starting point for the theological constructions of Paul, the author of Hebrews, and the Fourth Evangelist.'[4]

Dodd develops his thesis first by considering the 'testimonies' —OT passages used repetitively in the NT—and then by classifying those sections of the OT which these passages embrace. Though recognising the possibility of literary dependence between the NT writers, he thinks such a presumption overlooks the more probable hypothesis of a common oral tradition. Accordingly, he proceeds to treat such parallels as occur as reflecting a common tradition unless there is definite evidence to the contrary.[5] The portions of Scripture which emerge as a source of *testimonia* for the NT writers are classified as follows[6]:

Apocalyptic-Eschatological	New Israel	Servant of the Lord	Unclassified
Joel 2-3; Zech. 9-14; Dan. 7.	Hosea; Isa. 6. 1-9.7; 11.1-10; 28.16; 40.1-11; Jer. 31.10-34.	Isa. 42.1-44.5; 49.1-13; 50. 4-11; 52.13-53. 12; 61; Ps. 69, 22, 31, 38, 88, 34, 118, 41, 42-3, 80.	Ps. 8, 110, 2; Gen. 12.3; 22.18; Deut. 18.15; 18.19.

[1] Dodd, *According to the Scriptures*, p. 126; *The Old Testament in the New*, p. 7.
[2] Dodd, *The Old Testament in the New*, p. 9.
[3] Dodd, *According to the Scriptures*, p. 126.   [4] Ibid., p. 127.   [5] Ibid., pp. 29f.
[6] Ibid., pp. 62-108. Gen. 15.6 is omitted as not directly bearing on an understanding of the *kerygma* (p. 107). The primary and secondary sources are listed in order.

Apocalyptic-Eschatological	New Israel	Servant of the Lord	Unclassified
Mal. 3.1-6; Dan. 12.	Isa. 29; Jer. 7; Hab. 1, 2.	Isa. 58.6-10.	Ps. 132, 16; 2 Sam. 7.13f; Isa. 55.3; Amos 9.11f.

With the exception of the first category Dodd's 'text-plots' are well represented in the Pauline letters.[1] Their significance is not merely in being the source of a number of NT quotations or allusions; the impressive fact is that these NT references have a thematic unity and reveal that the writers went to common sources and interpreted them with a common understanding of their application to the facts of the Gospel.

Dodd's hypothesis gives a more comprehensive picture of the use of Scripture in the early Church than Harris' theory was able to do. Dodd does not reject the possibility of written testimonies in the apostolic period.[2] But they are not primary, but derivative from a particular method of Bible study; and in the early pre-canonical development they form only a small and fragmentary portion of the total 'testimony' exegesis.

As noted above Dodd views the process as growing out of an 'original coherent and flexible method of biblical exegesis' whose beginnings lead back to the very nascence of the Christian Church: 'This is a piece of genuinely creative thinking. Who was responsible for it? The early Church we are accustomed to say, and perhaps we can safely say no more. But creative thinking is rarely done by committees. . . . Among Christian thinkers of the first age known to us there are three of genuinely creative power: Paul, the author to the Hebrews, and the Fourth Evangelist. We are precluded from proposing any one of them for the honour of having originated the process, since even Paul, greatly as he contributed to its development, demonstrably did not originate it. . . . But the NT itself avers

---

[1] See Appendixes I and IV. There are only a very few from the apocalyptic-eschatological section (e.g. Rom. 10.13; cf. 1 Cor. 6.2; 1 Thess. 4.13); but since the section itself is small, this may not be particularly significant. Dodd's list is not exhaustive; and if 'testimonies' be taken in a broader sense, some other passages which are important for Paul might be added (e.g. Gen. 2, 15ff; Lev. 18, 19).

[2] Harris is to this extent confirmed by the discovery of *testimonia* among the Qumran texts. Cf. J. T. Milik, *Discoveries in the Judean Desert*, 1955, I, 121; F. F. Bruce, 'Qumran and Early Christianity,' NTS, II, 3, pp. 179f.

that it was Jesus Christ himself who first directed the minds of his followers to certain parts of the Scriptures as those in which they might find illumination upon the meaning of his mission and destiny. . . . To account for the beginning of this most original and fruitful process of rethinking the OT we found need to postulate a creative mind. The gospels offer us one. Are we compelled to reject the offer?'[1] The examination made earlier of material which Paul holds in common with other NT writers points in the very direction which Dodd has suggested.

Λέγει Κύριος Quotations

There are nine NT quotations—four of them in Pauline letters—within which the phrase 'saith the Lord' (λέγει κύριος) occurs[2]; the equivalent phrase, λέγει ὁ θεός occurs once.[3] Rom. 12.19 is a typical example: 'For it is written: Vengeance is mine, I will repay saith the Lord.' The phenomenon would ordinarily be of only passing interest since any number of OT texts include this seal of authority. However, two factors are present which warrant a second look: (1) All the citations vary, to one extent or another, both from the LXX and from the MT. Furthermore, the variations are not only in the addition or omission of words but in the rendering of the text as well. (2) On at least six occasions the phrase λέγει κύριος (as well as λέγει ὁ θεός in Acts 2.17) is a NT addition to the text[4]; the other five occurrences—all non-Pauline—have the phrase or its equivalent in the OT text.[5]

In the question of subject matter there is some affinity with *testimonia* already considered although only one λέγει κύριος passage is used more than once (Rom. 12.19; Heb. 10.30). The greater portion of the citations is related to the 'temple' typology in which the Christian community is viewed as God's new temple. This is the definite import of Stephen's words (Acts

---

[1] Dodd, *According to the Scriptures*, pp. 109f.

[2] Acts 7.49; 15.16f; Rom. 12.19; 14.11; 1 Cor. 14.21; 2 Cor. 6.16ff; Heb. 8.8-12; 10.16f; 10.30. The phrase occurs twice in 2 Cor. 6.16ff and three times in Heb. 8.8-12. Its presence in Heb. 10.30 (=Rom. 12.19) is textually uncertain; Codex *A* and the Antiochene texts have it, *B* and *C* omit it.   [3] Acts 2.17.

[4] If Heb. 10.30 be admitted, the total is seven. In Acts 7.49 the phrase may have been borrowed from the opening clause of the LXX and the MT.

[5] Acts 15.16f; Heb. 8.8, 9, 10; 10.16f. The passages quoted in Hebrews all have φησὶ κύριος in the LXX.

7.49),[1] and it is the explicit purpose for the adduction of the *catena* in 2 Cor. 6.16. Amos 9.11f (Acts 15.16f) is cited by James to show that the purpose of God includes the Gentiles; the introductory portion of the quotation concerns rebuilding 'the tabernacle of David'. As noted above, these themes are a part of a pattern, and their presence here suggests, at least, that this context of Scripture was understood as a part of the 'new temple' *testimonia*.[2]

The New Covenant prophecy (Jer. 31.31ff) cited in Hebrews (8.8-12; 10.16) also has more than a surface connexion with the other passages. The author of Hebrews sums up his argument by noting that Christ is the minister 'of the true tabernacle (τῆς σκηνῆς τῆς ἀληθινῆς), which the Lord pitched, not man',[3] and the mediator of a better covenant; then follows Jeremiah's prophecy concerning the New Covenant. It may be going too far to see in 'the house of Israel' (i.e. the Christian 'remnant') an allusion to the 'true tabernacle'[4] or to make a contrast between the law in the heart and the tablets (or scrolls) of the law in the temple. But the words, 'I shall be to them a God and they shall be to me a people', are a distinct echo of a verse in a Pauline 'new temple' quotation (2 Cor. 6.16ff); and the reference to the Old Covenant 'ready to vanish away' (v. 13) is probably an allusion to the old temple services.[5]

The other λέγει κύριος quotations concern (1) the principle of vengeance or judgment as the prerogative of God alone (Rom. 12.19; 14.11; Heb. 10.30) and (2) the judicial significance of 'tongues' (1 Cor. 14.21). The latter may be considered within the framework of anti-Jewish polemic to which Harris assigned the 'Testimony Book'.[6] The citation (Acts 2.17ff) λέγει ὁ θεός is from a section of the OT listed by Dodd as a primary testimony source, and from which Paul also draws a quotation (Rom. 10.13).

---

[1] Cf. *supra*, p. 90.   [2] Cf. *supra*, pp. 90ff.
[3] Heb. 8.2. It is an interpretive paraphrase of Num. 24.6 (LXX).
[4] Taken in terms of the Jewish concept of solidarity, there is a closer relation than is apparent at first. Cf. Paul's phrase, οἶκος θεοῦ, *supra*, pp. 89f; 1 Tim. 3:15; *KTW*, V, 128ff.   [5] Cf. Westcott, op. cit., p. 226. Cf. Rev. 21.2f.
[6] The passage is difficult. Robertson and Plummer give perhaps the best explanation (op. cit., pp. 316f): As the Jews who scorned Isaiah's clear and simple message were judged in God's speaking to them by means of a foreign-tongued Assyrian horde, so now those Jews rejecting the simple message of the Gospel are, in effect, judged by the incomprehensible words of the Holy Spirit.

Taken as a whole, the λέγει κύριος quotations represent only a fraction of NT citations, and some of these merely repeat the phrase from the OT text; and most of the passages inserting the phrase *ad hoc* are Pauline. Yet the usage appears to be more than an idiosyncracy of any individual NT writer. The 'testimony' pattern into which most of the passages fall, the ever-present textual variations, and the significance of the phrase in the OT suggest that λέγει κύριος may have been characteristic in the proclamation of elements of the *kerygma*. Even if Heb. 10.30 be excepted, the words of Stephen and the essentially identical λέγει ὁ θεός of Peter remain independent witnesses to the practice. Its employment in Paul is too sporadic to construe the verses in Acts as Lukan interpolation of Pauline phraseology. Nor is the explanation satisfying that the NT writers are merely stressing the fact that God is speaking. The IF performs this function; and the λέγει κύριος is always an integral part of the citation, apparently already present in the text when it is introduced by the writer.

Λέγει κύριος is the badge of prophetic pronouncement in the OT. Its presence in the NT probably has an equivalent significance and may give a clue to understanding the rôle which the NT exegete—or better, the NT prophet—considered himself to fill. The gift of prophecy was highly regarded in the apostolic age[1]; it was a specific gift or appointment of the Holy Spirit[2]; and it was not conferred upon all.[3] Early Christians without doubt used the word in full light of its OT significance, and, indeed, some of the functions most peculiar to OT prophets, such as predictive utterance, appear in their NT counterpart.[4]

It is not unreasonable to expect that the NT 'prophet' would, at times, employ the prophetic epigraph 'thus saith the Lord'. The equivalent phrase, 'thus saith the Holy Spirit' (τάδε λέγει

---

[1] Cf. Acts 2.17ff; 1 Cor. 14.1-5. Stress on the prophetic aspect is seen in the added phrase καὶ προφητεύσουσιν in Acts 2.18.   [2] Cf. 1 Cor. 12.4, 10, 28.

[3] Cf. 1 Cor. 12.28. Swete states that 'only a relatively small number of believers were "established to be prophets", forming a charismatic order to which a recognised position was given in the Church. Such persons were said ἔχειν προφητείαν (1 Cor. 13.2) and known as οἱ προφῆται (Eph. 2.20; 3.5; Rev. 18.20; 22.6), being thus distinguished from those who occasionally "prophesied" (Acts 19.6; 1 Cor. 11.4f; 14.31).' Swete, *The Holy Spirit in the New Testament*, p. 377. cf. H. B. Swete, *The Apocalypse of St. John*, London, 1909, pp. xvii-xxi.   [4] e.g. Acts 21.11.

τὸ πνεῦμα τὸ ἅγιον), introduces the prophecy of Agabus in Acts 21.11.[1] The occurrences in Revelation are even more noteworthy. In Rev. 14.13 the phrase 'saith the Spirit' appears in much the same fashion as λέγει κύριος in the passages mentioned above: 'And I heard a voice from heaven saying, Write: Blessed are the Dead who die in the Lord henceforth. Yea, saith the Spirit, that they may rest from their labours; for their deeds follow them.' In the beginning of John's prophecy[2] the Lord Christ is quoted as follows: 'I am the Alpha and the Omega, saith the Lord God (λέγει κύριος ὁ θεός), the One who is, and was, and is to come, the Almighty (ὁ παντοκράτωρ).'[3] This quotation has no IF and λέγει κύριος may only be the writer's way of introduction. If so, it evidences a type of IF of which there are very few in the NT; even the other λέγει κύριος quotations have an IF of the ordinary type.

At first sight one is inclined to dismiss the whole matter as the idiom of the NT writers as they quoted, and it may well be that some instances are only the writer's formula of quotation. Such a case could be made, for example, of the two citations in Revelation. This, however, does not explain why the pattern is not found more often; it certainly does not explain why Paul, whose IF are so consistently different, should have λέγει κύριος embedded in a few of his quotations which already contained an ordinary formula of introduction, and that he should do this without any warrant from the OT text. It is more probable that this was the form of the quotation most familiar to him. He may, certainly, have originated the particular form himself; but it is extremely doubtful that he did so as he wrote his epistle. That he introduced a double IF into his quotations sporadically and apparently without any reason is one of the least likely explanations of the matter.

The foregoing argument may be summed up as follows:

1. Λέγει κύριος is a characteristic phrase of prophetic pronouncement in the OT.

---

[1] Cf. Heb. 3.7.   [2] Cf. Rev. 1.3.
[3] Rev. 1.8. The phraseology differs from the more usual IF, e.g. 'these things saith he that . . .'. Cf. Rev. 2.1; 3.1. It is perhaps worth noting that ὁ παντοκράτωρ occurs only once in the NT outside Revelation; it is in the λέγει κύριος quotation in 2 Cor. 6.16ff.

2. The early Christian community also includes those with the office or appointment of 'prophet', and these 'prophets' sometimes use the same phrase, or its equivalent, in citing their own revelation.

3. The phrase also is inserted within some quotations in the NT in such a manner as to preclude its being considered an IF or a part of the cited OT text.

4. These λέγει κύριος quotations are consistently divergent from extant OT texts and their OT source is often within a 'testimony' pattern evident elsewhere.

It is not an unreasonable conclusion that at least some of the Pauline λέγει κύριος texts were quoted by the apostle in a form already known and used in the early Church. The most natural origination for such paraphrasis of the OT would be early Christian prophets—including not only leaders such as Paul but also many minor figures.

The use of testimonies may well have arisen, as Dodd suggests, from the selection of whole sections of the OT and their oral application to the facts of the Gospel. But this does not mean that no written and specific 'proof-texts' were in use in the pre-canonical testimony tradition.[1] Whether there was an actual 'school of the prophets' one can only speculate. But Stendahl has shown at least that many OT quotations in the NT evidence a careful working out of interpretive principles, and the incorporation of these principles into the text of the quotations themselves.[2]

There is an activity of the Holy Spirit in the early Church which may well explain the source of some of the interpretations. It is the exercise of prophecy, and it occurs both in ecstatic utterance (cf. 1 Cor. 12-14) and in the disclosure of the import of revelations from the Holy Spirit (e.g. Acts 21.11). There

---

[1] Dodd argues against the hypothesis of a pre-canonical 'Testimony Book', but he recognises the possibility of occasional testimonies in written form; cf. Dodd, *According to the Scriptures*, p. 126. The presence of OT *florilegia* among the recent Qumran discoveries witnesses to the practice; *supra*, p. 106n. Cf. C. Rabin, *The Zadokite Documents*, Oxford, 1954, p. ix.

[2] *Infra*, pp. 139ff. Stendahl's conclusions are concerned mainly with Matthew, but he finds similar evidence in the Fourth Gospel: 'Thus the Johannine method is not what is usually meant by loose citations, or those more or less freely quoted from memory. It is rather the opposite since the form of John's quotations is certainly the fruit of scholarly treatment of written OT texts' (op. cit., p. 163).

is no reason why it should not include elaboration, interpretation and application of OT Scriptures.[1] The fact that
the prophetic λέγει κύριος was already present in some OT
texts being used as *testimonia* may well have facilitated an *ad
hoc* employment elsewhere. This extension appears, at least
in some degree, to be related to *testimonia* of the same order
or perhaps arising from the same group or 'school'.[2] There
would be no hesitation in using these OT paraphrases—or any
other matter spoken 'in the Spirit', for they, as much as the OT
itself, were the words of God. This hypothesis is not without
its problems, but it does seem satisfactorily to explain at least
some of the phenomena found in NT quotation and to shed
further light on the genesis and development of OT exegesis in
the early Church.

Summary and Conclusion

It is evident from observations made in the above pages that
Paul does not quote the OT in isolation; and his relation to
other NT writings is not satisfactorily explained as merely a
borrowing by one writer from another. Some sort of mutual
connexion with a third source appears most probable. Queries
as to the nature of this connexion gave rise to the testimony-
book theory. There is at least one pre-canonical Christian
document known—the Jerusalem Decree (Acts 15.23-9), and
there can be no *a priori* objection to others. Harris supposed
that one of these was a 'Testimony Book' upon which NT and
patristic writers freely drew in quoting the OT. Harris depended
too much in his theory on the independence of patristic citations
from their NT parallels; but once established, the 'Testimony
Book' was seen lying behind parallels within the NT itself.
Dodd's objections to Harris' hypothesis are, for the most part,
well taken; and it is with his theory of an interpretative method
applied to selected OT 'text-plots' that future investigations

[1] There is something similar to this in the reflection of OT prophets upon earlier
Scriptures; cf. Ps. 2, 105; Isa. 48.21; *supra* p. 47n. The origin of some early
Christian hymns—a few of which are incorporated into the NT (cf, Selwyn, op. cit.,
p. 267; *supra*, p. 35)—may also have been included within the exercise of the
prophetic gift. Cf. 1 Cor. 14.15.

[2] e.g. the presence of λέγει κύριος (φησὶ κύριος) in Amos 9.11f (Acts 15.16f) and
Jer. 31.31ff (Heb. 8.8ff) may have occasioned the *ad hoc* usage in other 'new temple'
testimonia such as the *catena* in 2 Cor. 6.16ff.

will begin. Dodd believes that the key to OT interpretation was given by Christ Himself to His apostles, and a considerable portion of Pauline exegesis appears to find its origin in just this source. Relevant to the question are the words of C. F. Evans: 'When the Old Testament and rabbinic and hellenistic writings have been ransacked for parallels to, and possible sources of influence upon, the Gospel tradition, it still remains at least possible, if not probable, that by far the greatest single determinative source with which we have to reckon is the creative originality of Jesus Himself. . . .'[1]

The λέγει κύριος quotations and a few other striking parallels indicate that some OT texts were already in stereotyped form when Paul used them. It therefore appears that some texts from the testimony 'text-plots' had, previous to Paul's letters, received specific interpretation and application by others in the early Church. There are grounds for supposing that this may have arisen and been carried on in informal fashion by those filling the rôle of prophet in the early Church. Much of this activity probably took place in the course of preaching and missionary endeavour, as Michel and Manson have suggested, though Stendahl's hypothesis of a 'school' for OT interpretation cannot be disregarded.

Dodd has made the point that the Lord is probably the One who pointed out pertinent sections of the OT and gave His apostles certain interpretative principles whereby these passages were to be understood. One further question is closely connected with this: What is the nature of the interpretative principles employed by the NT writers? Some consideration of this question as it applies to the Pauline hermeneutic will be given in the following chapter.

[1] C. F. Evans, 'I will Go Before You Into Galilee', *JTS*, Second Series, 5 (April 1954), p. 3.

CHAPTER IV

PAULINE EXEGESIS

INTRODUCTION

IN the previous chapters an attempt has been made to determine the nature and significance of Paul's OT quotations and to relate his usage to contemporary Jewish and Christian exegesis. The following pages consider some of the emphases in Pauline exegesis and the hermeneutical principles which govern his citation and application of the OT. Quotations may be classified according to text,[1] purpose[2] or subject matter.[3] In the present study a topical classification has been followed with some particular attention given to the use of typology. The concluding section discusses two fundamental principles which are determinative for Paul's OT hermeneutic.

Paul's exegesis fits into a pattern which, when properly understood, forms a cogent and systematic whole. Even the more difficult passages take their place in the pattern when they are considered from the apostle's point of view.[4] Paul was a profound thinker and the OT was one subject on which his thought was in orderly array. His was no grasping for texts or waving of a talisman; and conclusions to that effect probably indicate a misunderstanding of his meaning. Dodd evaluates Paul's elaborate exegesis in Rom. 9-11 as follows: 'This is evidence of the thorough and extensive biblical research which lies behind Paul's exposition of the Gospel. It should be added that the argument, compressed and complex as it is, proceeds by

---

[1] Cf. Appendix I.   [2] e.g. proof, type, analogy, illustration, allegory.
[3] Bonsirven (op. cit., pp. 294-324) classifies Paul's exegesis as express and implicit.
[4] Quotations for illustration or language colour, although present, are not so prevalent as is usually supposed. 1 Cor. 15.32 repeats a proverb in Isaiah; 1 Cor. 10.26 also appears to be a convenient use of Scripture phraseology. Dodd (*The Old Testament in the New*, pp. 3f) allows for such allusion in the NT, as in any book, which serves no further purpose than to stimulate the fancy or give aesthetic enrichment; but he concludes that NT writers use such allusion 'less than might appear at first sight'.

strict sequence from step to step, and is, with one or two possible exceptions, completely cogent, granted the presuppositions common to Paul and to those whom he addressed. The qualification indeed is itself scarcely necessary; if one takes the pains to understand exactly what is implied in the various steps of the argument, there is very little which does not contribute to a strictly logical presentation of his case from first principles.'[1]

The discussion below does not pretend to be a commentary. It is an endeavour to form a synthesis of Pauline exegesis both from a topical and from a hermeneutical viewpoint. In a sense the whole NT is an exegesis of the Old; for it seeks throughout to explain the Christian movement as a fulfilment of the OT. So Luther wrote: ' ... All [the apostles'] preaching is based on the OT, and there is no word in the NT which does not look back to the Old wherein it was already declared. ... The OT is thus the testament of Christ—a letter which he caused to be opened after his death and read and proclaimed in the light of the gospel...'[2] It is 'the light of the Gospel' which determines Paul's approach to the OT. The demonstrable fact that Jesus is the promised Messiah—a major theme of OT citation in the Gospels—is assumed.[3] The apostle is chiefly concerned with the next step—the significance of the Scriptures for the Messianic Age and Messianic Community.

TOPICAL EMPHASES

Paul's devotion to Scripture was not that of a rabbi; he did not cite the Scriptures from a sense of duty or a love of theology or tradition, but because of their witness to Christ. For Paul, Christ was not only a factor giving added meaning to the OT but the only means whereby the OT could be rightly understood; it was not merely that he saw Christ in the OT but that he viewed the whole scope of OT prophecy and history from

[1] Dodd, *According to the Scriptures*, p. 18.
[2] Luther, Sermon on John 1.1-14; Weimar ed., X, 1, pp. 181f, cited in W. Vischer, *The Witness of the Old Testament to Christ*, London, 1949, p. 7.
[3] Stendahl, (op. cit. pp. 41f) notes also the many allusions to Elijah in the Gospels as contrasted with Paul (e.g. Mark 1.2, 3, 14; Matt. 17.10ff; Luke 1.17). Even more striking is the absence of Pauline messianic proof-texts, basically important for any Jewish Christian. Their existance, however, in the form of early 'Gospels' or of previous oral teaching, is presupposed.

the standpoint of the Messianic Age in which the OT stood open, fulfilled in Jesus Christ and in His new Creation.

Paul, like the other NT writers, uses the OT selectively; he makes no attempt to exploit even the whole corpus of messianic prediction either as it refers to Christ or to the Messianic Age.[1] Nevertheless, the subjects on which the apostle dwells read like an outline of biblical theology.[2] Something of the scope of his OT references may be seen in the following index:

1.	The Fall of Man and its Effects	Rom. 5.12ff
2.	The Universality of Sin	Rom. 3.10ff
3.	The Coming of Christ and the Gospel	Rom. 1.2; Gal. 3.8, 14
4.	The Obedience and Sufferings of Christ	Rom. 15.3
5.	The Resurrection of Christ	1 Cor. 15.1ff
6.	The Lordship and Dominion of Christ	1 Cor. 15.25, 27
7.	The Sovereignty of God	Rom. 9.15, 17, 20
8.	Divine Election	Rom. 9.7, 10ff; 11.4f
9.	The Rejection of Israel and Calling of the Gentiles	Rom. 9.25ff; 10.16ff
10.	The Universality of the Gospel	Rom. 10.18
11.	The Forgiveness of Sin	Rom. 4.6; 9.33; 10.11ff
12.	Justification by Faith	Rom. 1.17; 4.1ff; 10.5ff
13.	Baptism and the Lord's Supper	1 Cor. 10.1ff
14.	The Gifts of the Spirit	Eph. 4.8
15.	Christian Conduct	Rom. 12.19; 13.9 1 Cor. 9.9
16.	The Persecution of Christians	Rom. 8.36
17.	The Final Salvation of the Jews	Rom. 11.26
18.	The *Parousia* of Christ	2 Thess. 1.8-10
19.	The Final Judgment	Rom. 14.11
20.	The Final Overthrow of Death	1 Cor. 15.54ff

If some of the above topics are not the object of express OT prophecy, they are implicit in its history or typology as viewed

---

[1] C. H. Dodd, *History and the Gospel*, London, 1938, p. 61.
[2] Cf. T. Houghton, 'Testimony of the Epistle to the Romans to the Old Testament', *Evangelical Quarterly*, 7 (October 1935), pp. 424ff.

from the standpoint of the Messianic Age. The extent to which these motifs may be traced to the Pentateuch is striking. Most of the framework of Paul's theology rests upon the accounts of the Creation, the life of Abraham, and the Exodus. Unlike the rabbis, however, it is a Pentateuch illumined and interpreted by the Prophets and Psalms, not by the traditions of the Elders.

FAITH AND WORKS

The most important OT theme in Romans and Galatians is the basis of man's justification before God.[1] Paul argues that righteousness comes through faith and not through the law; to those who trust God's promise righteousness is imputed, but to those who seek righteousness through law perfect obedience to the law is required. While the law was good in that it made manifest God's will, it could not by the works it enjoined enable men to fulfil its commands.[2]

The *locus classicus* for this theme is Hab. 2.4 (Rom. 1.17; Gal. 3.11): 'The righteous shall live by faith.' The verse poses several problems: What is the content of the word faith ($\pi i\sigma\tau\iota\varsigma$)? Is the contrast between a 'faith-righteousness' and a 'law-righteousness' (i.e. the righteous-by-faith shall live) or is $\pi i\sigma\tau\iota\varsigma$ the sole factor which secures 'righteousness'? The Hebrew אמונה has primarily a passive idea of 'faithfulness' or 'trustworthiness', while the Greek $\pi i\sigma\tau\iota\varsigma$ stresses the active force of 'trust in'. Burney has observed that while אמונה is frequently used to denote the quality of character produced by $\pi i\sigma\tau\iota\varsigma$, the words 'to show steadfastness in' (ב האמין cf. Num. 14.11) are the regular Hebrew phrase denoting 'believe in' ($\pi i\sigma\tau\iota\varsigma$). Thus, Burney concludes, 'The statement that Hebrew has no term which can be regarded as the equivalent of $\pi i\sigma\tau\iota\varsigma$, and that therefore St Paul's use of Hab. 2.4 cannot be justified, hardly represents the fact.'[3] The meanings of the two words

---

[1] Cf. Rom. 1.17; 4; 10.4ff; Gal. 3.6ff; 4.22ff. The two principal sections, Rom. 4 and Gal. 3, may be classified as a Christian Midrash or commentary on Abraham's faith. Cf. Windisch, *Paulus und das Judentum*, pp. 52f.

[2] Cf. W. Fairweather, *The Background of the Epistles*, Edinburgh, 1935, p. 339.

[3] Burney, *The Gospel in the Old Testament*, pp. 129f. Cf. Lightfoot, *Galatians*, p. 138; J. S. Stewart, op. cit., pp. 173-86; D. M. Baillie, *Faith in God*, Edinburgh, 1927, p. 34: 'In apocalyptic literature the ideas of faith and fidelity merge into one.' *Contra*: S. R. Driver, *The Minor Prophets*, Edinburgh, 1906, p. 76; A. B. Davidson, *Nahum, Habakkuk and Zephaniah*, Cambridge, 1896, p. 76.

overlap and vary only in stressing different aspects of the larger
'whole'. Paul's rendering is paraphrastic and interpretive
but quite justifiable.[1] Epstein gives a particularly good definition of אמונה which could well serve as a 'harmony' of Paul
and James: 'The Hebrew word *Emunah* has a two-fold connotation—theological and human. It signifies alike faith—trust in
God, and faithfulness—honesty, integrity—in human relations.
These two concepts . . . do not conflict with each other; on the
contrary they complement and supplement each other. . . .
Faith . . . is of value only in so far as it is productive of faithful
action; nor is there any faithful action that is not rooted in
faith in God.'[2]

'Εκ πίστεως in Rom. 1.17 has usually been taken, in accordance with Habakkuk's meaning and Paul's grammar, as
modifying ζήσεται and pointing out the condition by which the
righteous live.[3] Nygren, on the other hand, views Paul as
establishing a 'faith-righteousness versus works-righteousness'
contrast which the apostle pursues throughout the epistle[4]: It
is the righteous-by-faith who shall live. 'It is not suggested',
writes Nygren, 'that Paul did not grasp the literal sense of the
statement, but rather that he saw in it a deeper significance.'[5]
But not only the grammar is against Nygren[6]; for Paul there is
no 'law-righteousness' or 'works-righteousness'. The universal-
ity of sin, which Paul takes such pains to point out (Rom. 3.10ff),
precludes the possibility of such; for the very principle from
which 'law-righteousness' proceeds is that 'he who does those
things shall live by them'.[7] The law fails and its adherents are
condemned, not because the righteousness it required is any
less acceptable, but because its adherents invariably 'continue

---

[1] Cf. Lightfoot, *Galatians*, p. 138. The Hebrew is so translated by Symmachus,
Aquila, Theodotion and other Greek versions.

[2] *SBT*, Seder Zera'im., I, p. xv.

[3] Lightfoot, *Notes*, pp. 250f; Sanday and Headlam, op. cit., pp. 28ff.

[4] A. Nygren, *Commentary on Romans*, London, 1952, pp. 87ff. Cf. A. Schweitzer,
The Mysticism of Paul the Apostle, London, 1931, pp. 208ff. Nygren, in good Lutheran
tradition, works out this contrast through the whole of Romans.

[5] Nygren, op. cit., p. 88.

[6] Sanday and Headlam (op. cit., p. 28) point out that if Paul had wished to
stress the contrast he could easily have written ὁ δὲ ἐκ πίστεως δίκαιος and removed
all ambiguity.

[7] Rom. 10.5; Gal. 3.11f. In Rom. 3.10ff Paul shows the Jews that the OT used
this language of them (v. 19); therefore, they are equally condemned with the
Gentiles.

not in the things which are written' (Gal. 3.10).[1] On the other hand faith secures, and maintains, righteousness, not because it is inherently superior to 'works' or law, but because it is the medium whereby a relationship is established with the One who is righteous.

Paul does not teach justification by faith in a vacuum. Faith does make one righteous both forensically[2] and, increasingly, in actuality,[3] because faith issues in the ἐν Χριστῷ relationship. For in Christ the law stands fulfilled; its goal (τέλος) is attained;[4] and for all who have passed from ἐν 'Αδάμ to ἐν Χριστῷ, Christ Himself is their 'righteousness, and sanctification and redemption' (1 Cor. 1.30). While 'the caption ἐν Χριστῷ may be placed above everything St Paul says',[5] its centrality does not displace the importance of *how* one becomes ἐν Χριστῷ. In Pauline thought the two concepts are one inseparable whole: 'One of the greatest mistakes of Albert Schweitzer has been to consider the doctrine of justification as a polemical by-product of Pauline thought, a theoretical auxiliary without practical significance. On the contrary, a proper understanding of St Paul must proceed from his teaching about how man is justified by faith in God's act of justification.'[6]

The place of the Habakkuk key-text in this motif may be better understood if approached from Paul's development of the theme in his earlier epistle to the Galatians.[7] Gal. 3 is largely a Midrash on the Abrahamic history, and of the seven quotations in the chapter all except the Habakkuk passage are from the Pentateuch.[8] It is virtually certain that the story of

[1] Paul does view the law as inferior (1) in being mediated through angels (Gal. 3.19), (2) in enticing men to make a claim on God (Rom. 4.3) and (3) in its transient character (2 Cor. 3.13). Cf. C. A. A. Scott, op. cit., pp. 41ff.

[2] 'Abraham believed God and it was counted to him for righteousness' (Rom. 4.3); 'Blessed is the man to whom the Lord will not impute sin' (Rom. 4.8).

[3] '[God sent His Son] that the righteousness of the law might be fulfilled in us who walk . . . after the Spirit' (Rom. 8.4). This is the force of the whole argument in Rom. 6-8; it is unthinkable that the unrighteous could be called righteous if the way and means of the creation and production of that righteousness were not in view and in operation. Cf. Rom. 8.29.

[4] Rom. 10.4. Sanday and Headlam (op. cit., p. 284) and Dodd (*Romans*, p. 165) take τέλος as 'termination', but the idea of fulfilment also seems to be present.

[5] A. Fridrichsen, 'Jesus, St Paul, and St John', *The Root of the Vine*, London, 1953, p. 41.　　　　　　　　　　　　　　　　　　　　[6] Ibid., p. 44.

[7] Schweitzer (*Mysticism of Paul*, pp. 208f) has rightly called attention to this distinction.

[8] Gen. 15.6; 12.3; 18.18; Deut. 27.26; Lev. 18.5; Deut. 21.23; Gen. 22.18.

Abraham forms the foundation for the 'righteousness by faith' motif in Pauline thought and that the verse from the 'Prophets' is adduced as an interpretation and application of the principle laid down in Genesis.[1] The lead-line position given Hab. 2.4 in the argument in Romans may be occasioned by its already popular connexion with Gen. 15.6, or its importance in Judaism as the summation of the law,[2] or, more probably, the place which it is likely to have had in the early Church as a 'pointer verse' to the whole faith-righteousness theme. The story of Abraham,[3] however, is the bedrock of Pauline thought on the question; and the faith therein expressed is determinative for the interpretation of 'faith' in Hab. 2.4. And this is an active faith, 'for Abraham's faith, according to St Paul, is faith in the miracle of the resurrection, which makes life out of death'.[4]

The transfer of Habakkuk's application to the status of a general principle arises from a selective interpretation of that passage. This exegetical moulding is present in the interpretation of 'faith' noted above, in the identification of the 'righteous', and in the whole point of reference involved in the vision. Whether the 'righteous' (צדיק) means every righteous individual, a particular righteous personage, righteous Israel, or the righteous in Israel, is left an open question by the grammar.[5] Paul, in accordance with the Targum and the Qumran commentary, interprets it of the righteous in Israel.[6] For the apostle, as for the Qumran community, the identity of the 'righteous' is bound up with the prophetic doctrine of the remnant. The NT writers understand the remnant to be the Christian Community; and it is to it that the prophecy refers.

It is important to remember that for Paul there is no discontinuity between Israel and the Church; his whole position depends upon the Christian remnant being the 'heir of the

---

[1] Similarly in Gal. 4, Isa. 54.1 apparently is cited as an elucidation of the Sarah-Hagar story.   [2] Cf. *supra*, p. 56n.

[3] The character of Isaac as 'the son of promise' (Rom. 4; Gal. 4.22ff) and the election of Jacob (Rom. 9.13) are a part of the same general theme: faith versus works, promise versus law. On Rom. 9-11 as also integral to it cf. Nygren, op. cit. p. 35.

[4] O. Cullmann *Baptism in the New Testament*, London, 1950, p. 66. Cf. Rom. 4.17; 10.9f; Heb. 11.17ff; Jas. 2.21ff.

[5] Cf. Manson, *The Argument from Prophecy*, pp. 133f.

[6] Ibid., p. 133; *supra*, p. 56.

Covenant'. The polemic against the Jewish nation for seeking righteousness apart from Christ 'must not conceal the fact that, in his opinion, righteousness is rooted in the Covenant itself, the New Covenant, the reality of faith. . . . For St Paul, to be righteous is to abide with one's whole being in this Covenant, to be "in Christ".'[1]

The vision in Hab. 2 is given in answer to the prophetic complaint that God has allowed the wicked (Chaldeans) to triumph. The vision is not to be fulfilled immediately,[2] and its fulfilment brings the final triumph of the righteous in which 'the earth shall be filled with the knowledge of the glory of the Lord, as the waters cover the sea' (Hab. 2.14). The 'wicked' in the vision are the Chaldeans, but the scope of the prophecy extends to a contrast of the wicked and righteous in general. In this wider context Paul finds the meaning of the vision. The Chaldean invasion is the occasion for the prophecy, but its fulfilment is in a wider and eschatological sphere. For the NT writers, the Messianic Age inaugurated by Jesus Christ's death and resurrection ushers in that fulfilment. This view of the prophecy understandably heightens the importance of Hab. 2.4 for the Christian Messianic Community.

JEW AND GENTILE

A second theme of primary importance in Pauline exegesis concerns the rejection of the Jews and 'calling' of the Gentiles. Both subjects find a place in the teaching of the pre-Pauline Church,[3] but Paul deals with the question more explicitly and extensively than do the other NT writers. The pertinent Pauline texts are found largely in Rom. 9-11, which Dodd terms a 'striking example' of the way Paul 'opens up' and applies the Scriptures.[4] The discussion grows out of the larger question of 'faith versus works' considered above, and (as Nygren contends) should be understood not as an arbitrarily inserted

---

[1] Fridrichsen, op. cit., pp. 50f.
[2] This is evidently the reason for writing it plainly 'upon tables' (Hab. 2.2). That it 'will not delay' emphasises not an immediacy but that it will occur exactly in its appointed time. Cf. 2 Sam. 20.5; Jud. 5.28; Driver, *The Minor Prophets*, p. 76. Davidson, *Habakkuk*, p. 75; G. W. Wade, *Habakkuk*, London, 1929, p. 182.
[3] Cf. *supra*, pp. 91f; *infra*, pp. 135ff.
[4] Dodd, *According to the Scriptures*, p. 18. There are a number of references elsewhere as, for example, Rom. 15.9-12, 21; Gal. 3.8; 1 Cor. 14.21.

pericope but as an integral part of the preceding argument.[1]

The apostle's analysis in Rom. 9-11 is intricate and interlaced throughout with OT 'proofs', but it follows an orderly sequence and gives a profound apologetic for a 'Christian' interpretation of the OT. Underlying the whole of the argument, and indeed the whole of Paul's OT exegesis, is the fundamental postulate that the 'true Israel', the heir of the promises, does not consist of physical descendants *ipso facto* but of 'children of the promise' sovereignly selected by God. This fact is clear (Rom. 9.6-13) in the selection of Isaac and rejection of Ishmael[2] and in the choice of Jacob instead of Esau,[3] even though all were physical descendants of Abraham. Paul proceeds (vv. 14-21) to justify such arbitrary decisions of God, and in doing so he assumes certain conclusions argued earlier: All men stand under a death judgment in Adam's sin and in their confirmation of Adam's rebellion in their own sins.[4] The favour of God even to the 'best' of men (Moses) is purely a matter of mercy, and His 'hardening' of wicked men (Pharaoh) is actually a moulding and directing of their evil 'in order to make known the riches of his glory on the vessels of mercy'.[5] Thus also (vv. 22-6) does the mercy given in calling Jews and Gentiles[6] in Christ apply only to a remnant of the Jewish nation, because they sought righteousness by works and found Christ, the way of faith, a rock of offence.[7]

[1] Whether the section did in fact have a separate existence is, of course, another question.

[2] Gen. 21.12.   [3] Gen. 18.10.   [4] Rom. 3.10ff; 5.12ff; *supra*, pp. 58ff.

[5] This section with its example of the potter and the clay is severely criticised by various commentators. Dodd (*Romans*, p. 159) calls it 'the weakest point in the whole epistle. . . . Man is not a pot; he will ask "why did you make me like this?" and he will not be bludgeoned into silence.' Cf. A. M. Hunter, *Interpreting Paul's Gospel*, London, 1954, p. 15. Such objections misconstrue Paul's argument; the moral question which Dodd labours is just not there. The character of the 'clay' is settled; it is in rebellion 'ripe and ready for destruction' (κατηρτισμένα v. 22, Moffatt), both personally and ἐν Ἀδάμ. The question is not 'Why did you create me thus?' but 'Why are you using me thus?' 'Why are you not showing me mercy?' God sovereignly makes the wrath of man to praise Him (cf. Ps. 76.10; Isa. 10.5); but it is for a merciful end, both in deferring judgment on the objects of wrath (v. 22) and in using their sins to bring objects—also sinful—of His mercy to Himself (v. 23).

[6] Rom. 9.25f; Hos. 2.23; 1.10. The application of this prophecy to Gentiles (as well as Jews) rests on the conception of 'Israel' argued in the earlier verses of Rom. 9. It is not the 'spiritualising' of a particular prophecy but the consistent application of a fundamental hermeneutical principle. Hosea has in view not physical Israel (Paul implies) but the regathered remnant of faith (cf. Rom. 9.27ff) irrespective of their lineage. Cf. *infra*, pp. 135ff.   [7] Isa. 10.22f; 1.9; 8.14; 28.16.

Rom. 10 contrasts the two ways, righteousness through works and through faith. The former requires perfect obedience to the law; the latter, a simple calling 'on the name of the Lord' in faith (vv. 6-11).[1] But Israel, as predicted, did not believe although the people knew the message and had ample warning of their impending rejection (vv. 16ff).[2] However, Paul concludes (Rom. 11), the rejection of Israel is not complete or final. As in Elijah's day there is a believing remnant; the rest, in judgment on their unbelief, are blinded (vv. 3f, 8ff).[3] After the full number of Gentiles are converted, the mass of Israel will turn to Messiah and be regrafted into the olive tree,[4] the Israel of God (vv. 26ff).[5] This purpose of salvation for Gentiles

[1] Lev. 18.5; Deut. 30.12ff; Joel 2.32. Rom. 10.6-8 is usually taken as a rhetorical application of a proverbial text. Cf. F. Johnson, op. cit., pp. 183ff; Prat, op. cit., I, p. 21; Davies, op. cit., pp. 153f; *supra*, pp. 54f. Others regard it as a misinterpretation of the OT passage; cf. Dodd, *Romans*, pp. 165ff; J. Weiss, op. cit., p. 436. While it is rhetorical (note the IF), the citation has more than a casual relation to the OT text. Deut. 30.6 speaks of the 'circumcision of the heart', which Jer. 31.31 identifies with the New Covenant. Deut. 30.11-14 does not merely concern the 'location' of the law but an attitude towards it, in which they love the Lord God 'with all their heart' (Deut. 30.6, 10, 16). Paul sees implicit in this an attitude of faith, which alone can fulfil the law (cf. Rom. 8.4), and so applies the principle to his own day.

[2] Isa. 53.1; Ps. 18.5; Deut. 32.21; Isa. 65.1.

[3] 3 Kings 19.14, 18; Isa. 29.10; Deut. 29.4; Ps. 68.23f. The 'unseeing eyes' motif (Isa. 29.10) reflects, and probably arises from, the teaching of Christ. Christ uses (Mark 4.11ff; cf. John 12.37) in this regard the prophecy in Isa. 6.9f, which Paul also cites in Acts 28.26ff. Cf. Rom. 10.16; John 12.38. On this passage Dodd (*Romans*, p. 176) aptly remarks: 'If we read the comments of a sober rabbi like Jochanan ben Zakki (cf. *SBK, ad loc.*) or of a political realist like Josephus, not to speak of the parables of Jesus, we are led to the conclusion that Paul did not exaggerate when he judged that the history of the eighth and seventh centuries B.C. was repeating itself in the half-century preceding the fall of Jerusalem.' Cf. 1 Thess. 2.16.

[4] As typifying Israel see Jer. 11.16; Men. 53b (*SBT*, p. 322). Cf. Hos. 14.7; A. Feldman, *The Parables and Similies of the Rabbis*, Cambridge, 1927, pp. 158-68. On the inclusion of the Gentiles in the 'olive tree' cf. Lev. R., I 2, (*SMR*, VI, 3).

[5] Isa. 59.20f; 27.9. The prophecy is applied not, as usual (e.g. Rom. 9.25f), to 'true Israel' but to the Jewish nation; cf. Dodd, *Romans*, p. 182. According to Delitzsch (*Isaiah*, II, p. 378), Isa. 59 gives a picture judgment (v. 18) resulting in a general turning to God and (v. 19) the coming of Jehovah for Zion, true Israel, and for Jacob, previously unfaithful Jews who then repent. The LXX rendering 'turn away from ungodliness from Jacob' reflects a variant text from the MT: 'to those turning from transgression in Jacob'; Ἐκ Σιὼν, Paul's only important variation from the LXX (ἕνεκεν Σιὼν), may arise from his contrast of Zion, true Israel, and Jacob, the nation Israel, and the resultant conviction that the Church as σῶμα Χριστοῦ and ναὸς θεοῦ is the *locus* (and perhaps the instrument) from which the Redeemer goes forth. Cf. Ps. 13(14).7; 52.7 (53.6). But cf. Ps. 77(78).68. Isa. 27.9 is in a similar messianic context. Paul probably uses both as 'pointer' texts, and his citation reveals an exegetical moulding by which his understanding of the prophecy is drawn out. Cf. *infra*, pp. 139ff.

and Jews—both disobedient, both rejected—arises totally from
God's mercy and draws from Paul's lips an exclamation of awe:
'O the depth of the riches and wisdom and knowledge of God.
How unsearchable his judgments and inscrutable his ways.'[1]

In conclusion, two points should be reiterated. First, the
doctrines of salvation by faith and the inclusion of the Gentiles,
so fully developed in Romans, as well as Paul's view of 'true
Israel', are found in one nucleus in Gal. 3. In the Galatians
passage most, if not all, of the points later 'spelled out' in
Romans either appear in abbreviated form or are assumed in
the argument: The Abrahamic Covenant is of faith (v. 6),[2]
includes the Gentiles (v. 8),[3] and has Christ for its true 'seed'
or heir (vv. 16, 29); neither physical descent nor works of law
avail to secure participation in it (vv. 10ff). Secondly, Paul's
theology stems primarily from the Pentateuch. The starting-
point of his thought is the story of Abraham; the citations from
the prophets appear to be interpreted in the light of the Genesis
narrative, and, *vice versa*, the Torah is understood in the light
of its interpretation by the prophets.[4]

MISCELLANEOUS

Eschatological quotations in Paul's letters are confined for
the most part to 1 Cor. 15,[5] but the principles expressed there

[1] Rom. 11.33. The section concludes with a quotation from Isa. 40.13; Job 41.3.
R. P. C. Hanson ('St. Paul's Quotations of the Book of Job', *Theology*, 53 (1950),
pp. 250-3) considers Paul's quotations from Job to reveal its true significance, not
the patience of the 'innocent sufferer' but the transcendence of God. Job, in short,
is 'the Epistle to the Romans of the OT' (p. 253).

[2] Gen. 15.6.

[3] Gen. 12.3; 18.18. Repetitions of the promise are given twice in the *hithpael*
(Gen. 22.18; 26.4), which has a reflexive connotation ('bless themselves'). 'But the
Niphal נברך (Gen. 12.3; 18.18; 28.14) has only the passive signification "to be
blessed"', and Paul's rendering, as an interpretation, is proper even for the others
(F. Delitzsch, *The Pentateuch*, Edinburgh, 1864, I, p. 195). Driver (*Genesis*, London,
1904, p. 145) regards the *Niphal* as ambiguous; E. Kautzsch (*Gesenius' Hebrew
Grammar*, Oxford, 1898, pp. 139-42), while defining the *Niphal* as primarily reflexive, grants that it may have a passive significance as well. This is probably
another instance in which Paul's application, although not contrary to the grammar, depends upon a particular interpretation of it within the whole Pauline
hermeneutic. Cf. *infra*, pp. 139ff.

[4] This pentateuchal emphasis may have been occasioned by the similar stress of
the Judaisers (Burton, op. cit., p. 159) or, more probably, by Paul's own view of
the OT: In the Pentateuch the basic pattern of God's plan appears; in the prophets one sees its development, interpretation, and predicted lines of fulfilment.

[5] 1 Cor. 15.27, 45, 54f. Rom. 14.11 is one other definite eschatological quotation. Cf. 1 Cor. 2.9; 2 Thess. 1.8-10.

are reflected throughout the Pauline corpus.[1] The quotations are applied more as typological interpretations than as 'proof-texts' in the strict sense. Ps. 8 implies the second Adam's lordship over death, 'for he has put all things under his feet' (1 Cor. 15.27); and this involves the power to grant life to others (1 Cor. 15.45).[2] Therefore, through Christ 'Israel' will be resurrected and the power of death vitiated.[3]

As for other topics, 1 Cor. 1-3 contains a number of citations from which the conclusion is drawn that 'Christ and His Cross' is the only true Wisdom[4]: Worldly wisdom is, in the long run, fruitless and vain, for it can never comprehend the plan of God either in the OT or in the Cross; the Christian, however, possesses true wisdom in the Lord Christ. The Pauline paraenesis contains a number of citations giving moral injunctions or applying New Covenant principles contained in or inferred from OT passages. Four concern 'giving',[5] and three the Decalogue and law of love[6]; the remainder cover a variety of subjects: avenging oneself, judging one's brother, fornication, idolatry, eating of meat, and marital relations.[7]

The following classification gives a résumé of major themes in Pauline quotation:

Faith and Works	Jew and Gentile	Ethics	Wisdom	Eschatology
Rom. 1.17; 4.3, 6f, 17f; 10.4ff; Gal. 3.6, 8-13, 16; 4.22ff	Rom. 9.7, 9, 12f, 15, 17, 25-29, 33; 10.16, 18-21; 11.3f, 8ff, 26f; 15.9ff, 21; Gal. 3.8	Rom. 12.19; 13.8; 14.11; 15.3; 1 Cor. 6.16; 9.9; 10.7, 26; 2 Cor. 6.16ff; 8.15; 9.9; Gal. 5.14, 31; 6.2f	Rom. 11.24f; 1 Cor. 1.19, 31; 2.9, 16; 3.19f	1 Cor. 15.27, 45, 54f

[1] e.g. the Adam-Christ typology provides the scaffolding for his doctrine of redemption and resurrection; cf. Black, *Second Adam*, p. 179.

[2] *Supra*, pp. 58ff, 95ff.

[3] 1 Cor. 15.54f (Isa. 25.8; Hos. 13.14). That Hos. 13.14 probably (as the grammar indicates) contains a promise and not (if taken interrogatively) a threat cf. *infra*, p. 138n.

[4] 1 Cor. 1.19, 31; 2.9, 16; 3.19f. Cf. Davies, op. cit., pp. 147-76.

[5] 1 Cor. 9.9; 2 Cor. 8.15; 9.9; 1 Tim. 5.18. [6] Rom. 13.8f; Gal. 5.14; Eph. 6.2f.

[7] Rom. 12.19; 14.11; 1 Cor. 6.16; 10.7, 26; Eph. 5.31. The 'temple' *catena* in 2 Cor. 6.16ff is used to enjoin 'separation' from the world; cf. further on the 'body of Christ', Dodd, *Gospel and Law*, pp. 33ff. In the citation in Rom. 15.3f the example of Christ is adduced as an ethical norm.

TYPOLOGY

As the above discussion shows, the stress of Pauline quotations is not upon predictive prophecy as it is usually understood[1] but upon the application of principles enunciated in the OT. These principles are often viewed as realised or fulfilled in a special way in the Messianic Age ushered in by Christ's resurrection.[2] In this context the significance of Pauline typology is readily apparent.

Τύπος occurs fifteen times in the NT. Primarily it signifies the imprint made by a blow, and from this the several NT meanings arise—imprint,[3] image,[4] form,[5] pattern or example.[6] Τύπος may be either the primary concept or the secondary image,[7] but in typological exegesis the 'type' is usually applied to the OT 'shadow' and the 'antitype' to the NT fulfilment. The NT writers see in certain OT persons, or institutions, and events prefigurations of New Covenant truths.[8] Thus Adam (Rom. 5.14), Jonah (Matt. 12.40), and the Paschal lamb (1 Cor. 5.7) are types of Christ; and the Flood (1 Pet. 3.18ff) and Exodus (1 Cor. 10.1ff) are typical of Christian experiences. In Hebrews Christ is presented as fulfilling the office of Moses (ch. 3), Aaron (ch. 5), and Melchizedek (cf. 7): 'The use which the author makes of Holy Scriptures is . . . not dialectic or rhetorical but interpretative. The quotations are not brought forward in order to prove anything, but to indicate the correspondence which exists between the several stages in the fulfilment of the Divine purpose from age to age.'[9] The 'type' used as an exegetical method has, then, a much more restricted meaning than τύπος would suggest—even in its NT usage.

[1] i.e. the prediction of a particular event, as, for example, that Messiah should be born in Bethlehem (Matt. 2.6).

[2] e.g. the inclusion of the Gentiles, the ἐκκλησία as God's temple, the gifts of the Holy Spirit.   [3] John 20.25.   [4] Acts 7.43.

[5] e.g. Rom. 6.17.   [6] e.g. 1 Cor. 10.6; Heb. 8.5.

[7] e.g. Acts 7.43; Heb. 8.5; 9.24. Cf. A. B. Davidson, *Old Testament Prophecy*, Edinburgh, 1903, pp. 224ff.

[8] Bonsirven (op. cit., pp. 269, 301ff) gives four classifications: a model of conduct, an example or parallel (Abraham and Christ), a prefiguration of the future order, and allegorical exegesis; this typology is quite distinct from rabbinical exegesis (ibid., p. 324). However, there is a resemblance in Jewish liturgy in which every OT event was 'regarded as prophetic, and every prophecy, whether by fact or by word . . . , as a light to cast its sheen on the future until the picture of the Messianic Age in the far background stood out. . . .' Edersheim, *Jesus the Messiah*, I, p. 163; cf. *Prophecy and History*, pp. 163ff.   [9] Westcott, *Hebrews*, p. 481.

NT typological exegesis is grounded firmly in the historical significance of the 'types'.[1] Even Pauline 'allegory' rests in a typological framework and is not allegory in the usual Jewish or Hellenistic sense.[2] The distinction between allegory and typology was expressed in 1762 by J. Gehard: 'Typus consistit in factorum collatione. Allegoria occupatur non tam in factis, quam in ipsis concionibus, e quibus doctrinam utilem et reconditam depromit.'[3] The historical character of this exegetical method evokes a further question: Are OT 'types' merely facts comparable to NT events, or is their typological character determined by Divine intent? Davidson maintained that a criterion of Divine intent was beside the point; it is not God's design but the 'similarity, identity, and predictiveness' which constitute the essential character—or 'typicalness'—of a type.[4] However, this definition does not fully meet the issue. For the NT writers a type has not merely the property of 'typicalness' or similarity; they view Israel's history as *Heilsgeschichte*,[5] and the significance of an OT type lies in its particular *locus* in the Divine plan of redemption. When Paul speaks of the Exodus events happening τυπικῶς and written 'for our admonition',[6] there can be no doubt that, in the apostle's mind, Divine intent is of the essence both in their occurrence and in their inscripturation.[7] The rationale of NT typological exegesis is not only 'the continuity of God's purpose throughout the

[1] Cf. Dodd, 'A Problem of Interpretation', p. 17: 'The writers of the NT, then, by their attitude to the older Scriptures, authorise an historical understanding of them as an indispensible element in their interpretation and application to contemporary situations.'

[2] Cf. *supra*, pp. 51ff; Bonsirven, op. cit., pp. 301f, 308. F. Buchsel (''Αλληγορέω', *KTW*, I, pp. 260-4) classifies alike as allegorical exegesis 1 Cor. 5.6-8; 9.8-10; 10.1-11; Gal. 4.21ff, but he notes an essential difference from Jewish (Palestinian and Alexandrian) allegory: The Scripture is fulfilled in *his* time (1 Cor. 10.11) and its true meaning is recognised only by Christians (2 Cor. 3.14).

[3] Quoted in L. Goppelt, *Typos. Die typologische Deutung des Alten Testaments im Neuen*, Gütersloh, 1939, p. 8: 'Typology consists in the comparison of facts. Allegory concerns itself not so much in facts as in their assembly, from which it draws out useful and hidden doctrine.' Cf. F. Johnson, op. cit., p. 117; Westcott, *Hebrews*, p. 200: 'Between type and antitype there is an historical and real correspondence in the main idea of each event or situation. . . . A type presupposes a purpose in history worked out from age to age. An allegory rests finally in the imagination.' [4] Davidson, *Prophecy*, pp. 235ff.

[5] On this concept of prophecy and fulfilment in the NT cf. O. Schmitz, 'Das Alte Testament im Neuen Testament', *Wort und Geist, Festschrift für K. Heim*, Berlin, 1934, pp. 49-74. [6] 1 Cor. 10.11; cf. Rom. 15.4; 1 Pet. 3.21.

[7] So M. S. Terry, *Biblical Hermeneutics*, New York, 1885, p. 337; Fairbairn, op. cit., p. 46; G. E. Wright, *God Who Acts*, London, 1952, pp. 61ff.

history of His Covenant',[1] but also His Lordship in moulding
and using history to reveal and illumine His purpose. God
writes His parables in the sands of time.

Although the 'type' has its own historical value, its real
significance typologically is revealed only in the 'anti-type' or
fulfilment.[2] Things which were hidden or only partially revealed are now revealed to the Church—the Messianic Community—in whom the fulfilment is realised. 'Die Typologie',
Goppelt concludes, 'zeigt nicht nur das Wesen des Neuen
gegenüber dem Alten, sondern auch, dass es gerade und nur
auf diesem heilsgeschichtlichen Grunde steht.'[3]

Yet a third factor is present in NT typology. Besides being
historical and in accordance with the Divine plan, the OT type
often has a dispensational or economic relationship to the
corresponding NT fact. For example, there is a pattern of
correspondence between the Old and New Covenants—the
shadow and the true[4]—so that the pattern outlines of the first
may be imposed upon the second. NT typology does not,
therefore, merely involve striking resemblances or analogies but
points to a correspondence which inheres in the Divine economy
of redemption.[5] And this appears to be true not only in the
Exodus typology, in which the two Covenants are so expressly
contrasted,[6] but in the other OT 'types' as well.[7]

Although Paul is sometimes cited as the originator of typological exegesis,[8] the presence of typological concepts in pre-

[1] G. W. H. Lampe, 'Typological Exegesis', *Theology*, 16 (June 1953), p. 202.
[2] Cf. ibid., pp. 207f. It is not without significance that the NT never seeks to
identify 'types' of future fulfilments though it does use parable and apocalyptic
imagery in this fashion.
[3] Goppelt, op. cit., p. 183: 'Typology shows not only the character of the new
vis-à-vis the old but also that it stands directly and solely on a "salvation-history"
foundation.'   [4] Cf. Col. 2.17; Heb. 8.5; 10.1.
[5] W. J. Pythian-Adams (*The Way of At-One-Ment*, London, 1944, p. 11) uses the
term 'homology' to express this meaning more clearly: 'By "homology" we mean
that there is between two things not a mere resemblance but a real and vital—in
this case an economic—correspondence.' *Contra*, Prat (op. cit., I, pp. 20f), who
dismisses the whole Covenant typology as accommodation or analogy.
[6] It is most explicitly formulated in Heb. 8-10. Cf. 2 Cor. 3.
[7] *Infra*, p. 134. Further on NT typology cf. H. Sahlin's *Zur Typologie des
Johannesevangeliums*, Uppsala und Leipzig, 1950, and the bibliography in H. H.
Rowley, *The Unity of the Bible*, London, 1953, pp. 19f.
[8] Cf. Wright, op. cit., p. 61. Harnack ('Paulinischen Briefen und Gemeinden',
p. 138) regards the inadvertent 'typological' usage in 1 Cor. 9.10 as the starting
point for the rise of the OT to *Erbauungsbuch* for Gentile Christianity; cf. *supra*,
p. 31.

Pauline strata of the NT precludes this.[1] Undoubtedly, however, the apostle contributed a great deal to its development in
the early Church. His typology is drawn chiefly from three
OT periods: the Creation, the Age of the Patriarchs, and the
Exodus.[2] From the Creation narratives Paul draws a typological
relation between Adam and Christ in which the whole scope
of cosmic redemption appears to be encompassed: Ἐν Χριστῷ
a man enters a new resurrection creation (καινὴ κτίσις) whose
head and sovereign is the Lord Christ[3]; and from Rom. 8 it
appears that the whole cosmic order is to be in this new redeemed creation.[4] These views are undoubtedly related to,
and probably in part derivative from, Paul's understanding of
the Adam-Christ typology. This typology finds express definition in Rom. 5 and 1 Cor. 15, where it is the rationale under
which the Christian's redemption—both in justification and in
final resurrection to immortality—is explained.[5] An extension
of the Adam-Christ parallel to Eve and the Church is apparently
the motif in Eph. 5.31f and possibly is implicit in 2 Cor. 11.2f.[6]
As τύπος τοῦ μέλλοντος Adam is typically related to Christ both
in comparison and in contrast: Both head a new creation; but
where Adam's failure brought sin and death to all ἐν Ἀδάμ,
Christ's victory brought righteousness and immortal life to all
ἐν Χριστῷ.[7] Also the historicity of Adam is quite as basic to
Paul's thought here as the historicity of Christ, and, as Goppelt
has noted, any theory which reduces the Adam typology to
speculation over a mythological *Urmensch* misses the point of
Paul's analysis: 'Die Beziehung Adam-Christus ist für Paulus
nicht Veranschaulichungsmittel oder Spekulation sondern

---

[1] *Supra*, pp. 90ff.
[2] This is generally true throughout the NT although there are notable exceptions, e.g. the Flood (1 Pet. 3.18ff), Jonah (Matt. 12.40; 1 Cor. 15.3?), Elijah (Matt.
11.14). Paul's interpretations of later OT events (e.g. the book of Hosea, the Exile)
often fall within a typological framework; but when this is true they usually point
back to principles or events originating in one of the earlier periods (e.g. the
Covenant, the faith-seed or remnant).
[3] 2 Cor. 5.17; Gal. 6.15; cf. Eph. 2.10, 15. See further Abbott (op. cit., p. 217)
and J. B. Lightfoot (*The Epistle to the Colossians and to Philemon*, London, 1875, pp.
212f, 222) on Col. 1.15-18. Cf. Rom. 1.4; Rev. 3.14.
[4] Rom. 8.19ff.
[5] *Supra*, pp. 58ff.
[6] Cf. Tasker, op. cit., p. 98; *contra*, Goppelt, op. cit., pp. 157f; Best, op. cit.,
p. 171. The Adam-Christ typology may underlie Phil. 2.5ff.
[7] Rom. 5.17; 1 Cor. 15.22.

Erleuchtung und Vergewisserung des Glaubens aus der Schrift, echte Typologie.'[1]

There are few typological parallels drawn from the patriarchal period. Such matters as the faith of Abraham stand in direct continuity with the New Covenant; they are not typology conceived of as a pattern of parallel and contrast, of shadow and true, of figure and fulfilment, of economic or dispensational correspondence.[2] There may be allusions in Rom. 3.25; 8.32 to the sacrifice of Isaac as typical of Christ's offering,[3] but the only definitive typological parallel is the Sarah-Hagar 'allegory' in Gal. 4.22ff.[4] This 'allegory of the two Covenants'[5] forms one picture with the Covenant typology drawn from the Exodus and later narratives. Although denominated 'allegory',[6] the passage differs from the symbolical use of Scripture in Philo and Origen, both in its view of history and in its epistemology. Its basis is not γνῶσις but πίστις, not the esoteric experience of a mystery religion but the 'heilsgeschichtliche Glaubenswirklichkeit'.[7] Although following an allegorical form in part, its subject matter places it within the framework of Pauline typology: Sarah and Hagar in their experiences foreshadow and manifest the principles seen in full flower in the Messianic Community versus legalistic Judaism.[8]

The two Covenants also provide the structural framework upon which the Exodus typology is built. The Abrahamic Covenant stands in continuity with the 'New Covenant' (καινὴ διαθήκη); the παλαιὰ διαθήκη of Sinai stands in contrast.[9] The

---

[1] Goppelt, op. cit., p. 162: 'The Adam-Christ relationship is for Paul not merely a medium of illustration or speculation but the illumination and confirmation of faith from the Scripture, genuine typology.'

[2] Goppelt (op. cit., pp. 164-7) treats the 'seed of Abraham' (Gal. 3.16, 29) as typology: As Abraham believed God would create life from his dead body (Rom. 4.18ff), so Christians believe God raised Christ from the dead (Rom. 4.24; 10.9f). But this is more a comparison of the faith-basis of the New Covenant in two situations than typological exegesis as defined above.

[3] Schoeps, op. cit., pp. 390ff; cf. *supra*, p. 95n.   [4] *Supra*, p. 51ff.

[5] Lightfoot, *Galatians*, pp. 192ff.   [6] Gal. 4.24.

[7] Goppelt, op. cit., p. 163: 'a redemptive-historical reality of faith.'

[8] Not only Isaac and Ishmael but also Jacob and Esau (Rom. 9.13) are treated in this fashion. Perhaps the apostle's application is merely illustrative, but it is more likely that he views the typological structure as proper to the history itself. Cf. Burton, op. cit., p. 256.

[9] 2 Cor. 3. It may be, as Goppelt maintains (op. cit., p. 171), that the Abrahamic Covenant is a positive 'type' of the later καινὴ διαθήκη. It is, then, a case of 'both-and', for Paul insists throughout that the Christian Community is in direct continuity with Abraham and heir to his Covenant promises. Goppelt's suggestion

events of the Exodus, the 'redemption' under the 'Old Covenant', provide a pattern of 'types, foreshadowing the redemption in Christ. As the Old Covenant was initiated in the Passover, so 'Christ our Passover is sacrificed for us', establishing a New Covenant in His blood.[1] As those redeemed by Moses were baptised εἰς τὸν Μωϋσῆν in the cloud and sea, so those redeemed in Christ's death and resurrection are baptised εἰς Χριστόν.[2] The Old Covenant like the New, had a food and drink in which Christ was (typically) present.[3] As the Old Covenant had a Law written in stone, so the New Covenant had a Torah, an ἐπιστολὴ Χριστοῦ, written on men's hearts.[4] Under the Old Covenant there was a tabernacle—and later a temple—in which the 'Presence' or *Shekinah* of God dwelt and where sacrifices for sin were offered; in the New Covenant Christ and His Church are the temple and Christ's Cross the altar of sacrifice.[5]

Exodus 'typology' was not original with Paul or even the early Church. The concept arises in the OT prophets who 'came to shape their anticipation of the great eschatological salvation through the Messiah according to the pattern of the historical Exodus under Moses'.[6] Sahlin probably overstates the case in describing Isa. 35, 40ff, as 'essentially variations on the Exodus story',[7] but the importance of the Exodus events is fundamental to all these prophecies. In Ps. 67(68) also, the

is congruous with Heb. 5.10, where Melchizedek provides a positive type and the Levitical priesthood a negative one (cf. ἀντίτυπον Heb. 9.24; 10.1). In the final analysis it is unwise to attempt to erect any integrated system of typology even within the Pauline writings; some elements were probably viewed as 'wholes' without reference to any larger scheme. Cf. *infra*, pp. 134f.

[1] 1 Cor. 5.7; 11.25ff.
[2] 1 Cor. 10.3; cf. Rom. 6.3; 1 Cor. 1.30; Gal. 3.27; Eph. 1.14; 4.30.
[3] 1 Cor. 10.4; cf. John 6.31f. The meaning is not clear. Πνευματικόν probably means 'in its typical or prophetic significance' (cf. Rev. 11.8; Gal. 4.25); Robertson and Plummer (op. cit., p. 200) interpret it as 'supernatural origin'.
[4] 2 Cor. 3.3. Christ's teaching is also considered 'Torah' by Paul. Cf. Dodd, "ΕΝΝΟΜΟΣ ΧΡΙΣΤΟΥ"; Davies, op. cit., pp. 147ff; *supra*, pp. 28ff.
[5] On 'temple typology' cf. *supra*, pp. 89ff. C. A. A. Scott (op. cit., pp. viiif) regards Paul's debt to the Levitical system as 'negligible' and refers ἱλαστήριον in Rom. 3.25 not to the tabernacle service but to the brazen serpent; Schoeps (op. cit., pp. 390ff) takes it to be a reference to Isaac's sacrifice. While this verse is uncertain, there is no reason to exclude the possibility of tabernacle sacrifice, especially in the light of the later typological development in Hebrews. Cf. Sanday and Headlam, op. cit., p. 87.
[6] H. Sahlin, 'The New Exodus of Salvation According to St Paul', *The Root of the Vine*, ed. A. Fridrichsen, p. 81. [7] Ibid.

Psalmist sees a greater messianic deliverance typified in the Exodus from Egypt.[1] The hundred-odd references to the Exodus in subsequent OT books evidence the central place it held in ancient Jewish thought.[2]

The same is true of the rabbis. Aside from the unique place of the *Pesach* in the Jewish religious calendar, this Passover feast served to impress the importance of the Exodus upon each individual Jew. The *Pesach* ritual required each participant to identify himself with the Exodus experience: '[This is what] the Lord did unto *me* when *I* came forth out of Egypt.'[3] The rabbis also drew a parallel between the 'first deliverer' (Moses) and the 'last deliverer' (the Messiah).[4] The Messiah was, like Moses, to bring plagues upon the oppressors of Israel,[5] bring forth water from the rock, and perform a miracle of manna.[6] The final deliverance, like the deliverance from Egypt, would take place at the Passover.[7]

The NT writers set forth the life, death and resurrection of Jesus of Nazareth as the fulfilment of these expectations. The picture of Christ in Matthew is particularly suggestive of the rabbinical parallels between Moses and Messiah: Like Moses, he is saved from Herod's slaughter, comes forth out of Egypt, calls out the 'twelve sons of Israel', gives the law from the mount, performs ten miracles (like Moses, ten plagues), provides 'manna' from heaven.[8] However, the picture is not certain; at least as good a case can be made out that Matthew has in mind Christ as the 'embodiment' of Israel.[9] No system-

---

[1] Cf. C. A. Briggs, *Messianic Prophecy*, Edinburgh, 1886, pp. 428ff; Ps. 77(78); Ps. 104(105).

[2] Cf. H. Englander, 'The Exodus in the Bible', *Studies in Jewish Literature, Festschrift for K. Kohler*, Berlin, 1913, pp. 108-16.

[3] Exod. 13.8; cf. Pes. 116b (*SBT*, pp. 595ff); Vischer, op. cit., p. 173.

[4] The rabbis seem to approach very closely here to a typological exegesis in the NT sense of the term. If so, it is an exception to the dictum of Bonsirven; cf. *supra*, pp. 51f.

[5] Pesikta 67b-68a; cf. *SBK*, I, pp. 85ff (Matt. 2.15); Weber, op. cit., p. 366.

[6] Pesikta 49b, Weber, op. cit., p. 364; Num. R. XI, 2 (*SMR*, V, pp. 415f); Eccl. R. I, 9 (*SMR*, VIII, p. 33) on Joel 3.18; Midrash on Ruth 2.14, Ps. 72.16, S. S. 2.9; cf. *SBK*, I, pp. 86f (Matt. 2.15); II, p. 481 (John 6.31).

[7] Cf. Sahlin. *New Exodus*, p. 82.

[8] Matt. 2.13ff; 10.2ff (cf. Mark 3.14); 5-7; 8-10; 14.15ff. The pattern is sporadic and mixed; in John 6 and 1 Cor. 10 it is Christ Himself who is the manna. Sahlin (*New Exodus*, p. 82) suggests that a Pentateuchal format is implicit in the first Gospel, viz., Matt. 1-7, 8-10, 11-18, 19-25, 26-28.

[9] This is almost certainly the meaning in Matt. 2.15; cf. also 'forty days in the wilderness' (Matt. 4.1ff). The Semitic concept of solidarity between the Messiah

atic formulation should be looked for in any case.[1] In other
NT contexts, John the Baptist's ministry as the fulfilment of
Isa. 40.3 (Mark 1.2f) carries an implicit reference to the Exodus
events; 'he is the forerunner, who now inaugurates the new
eschatological Exodus which is to be fulfilled by the Messiah'.[2]
In the new Exodus, as in the old, the redeemed 'sing the song
of Moses'.[3] The connexion of Christ's death with the Passover
is one of the cardinal points in the Passion narratives; Burney's
words well express its significance: 'It was not, we may believe,
a mere coincidence that 1200 years later at precisely the same
season, . . . that He, the true Passover Lamb, suffered and died
for our salvation at the very moment when the Jews were
making ready for their annual commemoration of the Passover
feast. . . .'[4]

The Pauline references to the Exodus events are not mere
illustrations or analogies but, as the above discussion demonstrates, are part of a system of OT interpretation reaching to
the heart of the Gospel. Paul specifically connects baptism and
the Lord's Supper with the Exodus.[5] In 1 Cor. 10.1ff and Rom.
6.3 Christian baptism is explained in terms of the Exodus
imagery. In the former passage the Red Sea crossing and
envelopment in the *Shekinah* cloud[6] are taken as typical of the
Christian's experience. A parallel to Jewish proselyte baptism
seems implicit in Rom. 6.3. In Judaism this baptism was essential to identify the proselyte with Israel; and this identification,
as the *Pesach* ritual stresses, signified an identification with
Israel's Exodus from Egypt, i.e. with the 'baptism' in the Red
Sea and *Shekinah* cloud. So Christian baptism identifies one
with the new Exodus—Christ's death and resurrection.
Sahlin's remark is pertinent: 'As through circumcision and
proselyte baptism the Jewish proselyte is incorporated into
the people of God and becomes a partaker of God's act of

and Israel, and Israel's leaders cautions against drawing any fine distinctions in
this regard.
    [1] Cf. *infra*, pp. 134f.   [2] Sahlin, *New Exodus*, p. 83.
    [3] Rev. 15.3.   [4] Burney, *The Gospel in the Old Testament*, p. 44.
    [5] See Sahlin, *New Exodus*, pp. 84-94. Cf. also A. H. McNeile, *New Testament
Teaching in the Light of St Paul's*, Cambridge, 1923, p. 145: 'Much of what St Paul
says about salvation and the Christian life he has before his mind the events of the
Exodus.'
    [6] Cf. Exod. 40.34-38. The rabbis expatiate considerably on this incident; cf.
SBK, III, p. 405.

salvation as recorded in the Exodus narrative, and primarily in the crossing of the Red Sea, so the Christian proselyte receiving Christian baptism, becomes a partaker in Christ's act of salvation, His death and resurrection. As the Jewish proselyte becomes by baptism *one* with the Exodus generation, so the Christian through baptism becomes *one* with Christ in His death and resurrection.'[1] Similarly, the Eucharist is compared with the manna and the water from the rock (1 Cor. 10.1ff); and in several passages there is an implicit reference to the *Pesach* feast with Christ as the true Paschal lamb.[2]

Some elements in Pauline typology are obscure, and it is sometimes difficult to determine whether a 'type' or merely an illustration is in mind. Some OT references which are probably no more than analogies or application of principles[3] may conform to a typological frame of reference. NT typology did not involve merely a catalogue of 'types'; it penetrated into the spirit of NT exegesis in all its forms.

In the Pauline writing two basic typological patterns appear —Adamic or Creation typology and Covenant typology. Each is related to a particular aspect of God's redemptive purpose in Christ,[4] and, over all, they unite to form one interrelated whole. Thus, becoming a Christian is spoken of as a new birth (Exodus typology) and a new creation (Adamic typology); sometimes (e.g. Rom. 6.3) both ideas are apparently joined in the figure of resurrection.

In a study and use of biblical typology two erroneous tendencies are ever present. Seeking to apply the 'truths' of typology one may 'de-historicise it, even while paying lip service to the historical context in which it is found'.[5] Further, the exegete is tempted to seek a logical extension of NT patterns and to mould them into a systematic and comprehensive hermeneutic. In this area particularly NT thought-forms are Semitic not Greek, and it is not without significance that Paul and other NT

---

[1] Sahlin, *New Exodus*, p. 91.
[2] 1 Cor. 5.7; 10.16ff; 11.2ff. According to J. Jeremias (*Die Abendmahlsworte Jesu*, Zurich, 1949, pp. 18ff) the Last Supper was a *Pesach* meal. If so, the Eucharist would probably be regarded as a continuation of the Jewish feast with Christ as the Passover lamb. Cf. Sahlin, *New Exodus*, p. 93.
[3] Cf. 1 Cor. 9.9ff; 2 Cor. 4.13; 8.15.
[4] These two ideas may be present in Rom. 1.3f, where Christ is described as σπέρματος Δαυὶδ and υἱοῦ θεοῦ.   [5] Wright, op. cit., p. 65.

writers were content to leave some typological elements in ambiguous form and apply others only in very limited fashion. Farrer's theory of image revelation may be helpful for the study of this NT discipline as well as biblical symbolism: 'Then each image will have its own conceptual conventions, proper to the figure it embodies: and a single overall conceptual analysis will be about as useful for the interpretation of the Apostle's writings as a bulldozer for the cultivation of a miniature landscape garden. The various images are not, of course, unconnected in the Apostle's mind; they attract one another and tend to fuse, but they have their own way of doing this, according to their own imagery laws, and not according to the principles of a conceptual system.'[1]

New Covenant Exegesis

Pauline exegesis employs a great deal of methodology found in rabbinical and other literature. IF, *Stichwort* combinations, and possibly 'pointer' citations are examples of such common stock usage. Yet, in other respects his exegetical methods appear to arise out of presuppositions peculiar to a particular segment of Jewish thought, if not to the NT exclusively. Two principles are fundamental to Paul's understanding of the OT. First, he reads the Scripture from the viewpoint of the 'End-time' in which OT history and prophecy have become realised and fulfilled in Christ. The OT is *Heilsgeschichte*, pregnant in anticipation of future fulfilment: The mystery of the Gospel, foretold in the OT, is now made manifest in Christ.[2] That the OT pointed to the Messiah and the Messianic Era was a familiar concept in Judaism. With this in mind the first century exegete had a twofold task, to 'search the Scriptures', and to discern 'the signs of the times'; he learned from the Scriptures the nature of God's purpose, and from current events he sought indication of the fulfilment[3]: 'When the Scripture rightly interpreted coincided with the event rightly understood, then you had the argument from prophecy. To rebut it in the early

---

[1] A. Farrer, *The Glass of Vision*, London, 1948, p. 45. Farrer applies the theory to the whole of biblical revelation.
[2] Rom. 16.26. Cf. T. Hoppe, *Die Idee der Heilsgeschichte bei Paulus*, Gütersloh, 1926, pp. 140-69; H. Vollmer, *Vom Lesen und Deuten Heiliger Schriften*, Tübingen, 1907, p. 25. [3] Manson, *The Argument from Prophecy*, p. 129.

centuries it was necessary to challenge the correctness of the exegesis or the justness of the interpretation of the event, or both.'[1] Paul assumes the validity of this principle, and his Christological interpretation of the OT proceeds from it.[2] As the OT itself notes, the 'last word' is not in it but in the New Covenant which fulfils and supersedes it. And with the inauguration of the New Covenant in Jesus Christ history enters 'the times of the End'. 'What had been predicted in Holy Scripture to happen to Israel in the *Eschaton* has happened to and in Jesus. The foundation-stone of the New Creation has come into position.'[3]

A second principle of deep consequence for Pauline exegesis is the Jewish concept of 'corporate solidarity'. For example, Israel the patriarch, Israel the nation, the king of Israel, and Messiah stand in such relationship to each other that one may be viewed as the 'embodiment' of the other. The precise nature of the relationship is not entirely clear, but the fact of it exercises a pronounced influence in NT exegesis. It is particularly important for Paul's understanding of such matters as original sin, the seed of Abraham, 'Israel', and the body of Christ.[4]

Two components in Paul's exegesis which are particularly revealing for his general hermeneutic are his concept of 'Israel' and his use of what Stendahl has called *Midrash pesher*.[5] The former clarifies many applications of the OT which would otherwise appear purely arbitrary; *Midrash pesher* gives a clue to Paul's understanding of the nature of 'quotation' and, consequently, throws light upon some of his textual variations.

The True Israel

Paul, like the other NT writers, regards the Christian *ecclesia* as the faithful remnant of Israel, the true people of God.[6]

---

[1] Ibid., p. 130.

[2] Cf. C. Clemen, 'Die Auffassung des Alten Testament bei Paulus', *Theologischen Studien und Kritiken* 75 (1902), pp. 173-87.

[3] W. Manson, 'Eschatology in the New Testament', *SJT*, Occasional Papers No. 2, pp. 1-16.   [4] Cf. *supra*, pp. 58ff, 70ff; *infra*, p. 139; Best, op. cit., pp. 203-7.

[5] Cf. Stendahl, op. cit., p. 35.

[6] Cf. Jas. 1.1; 1 Pet. 2.5, 9, 10; K. L. Schmidt, *The Church*, trans. J. E. Coates from *KTW*, London, 1950, p. 32; H. Strathmann, 'Λαός im Neuen Testament', *KTW*, IV, pp. 53f. Strathmann is mistaken in taking the concept, found also in 1 Pet. 2.9, as originating with Paul; cf. Dodd, *According to the Scriptures*, p. 43.

Christians are the true 'Jews' (Rom. 2.29),[1] Israel (Rom. 9.6), Israel after the Spirit (cf. 1 Cor. 10.18), the seed of Abraham (Gal. 3.29), the Israel of God (Gal. 6.16), the circumcision (Phil. 3.3), the peculiar people (Tit. 2.14).[2] The unbelieving majority of Jews are, in contrast, characterised by terms usually reserved for the heathen or Gentiles; a striking example is κύνας in Phil. 3.2.[3]

The early Church did not view itself as merely a sect within the larger 'Israel' of Judaism, or as a new or different people of God.[4] Gutbrot rightly observes that 'an all diesen Stellen ist nirgends eine Erweiterung von 'Ισραήλ in der Richtung auf Bezeichnung des neuen Gottesvolkes zu bemerken. . . .'[5] As the imagery of the olive tree in Rom. 11 shows, for Paul there is only one Israel into which the Gentiles are ingrafted; there is, therefore, no necessary contrast between Israel κατὰ σάρκα and the true Israel.[6] Paul's exclamation, 'I too am an Israelite' (Rom. 11.1), reveals how firmly he holds to the fact that the Christian *ecclesia* is the continuing body of OT Israel. As Flew expresses it: 'The proud claim [of the early Church] to the exclusive possession of the original Covenant is unmistakable. The Jews in those early years regarded Christianity as a Jewish sect, and modern writers have sometimes so described the early Church. But that was not the view of the original disciples. A sect is a party or school within Israel. But the disciples were Israel. They were the Church or People of God. They did not separate from Israel. They could not. It was the rebellious

---

[1] Cf. Rev. 2.9.

[2] Cf. Exod. 19.5. The term ἐκκλησία is itself of marked significance; cf. R. Bultmann, *Theology of the New Testament*, London, 1952, p. 38: 'In understanding themselves as Congregation or Church the disciples appropriate to themselves the title of the OT Congregation of God, the קְהַל־יְהוָה.' Ἐκκλησία (קְהַל־יְהוָה) is carefully distinguished from συναγωγή in Jewish literature.

[3] 'Dogs' was a choice Jewish epithet for Gentiles. E. Lohmeyer (*Der Brief an die Philipper*, 9th ed., Göttingen, 1953, pp. 124-6) contends that Paul's attack here is directed solely against 'jüdische Agitatoren' from the Jewish synagogue in Philippi. Even if, as is more probable, Judaisers are included, the figure is still revealing, i.e. not being true Christians they are not true Jews.

[4] *Contra*, Strathmann, op. cit., pp. 55f.

[5] W. Gutbrot, "Ἰουδαῖος, 'Ισραήλ, 'Εβραῖος im Neuen Testament', *KTW*, III, p. 390: '. . . in all these passages there is nowhere an enlargement of the concept "Israel" with the aim of denoting a new people of God.'

[6] Ibid., pp. 390f. As Gutbrot notes, Rom. 11.26 does not say πάντες οἱ 'Ιουδαῖοι σωθήσεται.

sons of Israel who forfeited their Covenant by rejecting Christ.'[1]

The true Israel, according to Paul, was constituted through a faith relationship and not merely on the basis of physical descent; and this criterion is operative in his view of OT Israel as well. This view of Israel has a greater effect on Pauline exegesis than is apparent on first observation. It is germane to the application of Hab. 2.4 (Rom. 1.17; Gal. 3.11), the status of the Christian believer, and the whole rationale of the Covenant promises.[2] Among the more obvious instances in his quotations, Rom. 9.25 (Hos. 2.23; 1.10) includes the Gentiles in a prophecy originally referring to faithless Israelites; that is, the unfaithful in Israel are in the category of Gentiles, and God's adoption of these 'Gentiles' implies the inbringing of other Gentiles into the true Israel—the Christian *ecclesia*. Another prophecy of Hosea (13.14; 1 Cor. 15.55) is similar: For their iniquities the nation Israel will suffer invasion and death, but God will redeem them from this death. Paul cites the passage as a description of the redemption of the true Israel in the resurrection.[3] Rom. 11.26 apparently assumes a distinction between 'Zion' and 'Jacob' or national Israel; from 'Zion', the true dwelling of God, the Redeemer shall come forth to the Jewish people.[4] The persecution of Israel by the Gentiles, described in Ps. 43(44).23, is applied by Paul (Rom. 8.36) to the persecution of Christians by Jews. In Ps. 67(68) God is described as a conqueror who redeems captive Israel and shares with them

---

[1] Flew, op. cit., p. 101. Cf. A. G. Hebert, *The Throne of David*, London, 1941, pp. 229-39; R. Smith, 'The Relevance of the Old Testament for the Doctrine of the Church', *SJT*, 5 (March 1952), 16ff; Schmidt, op. cit., pp. 48f: '[The Church's] own conviction was that it was the only synagogue entitled to claim that it embodied true Judaism, the true Israel.'

[2] *Supra*, pp. 70ff. The identification of Abraham's seed is especially pertinent.

[3] From Calvin onward (cf. C. F. Keil, *The Twelve Minor Prophets*, Edinburgh, 1868, I, p. 159) many commentators have viewed this verse, as its context, as a threat rather than a promise; consequently, Paul's citation should be understood as merely literary allusion (cf. Toy, op. cit., p. 181; F. Johnson, op. cit., p. 153; Hos. 13.14 RSV). But it may be interpreted, as the grammar suggests, in contrast with the general context of judgment (cf. Keil, op. cit., pp. 160ff), and there is evidence that the early Church so understood it. As the usage here and elsewhere in the NT (cf. Matt. 2.15; 1 Cor. 15.3?) indicates, Hosea in general and this passage in particular was understood as a description of God's deliverance of His people. Cf. Matt. 16.18; *supra*, p. 96n.

[4] Paul sets this view forth as a 'mystery', 'a truth given by special revelation rather than deduced by argument'. Dodd, *Romans*, p. 182; cf. 2 Cor. 3.15f. Whether Σιών refers to the heavenly Jerusalem (Sanday and Headlam, op. cit., p. 337) or the Church (God's temple) is uncertain. Cf. *supra*, pp. 123n.

the booty of his victory; Paul applies the Psalm (Eph. 4.8) to gifts Christ gives to the Church after His victory over the 'captivity' of death.[1]

The concept of solidarity has a bearing on a number of Paul's OT interpretations[2]: Ps. 68(69), which probably refers to Israel's king, is applied in Rom. 15.3 to Christ the true head of Israel.[3] The place of Solomon in the temple typology (2 Sam. 7.14; 2 Cor. 6.16ff) suggests a further interpretation along the same lines. An allusion to Hos. 6.2 may occur in 1 Cor. 15.4 ('the third day'); if so, it is another instance of solidarity in which Christ's resurrection is considered Israel's resurrection.[4] The NT allusions to Exod. 19.5f afford a very striking example of convergence[5]: Israel is appointed to be a nation of 'priest-kings'.[6] Within this nation of priest-kings there is a royal and priestly (Ps. 110.4) line of David; from this arises Christ, the messianic priest-king, in whom Israel is personified. The NT consequently views the Church, Christ's body, as the true Israel, the nation of priest-kings.

MIDRASH PESHER

Of the considerable number of Pauline quotations which vary from the LXX and/or the MT, some may be explained on the basis of a variant textual source. However, agreements with the Targum, Peshitta, and various Greek texts are sporadic; and in some of these texts, at least, a Christian influence is probable. In any case it is very doubtful that all of the apostle's textual aberrations can be accounted for in this manner.[7]

Several variant readings which have a direct bearing on the NT application suggest either an *ad hoc* rendering or an interpretative selection from the various known texts.[8] For ex-

[1] The Psalm may be a survey of the whole history of Israel; the Exodus typology is expressly in view in vv. 8-11. Cf. C. A. Briggs, *The Book of Psalms*, Edinburgh, 1907, I, p. 94. On the text of v. 19 cf. *supra*, pp. 35ff.   [2] Cf. *supra*, p. 136.
[3] The title 'of David' may or may not be genuine; perhaps is it a 'Servant' Psalm with a personification of Israel's remnant (v. 17). Either possibility is more suitable to Paul's typological application than Brigg's (*Psalms*, II, p. 115) conjecture of Jeremiah.
[4] Dodd, *According to the Scriptures*, pp. 77, 103; J. Weiss (op. cit., pp. 94ff) takes the phrase as a current idiom for a short interval of time.
[5] Cf. Col. 1.12f; Tit. 2.14; 1 Pet. 2.9.
[6] The Hebrew construct (מַמְלֶכֶת כֹּהֲנִים) is a 'closer relation than the genitive case. It is nearer the compound noun. . . .' (Briggs, *Messianic Prophecy*, pp. 101ff).   [7] See *supra*, pp. 19f.   [8] See Appendix II.

ample, the addition of πᾶς in Rom. 10.11 (Rom. 9.33 omits it) contributes directly to the argument; and there is little doubt that Paul is here inserting his own 'commentary' into the body of the text. In Rom. 12.19 the variation apparently follows the rendering of the Targum; by making this selection, Paul (or an earlier Christian exegete) secures the desired interpretation:

NT: Vengeance is mine, I will repay.
Heb: To me belongs vengeance and retribution.
Targ: Vengeance is before me and I will repay.

Also, לנצח in Isa. 25.8, which Paul (1 Cor. 15.54)—against the LXX and the Targum (לעלמין)—renders εἰς νῖκος, is usually translated 'forever' or 'utterly'.[1] The Aramaic נצח can mean 'excel' or 'overcome', and this connotation is probably not entirely absent from the Hebrew. The point of interest, however, is that Paul uses a selective interpretation; and this interpretation is essential for the application of the passage in 1 Cor. 15.

The same motive is apparently present in Rom. 11.26f. Where the MT reads 'to those who turn from transgression in Jacob', Romans, with the LXX, has 'and shall turn away ungodliness from Jacob'. The LXX itself is here an interpretative rendering of the Hebrew, an interpretation which accords with the argument in Romans. Possibly Paul merely follows the text which lay before him, but more likely he retains the LXX reading because it gives the sense which he himself finds in the passage. There are a number of indications favouring this supposition. In the same verse Paul departs from the LXX in the phrase ἐκ Σιών, evidently with a hermeneutical purpose in view.[2] Furthermore, where the LXX text is followed elsewhere a distinctive interpretation of the Hebrew is involved in it; and upon this interpretation Paul's argument is built. For example, in Rom. 1.17 πίστις stresses a particular aspect of אמונה; in Gal. 3.8 the NT and LXX 'be blessed' would, on the basis of statistical probability, better represent the Hebrew if it were reflexive rather than passive.[3] These variations should

---

[1] 2 Sam. 2.26; Job. 36.7; Amos 1.11.
[2] See *supra*, p. 123n. Cf. Rom. 12.19; 2 Cor. 6.16ff; 1 Cor. 15.54f.
[3] Cf. *supra*, p. 124n.

not be viewed as capricious, or arbitrary, or merely incidental. Similar features found in other writings of the NT and of the Qumran Sect indicate that this procedure has a more significant purpose: Paul utilises *ad hoc* renderings and the deliberate selection and rejection of known readings to draw out and express the true meaning of the OT passage as he understands it.

In a recent dissertation, K. Stendahl compared the texts of Matthew's 'formula' quotations with the MT, LXX, Targum, and other Greek and Syriac versions.[1] He found that, in contrast to other OT citations in the Gospels, the 'formula' quotations peculiar to Matthew follow no one textual tradition but represent a selective targumising procedure in which the interpretation is woven into the text itself. The rendering is not the result of a free paraphrase or looseness but arises out of a scholarly, detailed study and interpretation of the texts themselves.[2] Furthermore, the Matthaean type of midrashic interpretation closely approaches the *Midrash pesher* of the Qumran Sect.[3] To prove this contention Stendahl engages in a detailed examination of some of the exegetical procedures employed in *DSH*.

In *pesher* quotation or Midrash the interpretation or exposition is incorporated into the body of the text itself, thereby determining its textual form. Also, the method, as found in *DSH* and the NT, has an apocalyptic feature in which the prophetic passage is viewed as 'fulfilled' in the present time and is applied to contemporary events.[4] As Matthew's formula quotations view the OT as fulfilled in Christ, similarly the Habakkuk 'Commentary' applies Hab. 1-2 to the Teacher of Righteousness and the events surrounding him. Stendahl, however, is concerned chiefly with the way in which *pesher* interpretation affects the text-form (as contrasted with the exposition proper) of *DSH*. He finds more than fifty variants

---

[1] Stendahl, op. cit., Cf. *NTS*, I (November 1954), pp. 155ff.

[2] Ibid., pp. 195, 200f.

[3] Ibid., p. 35. *Pesher* (פשׁר) occurs as a technical term in *DSH*. Whether it should be rendered 'commentary', 'interpretation', or 'Midrash' is uncertain; Stendahl classifies it as a Midrash parallel to Halacha and Haggada. Cf. the discussion in B. J. Roberts, 'Some Observations on the Damascus Documents and the Dead Sea Scrolls', *BJRL* 34 (1951-2), pp. 367ff.

[4] Roberts ('Observations', pp. 367f) regards this factor as the chief link between *DSS* and the NT.

from the MT, most of which form 'such an intimate and organic part of the exposition of the text that they cannot possibly be dismissed as (scribal errors)'.[1] Even though many of these readings appear to be created *ad hoc*, they nevertheless frequently coincide with one or more of the known versions; 'such coincidences occur where adaption to the dogma and situation of the sect would sufficiently explain the text of *DSH*'.[2]

Stendahl classifies *DSH* variants according to (1) alterations of number and suffix, and (2) more substantial changes.[3] Among the former, in Hab. 1.13 MT has the singular (הביט), *DSH* the plural (הביטו); in Hab. 2.1 MT has מצור, *DSH* מצורי; in Hab. 1.10 MT has a feminine, *DSH* a masculine; MT a second person suffix, *DSH* a third person (Hab. 2.15); MT a suffix where *DSH* has none (Hab. 2.18). Other variations are of greater weight: MT in Hab. 1.9 has a locative *heh* with the idea 'eastward' or 'forward' (קדימה), *DSH* takes the word as a noun (קדים); in Hab. 2.5 MT has היין ('wine'), *DSH* הון ('riches'); Hab. 2.6 MT has מליצה ('taunt'), *DSH* מליצי ('scoffers' or 'interpreters'). In several places a reading or interpretation is omitted from the *DSH* text only to be taken up in the exposition, e.g. 'they shall come' in Hab. 1.8; this indicates the exegete's acquaintance with other readings or possible interpretations. Stendahl compares the divergent readings with other versions with the following results[4]:

	DSH	MT	Targ.	LXX	Pesh.	Vulg.
Hab. 1.9	קדים	קדימה	DSH	MT	—	DSH	Symm.=DSH
(1.17a	not interrog.	interrog.	MT	DSH	DSH	DSH)	Frag.=DSH
1.17b	חרבו	חרמו	(MT)	MT	MT	MT
2.1	מצורי	מצור	DSH	MT	MT	MT
2.5	הון	היין	MT	MT	DSH	MT
2.6	מליצי	מליצה	(DSH)	MT	(DSH)	MT
2.8	וישלוכה	ישלוך	MT	MT	MT	MT	Frag.=DSH
2.15	חמתו	חמתך	no suf.	no pron.	no suf.	DSH
2.16	הרעל	הערל	MT	DSH	DSH	(DSH)	Aq.=DSH

The data are then evaluated, with this conclusion: 'The peculiar

[1] Stendahl, op. cit., p. 185.   [2] Ibid., p. 189.
[3] Ibid., pp. 185-90.   [4] Ibid., p. 189.

way in which *DSH* coincides both with those readings differing from the MT and with the MT's own makes it inadequate to say that *DSH*'s Hebrew text was the one which is supported by the said versions. We must rather presume that *DSH* was conscious of various possibilities, tried them out and allowed them to enrich its interpretation of the prophet's message, which in all its forms was fulfilled in and through the Teacher of Righteousness.'[1]

Stendahl finds similar phenomena—variations in person and number, structural changes, and evident knowledge of divergent readings—in Matthew's quotations and regards this as arising from a scholarly interpretation of the texts by an early Christian 'school' of exegetes: They selected from various textual traditions, and at times created *ad hoc*, readings which best expressed the meaning of the text as they understood it.

There are a number of Pauline quotations which indicate that the *pesher* method was employed not only by the apostle but in the pre-Pauline period of the Church as well.[2] The apocalyptic outlook, in its messianic expression, is implicit in the whole Pauline hermeneutic, and is particularly obvious in 2 Cor. 6.2: 'For he saith, I have heard thee in a time accepted and in the day of salvation have I succoured thee: behold, now is the accepted time, behold now is the day of salvation.'[3] The interpreted or *pesher* text-form is also present in Paul's quotations. The apostle follows the LXX where it diverges from the MT in a number of places. Some of these probably have an exegetical purpose in view (e.g., $\pi i\sigma\tau\iota\varsigma$ in Rom. 1.17; $o\tilde{\iota}\varsigma$ in Rom. 15.21)[4]; but since the LXX is his usual *vade mecum*, it is difficult in most of these texts to show 'a selective rendering of a chosen text'.

---

[1] Ibid., p. 190.

[2] Stendahl recognises that this type of interpretation is present in apocalyptic writings and occasionally in the rabbis (ibid., p. 195) and that it is found in other NT writings, especially the Fourth Gospel. But he concludes that there were fewer intentional changes based on the Hebrew, and 'thus the elaborate stage of the *pesher* found in Matthew scarcely existed' (ibid., p. 202). Cf. Bonsirven, op. cit., pp. 77-83.

[3] The manner in which this citation is parenthetically inserted suggests that the whole verse—the OT text plus the interpretation—was taken as a quotation by Paul. Cf. 1 Cor. 15.45; 1 Tim. 5.18; 2 Tim. 2.19.

[4] On Rom. 1.17 cf. *supra*, pp. 117f; the LXX 'to whom' in Rom. 15.21 accords much more explicitly with Paul's application than the indefinite אֲשֶׁר of the MT.

In some twenty citations in which the LXX and Hebrew agree and Paul's text varies, the evidence of *pesher* quotation is more certain.[1] In almost all of these the variation seems to be a deliberate adaptation to the NT context; in some cases the alteration has a definite bearing on the interpretation of the passage. Changes in person and number are especially prevalent.[2] The deviations in the *catena* in 2 Cor. 6.16ff are evidently designed for a Messianic-Age interpretation of the prophecies. God's command to Israel regarding Babylon (αὐτῆς) is now applied to the relation of Christians with unbelievers (αὐτῶν); the promise given to Israel 'personified' in Solomon (αὐτῶ . . . αὐτός) is fulfilled in true Israel, the members of Christ's body (ὑμῖν . . . ὑμεῖς). Similarly, σοφῶν in 1 Cor. 3.20 and ὁ πρῶτος ἄνθρωπος Ἀδὰμ in 1 Cor. 15.45a show an elaboration or interpretation of the OT text to fit it to the NT context.

In a few instances the variations point to a selection from among various known readings. The present state of the whole textual problem cautions against any dogmatising in this regard,[3] and there appears to be no instance of a rejected reading being alluded to in the apostle's exposition. Nevertheless, the choice of a particular text for interpretive reasons appears probable in several Pauline quotations. Rom. 12.19 modifies the Hebrew with the Targum; the Targum also may be the source of the rendering 'confess' which is important for the sense of the citation in Rom. 14.11.[4] Eph. 4.8 substitutes the third person for the second and rejects the MT and LXX rendering 'take' or 'receive' in favour of the translation 'give' found in the Targum and Peshitta. Whether this represents an interpretation of לָקַח ('take', 'fetch') or a variant Hebrew textual tradition (e.g. חָלַק, 'apportion', 'distribute') is uncertain, but the former is more probable.

1 Cor. 15.54f is perhaps the most notable instance of *pesher* quotation in the Pauline literature:

---

[1] Cf. Appendix I.

[2] e.g. Rom. 3.18 (αὐτοῦ to αὐτῶν); 10.19 (αὐτούς to ὑμᾶς); 1 Cor. 15.27 (ὑπέταξας to ὑπέταξεν).

[3] e.g. Paul's citations from Job (Rom. 11.35; 1 Cor. 3.19) may follow the Hebrew simply because it is the most familiar text. The Vulgate in Job 41.3 also follows the Hebrew (and Romans). Cf. *supra*, pp. 14ff.

[4] So Toy, op. cit., p. 164. The *pael* תְּקַיֵּם, used in the Targum, may have the meaning 'vouch' or 'confirm'. Cf. Mt. 14.7.

Death is swallowed up in victory.
Where, O Death, is your victory?
Where, O Death, is your sting?

The interrogative of the LXX is followed (the MT אֵהִי is
uncertain), and for the MT לָנֶצַח ('forever') εἰς νῖκος ('in
victory') is substituted. The rendering εἰς νῖκος, which follows
a number of Greek texts,[1] may originate in the Hebrew (or
Aramaic) root itself (נצח, 'leader', 'success'). The Peshitta
conflation, 'to victory forever', witnesses to two known versions
of the passage[2]; but whether the Peshitta, Aquila and like
readings reflect a textual tradition known to and used by Paul,
or whether they represent a textual tradition derived from the
Pauline usage, is a moot point. The variant εἰς νῖκος is inter-
woven into Paul's exposition and indicates that the merged
quotation was probably known to him in this form. But the
idea of death being 'swallowed up in victory' is so intimately
connected with the 'victory' of Christ's resurrection that, if a
conjecture must be made, the probability is that this interpretation of the Hebrew is one created (or recovered) in the early
Church. As Manson has well remarked, the doctrinal and
liturgical traditions of the first century were very influential in
shaping the textual traditions themselves.[3]

Taken as a whole, the Pauline citations reflect in substantial
measure a *pesher*-type moulding of the text which in some cases
is determinative for the NT application of the passage. While
this at times involves a choosing and rejecting between texts
and/or Targums known to the apostle, more often the interpretative paraphrase appears to be created *ad hoc* by Paul or by
the early Church before him. This type of *pesher* arises from
the NT's attitude towards and understanding of the concept of
'quotation' itself, as Manson has noted: 'We are long accustomed to distinguish carefully between the text which—in more
senses than one—is sacred, and the commentary upon it and
exposition of it. We tend to think of the text as objective fact
and interpretation as subjective opinion. It may be doubted

---

[1] Cf. *supra*, p. 15. The Targum has 'forever' (לְעָלְמִין).
[2] Cf. Toy, op. cit., p. 180.
[3] Manson, 'The Cairo Geniza: A Review', p. 184. Other quotations such as
1 Cor. 2.9; 14.21; 15.45 also appear to involve interpretations which have a
distinctively Christian origin.

whether the early Jewish and Christian translators and exposi-
tors of Scripture made any such sharp distinction. For them
the meaning of the text was of primary importance; and they
seem to have had greater confidence than we moderns in their
ability to find it. Once found it became a clear duty to express
it; and accurate reproduction of the traditional wording of the
Divine oracles took second place to publication of what was
held to be their essential meaning and immediate application.
Odd as it may seem to us, the freedom with which they handled
the Biblical text is a direct result of the supreme importance
which they attached to it.'[1]

In selecting a particular version or in creating an *ad hoc*
rendering Paul views his citation as thereby more accurately
expressing the true meaning of the Scripture. For Paul, as for
the rabbis, the 'letter' was sacred; but unlike the rabbis, Paul
valued the 'letter' not for itself alone but for the meaning which
it conveyed. His idea of a quotation was not a worshipping of
the letter or 'parroting' of the text; neither was it an eisegesis
which arbitrarily imposed a foreign meaning upon the text.
It was rather, in his eyes, a quotation-exposition, a *Midrash
pesher*, which drew from the text the meaning originally implanted there by the Spirit and expressed that meaning in the
most appropriate words and phrases known to him.

The *pesher* method is not used extensively in Paul's quotations,
but where it does occur, it often appears to go behind the
Greek to reflect an interpretation of the Hebrew ur-text.
Further, some of the most significant instances appear to point
back to a pre-Pauline usage in the early Church. The presence
of the method in λέγει κύριος quotations (e.g. Rom. 12.19;
1 Cor. 14.21),[2] the temple typology *catena* (cf. 2 Cor, 6.16ff),[3]
and such citations as 1 Cor. 15.45[4] are cases in point. Stendahl's
valuable dissertation, by its comparison of *pesher* quotation in
Matthew and *DSH*, has clearly shown that NT writers and the
Christian exegetes behind them, in their use of this method, are

---

[1] Manson, 'The Argument from Prophecy', p. 135. Some of Manson's conclusions on the particular text in question (Heb. 10.37f; cf. Rom. 1.17) may be
open to qualification, but the fundamental principle which he here delineates is
clearly present in Pauline and NT exegesis; and it may explain some of the variations in parallel NT texts (e.g. the Synoptic sayings of Jesus).
[2] Cf. *supra*, pp. 107ff.   [3] Cf. *supra*, pp. 89ff.   [4] Cf. *supra*, pp. 95ff.

not indulging in a novelty. Converted priests and rabbis, especially those adhering to apocalyptic parties or sects, might be expected to be well acquainted with it. Having now the light of the Gospel and the gifts of the Spirit, it is no surprise that they apply a *Midrash pesher* method to the OT with conviction, confidence and thoroughness. Stendahl envisions this exposition in its NT form as the product of early Christian 'schools of the prophets'. He suggests that the development may form an 'unbroken line from the School of Jesus via "the teaching of the apostles", the "ways" of Paul, the basic teaching of Mark and other ὑπηρέται τοῦ λόγου, and the more mature School of John to the rather elaborate School of Matthew with its ingenious interpretation of the OT as the crown of its scholarship'.[1] While the predilection of different writers for particular IF, subject matter and text-forms does indicate different 'schools' of exegesis in the early Church, nevertheless the developmental progression posited by Stendahl for the use of *Midrash pesher* is open to some question. Since the method is not a Christian development, there is no reason why it could not have been employed even by individual exegetes (e.g. converted rabbis) from the earliest time. If *Midrash pesher* is understood as an interpretative moulding of the text within an apocalyptic framework, *ad hoc* or with reference to appropriate textual or targumic traditions, then there is some evidence for its use on a rather advanced scale even in the pre-Pauline strata of the NT.

Pauline Exegesis: An Added Factor

Pauline exegesis might be termed 'grammatical-historical plus'. The apostle does not ignore the historical significance of the text; neither does he play fast and loose with the grammar if care is taken to understand the precise purpose and meaning of his citation. The grammar and the historical meaning are assumed; and Pauline exegesis, in its essential character, begins where grammatical-historical exegesis ends. The latter discipline could say 'these' possibilities lie within the grammar, and 'this' is the probable historical significance. But Paul would probably begin by saying, 'The OT Scripture has a

[1] Stendahl, op. cit., p. 34.

wider meaning than its immediate historical application[1]; even OT history is God-moulded history whose significance does not lie merely in the event but in the meaning of the event for its later fulfilment. Furthermore, grammatical exegesis can only circumscribe the possibilities as to what a text *says*; to determine the *meaning* of a text one must not only select the proper grammatical possibility but also fit it into a proper interpretation of OT history as a whole.' This is precisely what Paul proceeds to do, integrating his exposition into the quotations themselves; and in doing so he is convinced that he thereby expresses the true meaning of the text. While his results do not always tally with the statistical probabilities of the grammar, they do lie within its possible meanings or reasonable inferences therefrom. The failure to recognise this 'added factor' is a notable weakness in nineteenth century criticism of the Pauline quotations. If Paul's presuppositions as to the nature of the OT and of its history are accepted, little fault can be found with his handling of the individual texts.

CONCLUSION

The problem posed by Pauline quotations lies in the variations of the Pauline text and the application given the passage by the apostle. As to textual variations, about half the citations follow the LXX, and a considerable number accord partially or fully with other texts or versions. Nevertheless, a textual investigation leaves several phenomena unaccounted for and is, in general, inconclusive. The essential problem appears to be more one of interpretation than of a purely textual nature.

In many cases the Pauline rendering is intimately connected with his application of the text. These applications make use of common stock interpretations, oral and targumic traditions, and rabbinic methodology. They are not, however, the product of rabbinic artifice; and in their essential character they are not rabbinic at all. In large measure they find their origin in the hermeneutical methods and topical emphases of the early Church.

Midrash pesher as a hermeneutical method is present not only in the Gospels of Matthew and John but in the Pauline writings

[1] Cf. Rom. 15.4; 1 Cor. 10.11.

as well. In this method the exposition of the text determined the textual form of the quotation itself. This was variously accomplished by (1) merging pertinent verses into one strongly expressive 'proof-text', (2) adapting the grammar to the NT context and application, (3) choosing appropriate renderings from known texts or Targums, and (4) creating *ad hoc* interpretations. All these devices were designed to best express the true meaning of the text as the NT writers understood it.

In conclusion, the significance of the OT for Paul's theology can hardly be overestimated. His experience on the Damascus road radically altered his understanding of the Book, but it in no way lessened its importance for the apostle to the Gentiles. Rather, his knowledge of Christ opened to him a New Way in which he found the true meaning of the Scriptures. The words of C. H. Dodd apply with special force to the use of the OT in the Pauline Epistles: 'I have here only hinted at the significance for Christian theology of a right understanding of the treatment of the Old Testament in the New. I believe it represents an intellectual achievement of remarkable originality, displaying penetration into the meaning that lies beneath the surface of the biblical text, and a power of synthesis which gathers apparently disparate elements into a many sided whole, not unsuitable to convey some idea of the manifold wisdom of God.'[1]

¹ Dodd, *The Old Testament in the New*, p. 21.

APPENDIX I (A)

QUOTATIONS IN THE PAULINE EPISTLES

Classification[1]:

1 —in agreement with the LXX and the Hebrew.
2 —in agreement with the LXX against the Hebrew.
3 —in agreement with the Hebrew against the LXX.
4[2]—at variance with the LXX and the Hebrew where they agree.
5[3]—at variance with the LXX and the Hebrew where they vary.
* —There is only a slight variation from the LXX.
** —There is a difference in word order.

NT	*OT*	*Classif.*
Rom. 1.17	Hab. 2.4	5*
2.24	Isa. 52.5	5
3.4	Ps. 50(51).6	4*
3.10-12	Ps. 13(14).1-3	4
3.13a	Ps. 5.10	1
3.13b	Ps. 139(140).4	1
3.14	Ps. 9.28(10.7)	5
3.15-17	Isa. 59.7-8	5
3.18	Ps. 35(36).2	4*
4.3 (9, 22)	Gen. 15.6	2
4.7-8	Ps. 31(32).1-2	2
4.17	Gen. 17.5	1
4.18	Gen. 15.5	1
7.7	Exod. 20.17 (Deut. 5.21)	1
8.36	Ps. 43(44).23	1
9.7	Gen. 21.12	1
9.9	Gen. 18.10, 14	5
9.12	Gen. 25.23	1
9.13	Mal. 1.2-3	4**
9.15	Exod. 33.19	1
9.17	Exod. 9.16	5

[1] Turpie (*Old Testament in New Testament*) gives a more detailed classification. Although containing a few readings later rejected, his work remains a valuable tool.

[2] The differences in Rom. 11.8 and 2 Cor. 6.17 affect clauses; the remaining texts vary in the addition, omission or rendering of words.

[3] Rom. 3.15-17; 9.33; 10.6-8; 14.11; 1 Cor. 2.9 vary as to clauses; the remaining texts vary as to words.

NT	OT	Classif.
Rom. 9.25	Hos. 2.23(25)	4
9.26	Hos. 1.10 (2.1)	5
9.27-8	Isa. 10.22-23	5
9.29	Isa. 1.9	2
9.33	Isa. 8.14+28.16	5
10.5	Lev. 18.5	4*
10.6-8	Deut. 30.12-14	5
10.11	Isa. 28.16	5
10.13	Joel 2.32 (3.5)	1
10.15	Isa. 52.7	5
10.16	Isa. 53.1	2
10.18	Ps. 18(19).5	2
10.19	Deut. 32.21	4*
10.20	Isa. 65.1	5* **
10.21	Isa. 65.2	2**
11.3	3(1) Kings 19.14	4
11.4	19.18	5
11.8	Isa. 29.10+Deut. 29.4(3)	4
11.9-10	Ps. 68(69).23-4	5
11.26-7	Isa. 59.20-1+27.9	5*
11.34	Isa. 40.13	5*
11.35	Job. 41.3	3
12.19	Deut. 32.35	5
12.20	Prov. 25.21-22	2
13.9	Deut. 5.17-21 (Exod. 20.13-17) +Lev. 19.18	1
14.11	Isa. 45.23 (+49.18)	5
15.3	Ps. 68(69).10	1
15.9	Ps. 17(18).50 (cf. 2 Kings 22.50)	4*
15.10	Deut. 32.43	2
15.11	Ps. 116(117).1	4*
15.12	Isa. 11.10	5*
15.21	Isa. 52.15	2**
1 Cor. 1.19	Isa. 29.14	5*
1.31	Jer. 9.24(23)	4
2.9	(Isa. 64.4+65.16)?	5
2.16	Isa. 40.13	5
3.19	Job 5.12-13	3
3.20	Ps. 93(94).11	4*
6.16	Gen. 2.24	2

NT	OT	Classif.
1 Cor. 9.9	Deut. 25.4	5*
10.7	Exod. 32.6	1
10.26	Ps. 23(24).1	1
14.21	Isa. 28.11-12	5
15.27	Ps. 8.7	4*
15.32	Isa. 22.13	2
15.45	Gen. 2.7	4
15.54	Isa. 25.8	5
15.55	Hos. 13.14	5
2 Cor. 4.13	Ps. 115(116).1(10)	1
6.2	Isa. 49.8	1
6.16	Lev. 26.11-12 (Ezek. 27.37)	4
6.17	Isa. 52.11-12	4
6.18	2 Kings (2 Sam.) 7.14	4
8.15	Exod. 16.18	3
9.9	Ps. 111(112).9	1
10.17	Jer. 9.24	4
13.1	Deut. 19.15	5*
Gal. 3.6	Gen. 15.6 (12.3; 18.18)	2
3.8	Gen. 12.3 (+18.18)	4
3.10	Deut. 27.26	5
3.11	Hab. 2.4	5*
3.12	Lev. 18.5	4*
3.13	Deut. 21.23	5
3.16	Gen. 22.18 (cf. 12.7; 13.15; 17.7)	1
4.27	Isa. 54.1	2
4.30	Gen. 21.10	4*
5.14	Lev. 19.18	1
Eph. 4.8	Ps. 67(68).19	4*
5.14	?	
5.31	Gen. 2.24	5
6.2-3	Deut. 5.16 (Exod. 20.12)	5
1 Tim. 5.18	Deut. 25.4 + (Matt. 10.10?)	2
2 Tim. 2.19	Num. 16.5 + (Isa. 26.13?)	3*

APPENDIX I (B)

OT ALLUSIONS AND PARALLELS IN THE PAULINE EPISTLES

* The allusion is manifestly intentional

	Allusion	Source or Parallel		Allusion	Source or Parallel
	Rom. 1.20-32	(Wis. 13.1ff)?		1 Cor. 5.13	Deut. 22.24; (24.7)
	1.23	Ps. 105(106).20		6.2	Dan. 7.22; Wis.
	2.6	Ps. 61(62).13			3.8 (?)
	2.9	(Isa. 8.22)?		6.12-13	(Sirach. 37.27, 28)?
	2.11	2 Chron. 19.7		6.17	Deut. 10.20
	3.4a	Ps. 115(116).2(11)		10.5	Num. 14.16
	3.20	Ps. 142(143).2		10.6	Num. 11.4, 34
	4.11	Gen. 17.10-11		10.20	Deut. 32.17
	4.25	Isa. 53.12, 4, 5		10.21	Mal. 1.7, 12
	5.5	Ps. 21(22).6		10.22	Deut. 32.21
*	5.12	Gen. 2.17; 3.19		11.3	Gen. 3.16
	7.2-3	Deut. 22.22		11.7	Gen. 1.27
	7.11	Gen. 3.13		11.25	Exod. 24.8; Zech.
	8.3	(Isa. 53.10)?			9.11
	8.33	Isa. 50.8-9		13.5	Zech. 8.17 (LXX)
	8.34	Ps. 109(110).1;		14.25	Isa. 45.14
		Isa. 53.12	*	14.34	Gen. 3.16
	9.18	Exod. 4.21; 7.3		15.25	Ps. 109 (110).1
	9.20	Isa. 29.16; 45.9			
	9.21	(Wis. 11.22-3)?		2 Cor. 3.3	Exod. 31.18; Ezk.
	11.1-2	Ps. 93(94).14			11.19
		94(95).4	*	3.7-18	Exod. 34.29-35,
		1 Sam. 12.22			etc.
	11.11	Deut. 32.21		5.10	Eccl. 12.14
	11.32	(Wis. 11.23)?		5.17	Isa. 43.18-19
	12.16-17	Prov. 3.7 + 3.4		6.9	Ps. 117(118).17-18
		(LXX)		6.11	Ps. 118(119).32
	14.13	Lev. 19.14 (Deut.		7.6	Isa. 49.13
		27.18)		8.21	Prov. 3.4 (LXX)
				9.7	Prov. 22.8 (LXX)
	1 Cor. 1.20	Isa. 19.11-12 +		9.10	Isa. 55.10 + Hos.
		33.18			10.12
	5.7	Exod. 12.21		11.2	(Isa. 61.10)?

Allusion	Source or Parallel	Allusion	Source or Parallel
2 Cor. 11.3	Gen. 3.4, 13	1 Thess. 2.4	Jer. 11.20
		2.16	Gen. 15.16; Ps. 78(79).6
Gal. 1.15-16	Isa. 49.1 + Jer. 1.5		(2. Macc. 6.14)
2.16	Ps. 142(143).2	4.5	Jer. 10.25
* 4.22ff	Gen. 16.15ff	4.6	Ps. 93(94).2;
6.16	Ps. 124(125).5		Deut. 32.35
		4.8	Ezek. 36.27; 37.14
Eph. 1.20	Ps. 109(110).1	4.13	(Wis. 3.18)?
1.22	Ps. 8.7	4.17	Dan. 7.13
2.13-17	Isa. 57.19; 52.7	5.8	Isa. 59.17
2.20	Isa. 28.16	5.22	Job. 1.1, 8; 2.3
* 4.25	Zech. 8.16	2 Thess. 1.8	Isa. 66.15
* 4.26	Ps. 4.5	1.9-10	Isa. 2.10, 11, 19, 21
5.2	Ps. 39(40).7; Ezek. 20.41	1.10	Zech. 14.5 + Ps. 67.36
5.18	Prov. 23.31 (LXX)	1.12	Isa. 66.15
5.25ff	(Isa. 61.10)?	2.4	Dan. 11.36; Ezek. 28.2
* 6.14a	Isa. 11.5	2.8	Isa. 11.4
* 6.14b	Isa. 59.17	2.13	Deut. 33.12
6.17	Isa. 49.2	1 Tim. 2.6	Isa. 53.11-12
		2.12-14	Gen. 3.16
Phil. 1.19	Job. 13.16 (LXX)	2.13	Gen. 2.7
2.7f	Isa. 53.12	2.14	Gen. 3.6
2.9	Isa. 52.13	* 5.19	Deut. 19.15
2.10-11	Isa. 45.23, 49.3	6.1	Isa. 52.5
2.15	Deut. 32.5 (LXX)	6.15	Deut. 10.17; Dan. 2.47
2.16	Isa. 49.4; 65.23 (LXX)	2 Tim. 4.14	Ps. 61.13; Prov. 24.12
4.3	Ps. 68(69).29	Tit. 2.5	Isa. 52.5
4.18	Ezek. 20.41	2.14	Isa. 53.12; Ps. 129(130).8
Col. 2.3	Isa. 45.3		
2.22	Isa. 29.13		
3.1	Ps. 109(110).1		
3.10	Gen. 1.27		

APPENDIX II

TEXTS OF
OLD TESTAMENT CITATIONS

Text	IF	NT
Rom. 1.17 For therein is the right- eousness of God revealed from faith to faith; as it is written, The just shall live by faith.	καθὼς γέγραπται	*Rom.* 1.17 ὁ δὲ δίκαιος ἐκ πίστεως ζήσεται
Rom. 2.24 For the name of God is blasphemed among the Gentiles through you, as it is written.	καθὼς γέγραπται	*Rom.* 2.24 τὸ γὰρ ὄνομα τοῦ θεοῦ δι' ὑμᾶς βλασφημεῖται ἐν τοῖς ἔθνεσιν
Rom. 3.4 God forbid; yea, let God be true, but every man a liar; as it is written, That thou mightest be justi- fied in thy sayings, and mightest overcome when thou art judged.	καθάπερ γέγραπται	*Rom.* 3.4 ὅπως ἂν δικαιωθῇς ἐν τοῖς λόγοις σου καὶ νικήσεις ἐν τῷ κρίνεσθαί σε
Rom. 3.10-12 As it is written, there is none righteous, no, not one; There is none that understandeth, there is none that seeketh after God. They are all gone out of the way, they are together become un- profitable; there is none that doeth good, no, not one.	καθὼς γέγραπται ὅτι	*Rom.* 3.10-12 οὐκ ἔστιν δίκαιος οὐδὲ εἷς οὐκ ἔστιν ὁ συνίων, οὐκ ἔστιν ὁ ἐκζητῶν τὸν θεόν· πάντες ἐξέκλιναν ἅμα ἠχρεώθησαν, οὐκ ἔστιν ὁ ποιῶν χρηστότητα, οὐκ ἔστιν ἕως ἑνός.
Rom. 3.13*a* Their throat is an open sepulchre; with their tongues they have used deceit; . . .		*Rom.* 3.13*a* τάφος ἀνεῳγμένος ὁ λάρυγξ αὐτῶν ταῖς γλώσσαις αὐτῶν ἐδολιοῦσαν
Rom. 3.13*b* . . . the poison of asps is under their lips:		*Rom.* 3.13*b* ἰὸς ἀσπίδων ὑπὸ τὰ χείλη αὐτῶν

LXX   NT Parallels

Hab. 2.4   *Gal.* 3.11
ὁ δὲ δίκαιος ἐκ πίστεώς μου ζήσεται   ὅτι ὁ δίκαιος ἐκ πίστεως ζήσεται

Heb. 10.38
ὁ δὲ δίκαιός μου ἐκ πίστεως ζήσεται

Isa. 52.5
δι᾽ ὑμᾶς διὰ παντὸς τὸ ὄνομά μου
βλασφημεῖται ἐν τοῖς ἔθνεσιν

Ps. 50.6
ὅπως ἂν δικαιωθῇς ἐν τοῖς λόγοις
σου καὶ νικήσῃς ἐν τῷ κρίνεσθαί σε

Ps. 13.1ff (*Eccl.* 7.21)
οὐκ ἔστιν ποιῶν χρηστότητα, οὐκ ἔστιν
[ἕως ἑνός . . .]
τοῦ ἰδεῖν εἰ ἔστιν συνίων ἢ ἐκζητῶν
    τὸν θεόν· πάντες ἐξέκλιναν
ἅμα ἠχρεώθησαν, οὐκ ἔστιν ποιῶν
χρηστότητα, οὐκ ἔστιν ἕως ἑνός.

Ps. 5.10
τάφος ἀνεῳγμένος ὁ λάρυγξ αὐτῶν
ταῖς γλώσσαις αὐτῶν ἐδολιοῦσαν

Ps. 139.4
ἰὸς ἀσπίδων ὑπὸ τὰ χείλη αὐτῶν

Text	IF	NT
Rom. 3.14 Whose mouth is full of cursing and bitterness:		*Rom.* 3.14 ὧν τὸ στόμα ἀρᾶς καὶ πικρίας γέμει
Rom. 3.15-17 Their feet are swift to shed blood: Destruction and misery are in their ways: And the way of peace have they not known.		*Rom.* 3.15-17 ὀξεῖς οἱ πόδες αὐτῶν ἐκχέαι αἷμα, σύντριμμα καὶ ταλαιπωρία ἐν ταῖς ὁδοῖς αὐτῶν καὶ ὁδὸν εἰρήνης οὐκ ἔγνωσαν
Rom. 3.18 There is no fear of God before their eyes.		*Rom.* 3.18 οὐκ ἔστιν φόβος θεοῦ ἀπέναντι τῶν ὀφθαλμῶν αὐτῶν
Rom. 4.3 For what saith the Scripture? Abraham believed God, and it was counted unto him for righteousness.	*(τί γὰρ) ἡ* *γραφὴ λέγει;*	*Rom.* 4.3 ἐπίστευσεν δὲ ᾿Αβραὰμ τῷ θεῷ, καὶ ἐλογίσθη αὐτῷ εἰς δικαιοσύνην
Rom. 4.7-8 Blessed are they whose iniquities are forgiven, and whose sins are covered. Blessed is the man to whom the Lord will not impute sin.	*καθάπερ καὶ* *Δαυὶδ λέγει*	*Rom.* 4.7-8 μακάριοι ὧν ἀφέθησαν αἱ ἀνομίαι, καὶ ὧν ἐπεκαλύφθησαν αἱ ἁμαρτίαι. μακάριος ἀνὴρ οὗ οὐ μὴ λογίσηται κύριος ἁμαρτίαν
Rom. 4.17 (As it is written, I have made thee a father of many nations.)	*καθὼς γέγραπται*	*Rom.* 4.17 ὅτι πατέρα πολλῶν ἐθνῶν τέθεικά σε
Rom. 4.18 So shall thy seed be.	*κατὰ τὸ* *εἰρημένον*	*Rom.* 4.18 οὕτως ἔσται τὸ σπέρμα σου
Rom. 7.7 Thou shalt not covet.	*ὁ νόμος ἔλεγεν*	*Rom.* 7.7 οὐκ ἐπιθυμήσεις

LXX

NT Parallels

Ps. 9.28 (10.7)
οὗ ἀρᾶς τὸ στόμα αὐτοῦ
γέμει καὶ πικρίας καὶ δόλου

Isa. 59.7-8
οἱ δὲ πόδες αὐτῶν ἐπὶ πονηρίαν τρέ-
χουσιν, ταχινοὶ ἐκχέαι αἷμα, καὶ οἱ
διαλογισμοὶ αὐτῶν διαλογισμοὶ ἀπὸ
φόνων· σύντριμμα καὶ ταλαιπωρία ἐν
ταῖς ὁδοῖς αὐτῶν καὶ ὁδὸν εἰρήνης
οὐκ οἴδασιν

Ps. 35.2
οὐκ ἔστιν φόβος θεοῦ ἀπέναντι τῶν
ὀφθαλμῶν αὐτοῦ

Gen. 15.6
καὶ ἐπίστευσεν Ἀβρὰμ τῷ θεῷ, καὶ
ἐλογίσθη αὐτῷ εἰς δικαιοσύνην

Jas. 2.23
ἐπίστευσεν δὲ Ἀβραὰμ τῷ θεῷ, καὶ
ἐλογίσθη αὐτῷ εἰς δικαιοσύνην

Gal. 3.6
Ἀβραὰμ ἐπίστευσεν   τῷ θεῷ
καὶ ἐλογίσθη αὐτῷ εἰς δικαιοσύνην

Ps. 31.1-2
μακάριοι ὧν ἀφέθησαν αἱ ἀνομίαι,
καὶ ὧν ἐπεκαλύφθησαν αἱ ἁμαρ-
τίαι. μακάριος ἀνὴρ οὗ οὐ μὴ
λογίσηται κύριος ἁμαρτίαν.

Gen. 17.5
ὅτι πατέρα πολλῶν ἐθνῶν τέθεικά σε.

Gen. 15.5
οὕτως ἔσται τὸ σπέρμα σου

(Cf. *Heb.* 11.12)

Exod. 20.17 (*Deut.* 5.21)
οὐκ ἐπιθυμήσεις

Rom. 13.9 (cf. *Matt.* 19.18ff)
... οὐκ ἐπιθυμήσεις

Text	IF	NT
Rom. 8.36 As it is written, For thy sake we are killed all the day long; we are accounted as sheep for the slaughter.	καθὼς γέγραπται	**Rom. 8.36** ὅτι ἕνεκεν σοῦ θανατούμεθα ὅλην τὴν ἡμέραν, ἐλογίσθημεν ὡς πρόβατα σφαγῆς
Rom. 9.7 . . . but, In Isaac shall thy seed be called.	ἀλλά	**Rom. 9.7** ἐν Ἰσαὰκ κληθήσεταί σοι σπέρμα
Rom. 9.9 At this time will I come, and Sarah shall have a son.	(special)	**Rom. 9.9** κατὰ τὸν καιρὸν τοῦτον ἐλεύσομαι καὶ ἔσται τῇ Σάρρᾳ υἱός.
Rom. 9.12 . . . The elder shall serve the younger.	ἐρρέθη αὐτῇ	**Rom. 9.12** ὅτι ὁ μείζων δουλεύσει τῷ ἐλάσσονι
Rom. 9.13 As it is written, Jacob have I loved, but Esau have I hated.	καθάπερ γέγραπται	**Rom. 9.13** τὸν Ἰακὼβ ἠγάπησα, τὸν δὲ Ἠσαῦ ἐμίσησα
Rom. 9.15 For he saith to Moses, I will have mercy on whom I will have mercy, and I will have compassion on whom I will have compassion.	τῷ Μωϋσεῖ γὰρ λέγει	**Rom. 9.15** ἐλεήσω ὃν ἂν ἐλεῶ, καὶ οἰκτειρήσω ὃν ἂν οἰκτείρω
Rom. 9.17 For the scripture saith unto Pharaoh, Even for this same purpose have I raised thee up, that I might shew my power in thee, and that thy name might be declared throughout all the earth.	λέγει . . . ἡ γραφὴ	**Rom. 9.17** εἰς αὐτὸ τοῦτο ἐξήγειρά σε, ὅπως ἐνδείξωμαι ἐν σοὶ τὴν δύναμίν μου, καὶ ὅπως διαγγελῇ τὸ ὄνομά μου ἐν πάσῃ τῇ γῇ

LXX   NT Parallels

Ps. 43.23
ὅτι ἕνεκα σοῦ θανατούμεθα ὅλην τὴν
ἡμέραν, ἐλογίσθημεν ὡς πρόβατα
σφαγῆς.

Gen. 21.12   *Heb.* 11.18
(ὅτι) ἐν Ἰσαὰκ κληθήσεταί σοι σπέρμα   (ὅτι) ἐν Ἰσαὰκ κληθήσεταί σοι σπέρμα

Gen. 18.10
ἐπαναστρέφων ἥξω πρὸς σὲ
  κατὰ τὸν καιρὸν τοῦτον εἰς ὥρας,
  καὶ ἕξει υἱὸν Σάρρα ἡ γυνή σου.

Gen. 25.23
καὶ ὁ μείζων δουλεύσει τῷ ἐλάσσονι

Mal. 1.2-3
καὶ ἠγάπησα τὸν Ἰακώβ
  τὸν δὲ Ἠσαῦ ἐμίσησα

Exod. 33.19
καὶ ἐλεήσω ὃν ἂν ἐλεῶ,
  καὶ οἰκτειρήσω ὃν ἂν οἰκτείρω

Exod. 9.16
καὶ ἕνεκεν τούτου διετηρήθης ἵνα
  ἐνδείξωμαι ἐν σοὶ τὴν ἰσχύν
  μου, καὶ ὅπως διαγγελῇ τὸ ὄνομά
  μου ἐν πάσῃ τῇ γῇ

Text	IF	NT
Rom. 9.25-6		*Rom.* 9.25-6

Rom. 9.25-6

As he saith also in Osee, I will call them my people, which were not my people; and her beloved, which was not beloved. And it shall come to pass, that in the place where it was said unto them, Ye are not my people; there shall they be called the children of the living God.

ἐν τῷ Ὡσηὲ λέγει

καλέσω τὸν οὐ λαόν μου λαόν μου καὶ τὴν οὐκ ἠγαπημένην ἠγαπημένην

καὶ ἔσται ἐν τῷ τόπῳ οὗ ἐρρέθη αὐτοῖς οὐ λαός μου ὑμεῖς, ἐκεῖ κληθήσονται υἱοὶ θεοῦ ζῶντος

Rom. 9.27-8

Esaias also cried concerning Israel, Though the number of the children of Israel be as the sand of the sea, a remnant shall be saved: For he will finish the work, and cut it short in righteousness: because a short work will the Lord make upon the earth.

Ἡσαΐας κράζει

Rom. 9.27-8

ἐὰν ᾖ ὁ ἀριθμὸς τῶν υἱῶν Ἰσραὴλ ὡς ἡ ἄμμος τῆς θαλάσσης τὸ ὑπόλειμα σωθήσεται. ῾λόγον γὰρ συντελῶν καὶ συντέμνων

ποιήσει κύριος ἐπὶ τῆς γῆς

Rom. 9.29

And as Esaias said before, Except the Lord of Sabaoth had left us a seed, we had been as Sodoma, and been made like unto Gomorrha.

καθὼς προείρηκεν Ἡσαΐας

Rom. 9.29

εἰ μὴ κύριος σαβαὼθ ἐγκατέλιπεν ἡμῖν σπέρμα, ὡς Σόδομα ἄν ἐγενήθημεν καὶ ὡς Γόμορρα ἄν ὡμοιώθημεν

LXX   NT Parallels

Hos. 2.23   (Cf. 1 *Pet.* 2.10)

καὶ ἀγαπήσω τὴν οὐκ ἠγαπημένην, καὶ
ἐρῶ τῷ οὐ λαῷ μου λαός μου εἶ σύ

Hos. 1.10

καὶ ἔσται ἐν τῷ τόπῳ οὗ ἐρρέθη
   αὐτοῖς
οὐ λαός μου ὑμεῖς
κληθήσονται καὶ αὐτοὶ υἱοὶ θεοῦ ζῶντος

Isa. 10.22-3

καὶ ἐὰν γένηται   ὁ λαὸς Ἰσραὴλ
   ὡς ἡ ἄμμος τῆς θαλάσσης
   τὸ κατάλιμμα αὐτῶν σωθήσεται.
λόγον   συντελῶν καὶ συντέμνων
ἐν δικαιοσύνῃ, ὅτι λόγον συντετμη-
   μένον
ποιήσει κύριος ἐν τῇ οἰκουμένῃ ὅλῃ

Isa. 1.9

καὶ εἰ μὴ κύριος σαβαὼθ ἐγκατέλιπεν
   ἡμῖν σπέρμα ὡς Σόδομα ἂν
ἐγενήθημεν καὶ ὡς Γόμορρα
   ἂν ὡμοιώθημεν

Text	IF	NT
Rom. 9.33		*Rom.* 9.33
As it is written, Behold I lay in Sion a stumbling-stone and rock of offence: and whosoever believeth on him shall not be ashamed.	καθὼς γέγραπται	Ἰδοὺ τίθημι ἐν Σιὼν λίθον προσκόμματος καὶ πέτραν σκανδάλου
		καὶ ὁ πιστεύων ἐπ' αὐτῷ οὐ καταισχυνθήσεται
Rom. 10.5		*Rom.* 10.5
That the man which doeth those things shall live by them.	Μωϋσῆς γράφει	ὁ ποιήσας ἄνθρωπος ζήσεται ἐν αὐτῇ
Rom. 10.6-8		*Rom.* 10.6-8
But the righteousness which is of faith speaketh on this wise, Say not in thine heart Who shall ascend into heaven? (that is, to bring Christ down from above:) Or, Who shall descend into the deep? (that is, to bring up Christ again from the dead.) But what saith it? The Word is nigh unto thee, even in thy mouth, and in thy heart: ...	ἡ δὲ ἐκ πίστεως δικαιοσύνη οὕτως λέγει (ἀλλὰ τί λέγει;)	τίς ἀναβήσεται εἰς τὸν οὐρανόν; ... ... τίς καταβήσεται εἰς τὴν ἄβυσσον; ... ... ἐγγύς σου τὸ ῥῆμά ἐστιν, ἐν τῷ στόματί σου, καὶ ἐν τῇ καρδίᾳ σου ...
Rom. 10.11		*Rom.* 10.11
For the scripture saith, Whosoever believeth on him shall not be ashamed.	ἡ γραφή λέγει	πᾶς ὁ πιστεύων ἐπ' αὐτῷ οὐ καταισχυνθήσεται
Rom. 10.13		*Rom.* 10.13
For whosoever shall call upon the name of the Lord shall be saved.	γάρ	πᾶς (γὰρ) ὃς ἂν ἐπικαλέσηται τὸ ὄνομα κυρίου σωθήσεται

LXX	NT Parallels
Isa. 8.14	1 *Pet.* 2.6 (cf. *Matt.* 21.42)
καὶ οὐχ ὡς	ἰδοὺ τίθημι ἐν Σιὼν
λίθου προσκόμματι συναντήσεσθε	(1 *Pet.* 2.8—λίθος προσκόμματος
οὐδὲ ὡς πέτρας πτώματι	καὶ πέτρα σκανδάλου) λίθον
Isa. 28.16	ἐκλεκτὸν ἀκρογωνιαῖον ἔντιμον,
ἰδοὺ ἐγὼ ἐμβάλλω εἰς τὰ θεμέλια	καὶ ὁ πιστεύων ἐπ᾽ αὐτῷ οὐ μὴ καται-
Σειὼν λίθον	σχυνθῇ.
πολυτελῆ ἐκλεκτὸν ἀκρογωνιαῖον ἔντι-	*Rom.* 10.11
μον εἰς τὰ θεμέλια αὐτῆς,	πᾶς ὁ πιστεύων ἐπ᾽ αὐτῷ οὐ καται-
καὶ ὁ πιστεύων οὐ μὴ καταισχυνθῇ.	σχυνθήσεται.

Lev. 18.5	*Gal.* 3.12 (cf. *Luke* 10.28)
ἃ ποιήσας ἄνθρωπος ζήσεται ἐν αὐτοῖς	ὁ ποιήσας αὐτὰ ζήσεται ἐν αὐτοῖς

Deut. 30.12-14
τίς ἀναβήσεται ἡμῖν εἰς τὸν οὐρανὸν . . .
. . . τίς διαπεράσει ἡμῖν εἰς τὸν πέραν
τῆς θαλάσσης, . . .
. . . ἔστιν σου ἐγγὺς τὸ ῥῆμα σφόδρα
ἐν τῷ στόματί σου καὶ ἐν τῃ καρδίᾳ
σου,

Isa. 28.16	*Rom.* 9.33
καὶ ὁ πιστεύων οὐ μὴ καταισχυνθῇ	καὶ ὁ πιστεύων ἐπ᾽ αὐτῷ οὐ καται-
	σχυνθήσεται
	1 *Pet.* 2.6
	καὶ ὁ πιστεύων ἐπ᾽ αὐτῷ οὐ μὴ
	καταισχυνθῇ

Joel 2.32	*Acts* 2.21
καὶ ἔσται πᾶς ὃς ἂν ἐπικαλέσηται τὸ	. . . καὶ ἔσται πᾶς ὃς ἐὰν ἐπικαλέσηται
ὄνομα κυρίου σωθήσεται	τὸ ὄνομα κυρίου σωθήσεται.

Text	IF	NT
Rom. 10.15		*Rom.* 10.15

Rom. 10.15
. . . as it is written, How
beautiful are the feet of
them that preach [the
gospel of peace, and
bring glad tidings of]
good things!

καθάπερ
γέγραπται

Rom. 10.15
ὡς ὡραῖοι
οἱ πόδες τῶν εὐαγγελιζομένων
ἀγαθά

Rom. 10.16
. . . For Esaias saith,
Lord, who hath believed
our report?

('Ησαΐας λέγει)

Rom. 10.16
κύριε, τίς ἐπίτευσεν τῇ ἀκοῇ ἡμῶν;

Rom. 10.18
Yes, verily, their sound
went into all the earth,
and their words unto
the ends of the world.

μενοῦν γε

Rom. 10.18
εἰς πᾶσαν τὴν γῆν ἐξῆλθεν ὁ φθόγγος
αὐτῶν, καὶ εἰς τὰ πέρατα τῆς
οἰκουμένης τὰ ῥήματα αὐτῶν

Rom. 10.19
But I say, Did not Israel
know? First Moses saith,
I will provoke you to
jealousy by them that
are no people, and by a
foolish nation I will
anger you.

Μωϋσῆς λέγει

Rom. 10.19
ἐγὼ παραζηλώσω   ὑμᾶς ἐπ' οὐκ
ἔθνει, ἐπ' ἔθνει ἀσυνέτῳ παροργιῶ
ὑμᾶς.

Rom. 10.20
But Esaias is very bold,
and saith, I was found of
them that sought me not;
I was made manifest
unto them that asked
not after me.

'Ησαΐας λέγει

Rom. 10.20
εὑρέθην τοῖς ἐμὲ μὴ ζητοῦσιν,

ἐμφανὴς ἐγενόμην τοῖς ἐμὲ μὴ
ἐπερωτῶσιν

Rom. 10.21
But to Israel he saith,
All day long I have
stretched forth my hands
unto a disobedient and
gainsaying people.

(πρὸς δὲ τὸν
'Ισραὴλ) λέγει

Rom. 10.21
ὅλην τὴν ἡμέραν ἐξεπέτασα τὰς
χεῖράς μου πρὸς λαὸν ἀπειθοῦντα
καὶ ἀντιλέγοντα

LXX   NT Parallels

Isa. 52.7
ὡς ὥρα ἐπὶ τῶν ὀρέων,
ὡς πόδες εὐαγγελιζομένου ἀκοὴν
  εἰρήνης,
ὡς εὐαγγελιζόμενος ἀγαθά,
ὅτι ἀκουστὴν ποιήσω τὴν σωτηρίαν σου

Isa. 53.1   *John* 12.38
κύριε, τίς ἐπίστευσεν τῇ ἀκοῇ ἡμῶν;   κύριε, τίς ἐπίστευσεν τῇ ἀκοῇ ἡμῶν; . . .

Ps. 18.5
εἰς πᾶσαν τὴν γῆν ἐξῆλθεν ὁ φθόγγος
  αὐτῶν, καὶ εἰς τὰ πέρατα τῆς
  οἰκουμένης τὰ ῥήματα αὐτῶν

Deut. 32.21
κἀγὼ παραζηλώσω αὐτοὺς   ἐπ᾽ οὐκ
  ἔθνει· ἐπ᾽ ἔθνει ἀσυνέτῳ παροργιῶ
  αὐτούς

Isa. 65.1
ἐμφανὴς ἐγενήθην τοῖς ἐμὲ μὴ ἐπερωτῶσιν,
    εὑρέθην τοῖς ἐμὲ μὴ ζητοῦσιν . .

Isa. 65.2
ἐξεπέτασα τὰς χεῖράς μου ὅλην τὴν
  ἡμέραν πρὸς λαὸν ἀπειθοῦντα καὶ
  ἀντιλέγοντα

Text	IF	NT

Rom. 11.3
Lord, they have killed thy prophets, and digged down thine altars; and I am left alone, and they seek my life.

(ἐν Ἠλίᾳ) . .
λέγει ἡ γραφή
. . .

Rom. 11.3
κύριε, τοὺς προφήτας σου ἀπέκτειναν, τὰ θυσιαστήριά σου κατέσκαψαν
κἀγὼ ὑπελείφθην
μόνος καὶ ζητοῦσιν τὴν ψυχήν μου.

Rom. 11.4
But what saith the answer of God unto him? I have reserved to myself seven thousand men, who have not bowed the knee to the image of Baal.

(τί) λέγει . . . ὁ
χρηματισμός ;

Rom. 11.4
κατέλιπον ἐμαυτῷ ἑπτακισχιλίους ἄνδρας, οἵτινες οὐκ ἔκαμψαν γόνυ τῇ βάαλ

Rom. 11.8
(According as it is written, God hath given them the spirit of slumber, eyes that they should not see, and ears that they should not hear;) unto this day.

καθάπερ
γέγραπται

Rom. 11.8
ἔδωκεν αὐτοῖς ὁ θεὸς πνεῦμα κατανύξεως,

ὀφθαλμοὺς τοῦ μὴ βλέπειν καὶ ὦτα τοῦ μὴ ἀκούειν, ἕως τῆς σήμερον ἡμέρας

Rom. 11.9-10
And David saith Let their table be made a snare, and a trap, and a stumblingblock, and a recompence unto them: Let their eyes be darkened, that they may not see, and bow down their back alway.

Δαυὶδ λέγει

Rom. 11.9-10
γενηθήτω ἡ τράπεζα αὐτῶν εἰς παγίδα καὶ εἰς θήραν καὶ εἰς σκάνδαλον καὶ εἰς ἀνταπόδομα αὐτοῖς,

σκοτισθήτωσαν οἱ ὀφθαλμοὶ αὐτῶν τοῦ μὴ βλέπειν, καὶ τὸν νῶτον αὐτῶν διὰ παντὸς σύγκαμψον.

Rom. 11.26-7
And so all Israel shall be saved: as it is written, There shall come out of Sion the Deliverer, and shall turn away ungodliness from Jacob: For this is my covenant unto them, when I shall take away their sins.

καθὼς γέγραπται

Rom. 11.26-7
ἥξει ἐκ Σιὼν ὁ ῥυόμενος, ἀποστρέψει ἀσεβείας ἀπὸ Ἰακώβ. καὶ αὕτη αὐτοῖς ἡ παρ' ἐμοῦ διαθήκη,

ὅταν ἀφέλωμαι τὰς ἁμαρτίας αὐτῶν

3 Kings 19.14
καὶ τὰ θυσιαστήριά σου καθεῖλαν, καὶ
τοὺς προφήτας σου ἀπέκτειναν

ἐν ῥομφαία καὶ ὑπολέλιμμαι ἐγὼ μονώ-
τατος, καὶ ζητοῦσι τὴν ψυχήν μου
λαβεῖν αὐτήν

3 Kings 19.18
καὶ καταλείψεις ἐν Ἰσραὴλ ἑπτὰ χιλι-
άδας ἀνδρῶν, πάντα γόνατα ἃ οὐκ
ὤκλασαν γόνυ τῷ βάαλ

Isa. 29.10   (Cf. Matt. 13.14f; John 12.40;
(ὅτι πεπότικεν ὑμᾶς κύριος πνεύματι   Acts 28.26f)
κατανύξεως καὶ καμμύσει τοὺς
ὀφθαλμοὺς αὐτῶν.)
Deut. 29.4
(καὶ οὐκ ἔδωκεν κύριος ὁ θεὸς
ὑμῖν καρδίαν εἰδέναι καὶ ὀφθαλμοὺς
βλέπειν καὶ ὦτα
ἀκούειν ἕως τῆς ἡμέρας ταύτης)
Ps. 68.23-4
γενηθήτω ἡ τράπεζα αὐτῶν ἐνώπιον
αὐτῶν εἰς παγίδα καὶ εἰς ἀνταπόδοσιν
καὶ εἰς σκάνδαλον.

σκοτισθήτωσαν
οἱ ὀφθαλμοὶ αὐτῶν τοῦ μὴ
βλέπειν, καὶ τὸν νῶτον αὐτῶν
διὰ παντὸς σύνκαμψον.

Isa. 59.20-1
καὶ ἥξει ἕνεκεν Σιὼν ὁ ῥυόμενος καὶ
ἀποστρέψει ἀσεβείας ἀπὸ Ἰακώβ.
καὶ αὕτη αὐτοῖς ἡ παρ' ἐμοῦ διαθήκη,
εἶπεν κύριος.
Isa. 27.9
... ὅταν ἀφέλωμαι αὐτοῦ τὴν ἁμαρτίαν

Text	IF	NT
Rom. 11.34-5		*Rom.* 11.34-5

Rom. 11.34-5

For who hath known the mind of the Lord? or who hath been his counsellor? Or who hath first given to him, and it shall be recompensed unto him again?

(γαρ)

Rom. 11.34-5

τίς γὰρ ἔγνω νοῦν κυρίου; ἢ τίς σύμβουλος αὐτοῦ ἐγένετο;

ἢ τίς προέδωκεν αὐτῷ, καὶ ἀνταποδοθήσεται αὐτῷ;

Rom. 12.19

. . . for it is written, Vengeance is mine; I will repay, saith the Lord.

γέγραπται γάρ (λέγει κύριος)

Rom. 12.19

ἐμοὶ ἐκδίκησις ἐγὼ ἀνταποδώσω λέγει κύριος.

Rom. 12.20

Therefore if thine enemy hunger feed him; if he thirst, give him drink; for in so doing thou shalt heap coals of fire on his head.

(ἀλλά)

Rom. 12.20

ἐὰν πεινᾷ ὁ ἐχθρός σου, ψώμιζε αὐτόν· ἐὰν διψᾷ πότιζε αὐτόν· τοῦτο γὰρ ποιῶν ἄνθρακας πυρὸς σωρεύσεις ἐπὶ τὴν κεφαλὴν αὐτοῦ.

Rom. 13.9

For this, Thou shalt not commit adultery, Thou shalt not kill, Thou shalt not steal, Thou shalt not bear false witness, Thou shalt not covet; and if there be any other commandment, it is briefly comprehended in this saying namely, Thou shalt love thy neighbour as thyself.

τὸ γάρ

Rom. 13.9

οὐ μοιχεύσεις, οὐ φονεύσεις, οὐ κλέψεις,

οὐκ ἐπιθυμήσεις . . .

ἀγαπήσεις τὸν πλησίον σου ὡς σεαυτόν.

Rom. 14.11

For it is written, As I live, saith the Lord, every knee shall bow to me, and every tongue shall confess to God.

γέγραπται γάρ (λέγει κύριος)

Rom. 14.11

ζῶ ἐγώ, λέγει κύριος, ὅτι ἐμοὶ κάμψει πᾶν γόνυ, καὶ πᾶσα γλῶσσα ἐξομολογήσεται τῷ θεῷ

LXX	NT Parallels
Isa. 40.13	1 *Cor.* 2.16

τίς ἔγνω νοῦν κυρίου; καὶ τίς αὐτοῦ   τίς γὰρ ἔγνω νοῦν κυρίου;
σύμβουλος ἐγένετο ὃς συμβιβᾷ αὐτόν;   ὃς συμβιβάσει αὐτόν;

Job 41.3
ἢ τίς ἀντιστήσεταί μοι καὶ ὑπομενεῖ;

Deut. 32.35 (cf. *Ps.* 93(94).1f)	*Heb.* 10.30

ἐν ἡμέρᾳ ἐκδικήσεως ἀνταποδώσω   ἐμοὶ ἐκδίκησις ἐγὼ ἀνταποδώσω
ὅταν σφαλῇ ὁ ποὺς αὐτῶν   (λέγει κύριος)

Prov. 25.21-2
ἐὰν πεινᾷ ὁ ἐχθρός σου, ψώμιζε
αὐτόν· ἐὰν διψᾷ πότιζε αὐτόν·
τοῦτο γὰρ ποιῶν ἄνθρακας πυρὸς
σωρεύσεις ἐπὶ τὴν κεφαλὴν αὐτοῦ.

Deut. 5.17-21	*Matt.* 19.18 (cf. *Matt.* 5.21, 27)

οὐ μοιχεύσεις, οὐ φονεύσεις, οὐ   οὐ φονεύσεις, οὐ μοιχεύσεις, οὐ κλέψεις,
κλέψεις.   οὐ ψευδομαρτυρήσεις, . . .
οὐ ψευδομαρτυρήσεις . . .   *Mark* 10.19
              οὐκ ἐπιθυμήσεις . .   μὴ φονεύσῃς, μὴ μοιχεύσῃς, μὴ κλέψῃς,
Exod. 20.13-17   μὴ ψευδομαρτυρήσῃς, . . .
οὐ μοιχεύσεις, οὐ κλέψεις, οὐ φονεύσεις.   *Luke* 18.20
οὐ ψευδομαρτυρήσεις . . . οὐκ ἐπι-   μὴ μοιχεύσῃς, μὴ φονεύσῃς, μὴ κλέψῃς,
θυμήσεις   μὴ ψευδομαρτυρήσῃς, . . .

Lev. 19.18	*Gal.* 5.14; *Matt.* 19.19; *Mark* 12.31

ἀγαπήσεις τὸν πλησίον σου ὡς   ἀγαπήσεις τὸν πλησίον σου ὡς
σεαυτόν   σεαυτόν

Isa. 45.23	*Mark* 12.31 (cf. *Luke* 10.27)

κατ᾽ ἐμαυτοῦ ὀμνύω, . . . ὅτι ἐμοὶ κάμψει πᾶν γόνυ καὶ ὀμεῖται πᾶσα γλῶσσα
τὸν θεόν.

Text	IF	NT
Rom. 15.3 ... but, as it is written, The reproaches of them that reproached thee fell on me.	καθὼς γέγραπται	**Rom. 15.3** οἱ ὀνειδισμοὶ τῶν ὀνειδιζόντων σε ἐπέπεσαν ἐπ' ἐμέ
Rom. 15.9-12 ... it is written, For this cause, I will confess to thee among the Gentiles, and sing unto thy name.	καθὼς γέγραπται	**Rom. 15.9-12** διὰ τοῦτο ἐξομολογήσομαί σοι ἐν ἔθνεσιν καὶ τῷ ὀνόματί σου ψαλῶ.
And again he saith, Rejoice, ye Gentiles, with his people.	(καὶ πάλιν λέγει)	εὐφράνθητε ἔθνη μετὰ τοῦ λαοῦ αὐτοῦ
And again, Praise the Lord, all ye Gentiles; and laud him all ye people.	(καὶ πάλιν)	αἰνεῖτε πάντα τὰ ἔθνη τὸν κύριον, καὶ ἐπαινεσάτωσαν αὐτὸν πάντες οἱ λαοί.
And again, Esaias saith, There shall be a root of Jesse, and he that shall rise to reign over the Gentiles; in him shall the Gentiles trust.	(καὶ πάλιν Ἡσαΐας λέγει)	ἔσται ἡ ῥίζα τοῦ Ἰεσσαί καὶ ὁ ἀνιστάμενος ἄρχειν ἐθνῶν, ἐπ' αὐτῷ ἔθνη ἐλπιοῦσιν.
Rom. 15.21 But as it is written, To whom he was not spoken of they shall see; and they that have not heard shall understand.	καθὼς γέγραπται	**Rom. 15.21** ὄψονται οἷς οὐκ ἀνηγγέλη περὶ αὐτοῦ, καὶ οἱ οὐκ ἀκηκόασιν, συνήσουσιν.
1 Cor. 1.19 For it is written, I will destroy the wisdom of the wise, and will bring to nothing the understanding of the prudent.	γέγραπται γάρ	**1 Cor. 1.19** ἀπολῶ τὴν σοφίαν τῶν σοφῶν, καὶ τὴν σύνεσιν τῶν συνετῶν ἀθετήσω
1 Cor. 1.31 That, according as it is written, He that glorieth, let him glory in the Lord.	καθὼς γέγραπται	**1 Cor. 1.31** ὁ καυχώμενος ἐν κυρίῳ καυχάσθω

LXX

NT Parallels

Ps. 68.10

(Cf. *John* 2.17)

οἱ ὀνειδισμοὶ τῶν ὀνειδιζόντων σε
ἐπέπεσαν ἐπ' ἐμέ

Ps. 17.50

διὰ τοῦτο ἐξομολογήσομαί σοι ἐν
ἔθνεσιν, κύριε,
καὶ τῷ ὀνόματί σου ψαλῶ.

Deut. 32.43

(Cf. *Heb.* 1.6)

εὐφράνθητε ἔθνη μετὰ τοῦ λαοῦ
αὐτοῦ.

Ps. 116.1

αἰνεῖτε τὸν κύριον πάντα τὰ ἔθνη
αἰνεσάτωσαν αὐτὸν πάντες
οἱ λαοί.

Isa. 11.10

(Cf. *Matt.* 2.23)

καὶ ἔσται ἐν τῇ ἡμέρᾳ ἐκείνῃ ἡ ῥίζα
τοῦ Ἰεσσαὶ καὶ ὁ ἀνιστάμενος ἄρχειν
ἐθνῶν, ἐπ' αὐτῷ ἔθνη ἐλπιοῦσιν.

Isa. 52.15

ὅτι οἷς οὐκ ἀνηγγέλη περὶ αὐτοῦ
ὄψονται, καὶ οἳ οὐκ ἀκηκόασιν
συνήσουσιν.

Isa. 29.14

(Cf. *Matt.* 15.8f; *Rom.* 11.8)

ἀπολῶ τὴν σοφίαν τῶν σοφῶν, καὶ
τὴν σύνεσιν τῶν συνετῶν   κρύψω.

Jer. 9.24

2 *Cor.* 10.17

ἀλλ' ἢ ἐν τούτῳ καυχάσθω ὁ καυχώμενος,

ὁ δὲ καυχώμενος

συνίειν καὶ γινώσκειν ὅτι ἐγώ εἰμι
κύριος . . .

ἐν κυρίῳ καυχάσθω

Text	IF	NT
1 *Cor.* 2.9 But as it is written, Eye hath not seen, nor ear heard, neither have entered into the heart of man, the things which God hath prepared for them that love him.	καθὼς γέγραπται	1 *Cor.* 2.9 ἃ ὀφθαλμὸς οὐκ εἶδεν καὶ οὖς οὐκ ἤκουσεν καὶ ἐπὶ καρδίαν ἀνθρώπου οὐκ ἀνέβη, ὅσα ἡτοίμασεν ὁ θεὸς τοῖς ἀγαπῶσιν αὐτόν
1 *Cor.* 2.16 For who hath known the mind of the Lord, that he may instruct him?...	(γὰρ)	1 *Cor.* 2.16 τίς γὰρ ἔγνω νοῦν κυρίου; ὃς συμβιβάσει αὐτόν;
1 *Cor.* 3.19-20 For it is written, He taketh the wise in their own craftiness. And again, the Lord knoweth the thoughts of the wise, that they are vain.	γέγραπται γάρ (καὶ πάλιν)	1 *Cor.* 3.19-20 ὁ δρασσόμενος τοὺς σοφοὺς ἐν τῇ πανουργίᾳ αὐτῶν. κύριος γινώσκει τοὺς διαλογισμοὺς τῶν σοφῶν ὅτι εἰσὶν μάταιοι
1 *Cor.* 6.16 . . . for two, saith he, shall be one flesh.	(γάρ φησίν)	1 *Cor.* 6.16 ἔσονται γάρ, φησίν, οἱ δύο εἰς σάρκα μίαν
1 *Cor.* 9.9 For it is written in the law of Moses, that thou shalt not muzzle the mouth of the ox that treadeth out the corn.	ἐν γὰρ τῷ Μωϋσέως νόμῳ γέγραπται	1 *Cor.* 9.9 οὐ κημώσεις βοῦν ἀλοῶντα
1 *Cor.* 10.7 . . . as it is written, The people sat down to eat and drink, and rose up to play.	ὥσπερ γέγραπται	1 *Cor.* 10.7 ἐκάθισεν ὁ λαὸς φαγεῖν καὶ πεῖν, καὶ ἀνέστησαν παίζειν
1 *Cor.* 10.26 For the earth is the Lord's, and the fulness thereof.	(γὰρ)	1 *Cor.* 10.26 τοῦ κυρίου γὰρ ἡ γῆ καὶ τὸ πλήρωμα αὐτῆς

LXX   NT Parallels

Isa. 64.4
ἀπὸ τοῦ αἰῶνος οὐκ ἠκούσαμεν οὐδὲ
οἱ ὀφθαλμοὶ ἡμῶν εἶδον
θεὸν πλὴν σοῦ καὶ τὰ ἔργα σου
            (*Isa.* 65.16
ἐπιλήσονται γὰρ τὴν θλίψεν τὴν πρώτην
καὶ οὐκ ἀναβήσεται αὐτῶν ἐπὶ τὴν
     καρδίαν;)
ἃ ποιήσεις τοις ὑπομένουσιν ἔλεον

            Isa. 40.13   *Rom.* 11.34
τίς ἔγνω νοῦν κυρίου; καὶ τίς αὐτοῦ   τίς γὰρ ἔγνω νοῦν κυρίου; ἤ τίς
σύμβουλος ἐγένετο ὃς συμβιβᾷ αὐτόν;   σύμβουλος αὐτοῦ ἐγένετο;

            Job 5.13
ὁ καταλαμβάνων σοφοὺς ἐν τῇ φρονήσει

            Ps. 93.11
κύριος γινώσκει τοὺς διαλογισμοὺς
τῶν ἀνθρώπων ὅτι εἰσὶν μάταιοι

            Gen. 2.24   *Matt.* 19.5; *Mark* 10.7-8; *Eph.* 5.31
καὶ ἔσονται   οἱ δύο εἰς σάρκα   καὶ ἔσονται   οἱ δύο εἰς σάρκα
μίαν   μίαν

            Deut. 25.4   1 *Tim.* 5.18
οὐ φιμώσεις βοῦν ἀλοῶντα   βοῦν ἀλοῶντα οὐ φιμώσεις . . .

            Exod. 32.6
ἐκάθισεν ὁ λαὸς φαγεῖν καὶ πιεῖν
καὶ ἀνέστησαν παίζειν

            Ps. 23.1
τοῦ κυρίου   ἡ γῆ καὶ τὸ πλήρωμα
αὐτῆς

Text	IF	NT
1 *Cor.* 14.21 In the law it is written, With men of other tongues and other lips will I speak unto this people; and yet for all that will they not hear me, saith the Lord.	ἐν τῷ νόμῳ γέγραπται (λέγει κύριος)	1 *Cor.* 14.21 ὅτι ἐν ἑτερογλώσσοις καὶ ἐν χείλεσιν ἑτέρων λαλήσω τῷ λαῷ τούτῳ, καὶ οὐδ' οὕτως εἰσακούσονταί μου, λέγει κύριος
1 *Cor.* 15.27 For he hath put all things under his feet.	(γὰρ)	1 *Cor.* 15.27 πάντα γὰρ ὑπέταξεν ὑπὸ τοὺς πόδας αὐτοῦ.
1 *Cor.* 15.32 ... let us eat and drink; for tomorrow we die.		1 *Cor.* 15.32 φάγωμεν καὶ πίωμεν, αὔριον γὰρ ἀποθνῄσκομεν
1 *Cor.* 15.45 And so it is written, The first man Adam was made a living soul; the last Adam was made a quickening spirit.	οὕτως καὶ γέγραπται	1 *Cor.* 15.45 ἐγένετο ὁ πρῶτος ἄνθρωπος Ἀδὰμ εἰς ψυχὴν ζῶσαν· (ὁ ἔσχατος Ἀδὰμ εἰς πνεῦμα ζωοποιοῦν.)
1 *Cor.* 15.54-5 ... then shall be brought to pass the saying that is written, Death is swallowed up in victory. O death, where is thy sting? O grave, where is thy victory?	τότε γενήσεται ὁ λόγος ὁ γεγραμμένος	1 *Cor.* 15.54-5 κατεπόθη ὁ θάνατος εἰς νῖκος. ποῦ σου, θάνατε. τὸ νῖκος; ποῦ σου, θάνατε, τὸ κέντρον;
2 *Cor.* 4.13 ... according as it is written, I believed, and therefore have I spoken.	κατὰ τὸ γεγραμμένον	2 *Cor.* 4.13 ἐπίστευσα, διὸ ἐλάλησα
2 *Cor.* 6.2 For he saith, I have heard thee in a time accepted and in the day of salvation have I succoured thee:	λέγει γάρ	2 *Cor.* 6.2 καιρῷ δεκτῷ ἐπήκουσά σου καὶ ἐν ἡμέρᾳ σωτηρίας ἐβοήθησά σοι

LXX   NT Parallels

Isa. 28.11-12
διὰ φαυλισμὸν χειλέων,
διὰ γλώσσης ἑτέρας, ὅτι
            λαλήσουσιν τῷ λαῷ
τούτῳ . . . καὶ οὐκ ἠθέλησαν ἀκούειν

Ps. 8.7   *Heb.* 2.8 (cf. *Eph.* 1.22)
πάντα ὑπέταξας ὑποκάτω τῶν ποδῶν   . . . πάντα ὑπέταξας ὑποκάτω τῶν
   αὐτοῦ   ποδῶν αὐτοῦ

Isa. 22.13
φάγωμεν καὶ πίωμεν, αὔριον γὰρ
ἀποθνήσκομεν

Gen. 2.7
ἐγένετο ὁ   ἄνθρωπος
   εἰς ψυχὴν ζῶσαν.

Isa. 25.8
κατέπιεν ὁ θάνατος ἰσχύσας

Hos. 13.14
ποῦ ἡ δίκη σου, θάνατε;
ποῦ τὸ κέντρον σου, ᾅδη;

Ps. 115.1
ἐπίστευσα, διὸ ἐλάλησα

Isa. 49.8
καιρῷ δεκτῷ ἐπήκουσά σου καὶ ἐν
ἡμέρᾳ σωτηρίας ἐβοήθησά σοι.

Text	IF	NT
2 *Cor.* 6.16-18		2 *Cor.* 6.16-18

2 *Cor.* 6.16-18

... as God hath said, I will dwell in them; and I will be their God, and they shall be my people. Wherefore come out from among them and be ye separate, saith the Lord, and touch not the unclean thing; and I will receive you. And will be a Father unto you, and ye shall be my sons and daughters, saith the Lord Almighty.

καθὼς εἶπεν ὁ θεὸς

(διὸ) (λέγει κύριος)

(λέγει κύριος παντοκράτωρ)

2 *Cor.* 6.16-18

ὅτι ἐνοικήσω ἐν αὐτοῖς καὶ ἐμπεριπατήσω
καὶ ἔσομαι αὐτῶν θεὸς καὶ αὐτοὶ ἔσονταί μου λαός

διὸ ἐξέλθετε ἐκ μέσου αὐτῶν καὶ ἀφορίσθητε, λέγει κύριος, καὶ ἀκαθάρτου μὴ ἅπτεσθε κἀγὼ εἰσδέξομαι ὑμᾶς,

καὶ ἔσομαι ὑμῖν εἰς πατέρα, καὶ ὑμεῖς ἔσεσθέ μοι εἰς υἱοὺς καὶ θυγατέρας, λέγει κύριος παντοκράτωρ.

2 *Cor.* 8.15

As it is written, He that had gathered much had nothing over; and he that had gathered little had no lack.

καθὼς γέγραπται

2 *Cor.* 8.15

ὁ τὸ πολὺ οὐκ ἐπλεόνασεν, καὶ ὁ τὸ ὀλίγον οὐκ ἠλαττόνησεν

2 *Cor.* 9.9

As it is written, He hath dispersed abroad; he hath given to the poor: his righteousness remaineth for ever.

καθὼς γέγραπται

2 *Cor.* 9.9

ἐσκόρπισεν, ἔδωκεν τοῖς πένησιν, ἡ δικαιοσύνη αὐτοῦ μένει εἰς τὸν αἰῶνα

2 *Cor.* 10.17

But he that glorieth, let him glory in the Lord.

(δὲ)

2 *Cor.* 10.17

ὁ δὲ καυχώμενος ἐν κυρίῳ καυχάσθω

LXX   NT Parallels

Lev. 26.11-12
καὶ θήσω τὴν διαθήκην μου ἐν ὑμῖν
. . . καὶ ἐνπεριπατήσω ἐν ὑμῖν
καὶ ἔσομαι ὑμῖν θεός, καὶ ὑμεῖς ἔσθεσθέ
μου λαός

Ezek. 37.27
(καὶ ἔσται ἡ κατασκήνωσίς μου ἐν
αὐτοῖς
καὶ ἔσομαι αὐτοῖς θεὸς, καὶ αὐτοί μου
ἔσονται λαός)

Isa. 52.11-12
ἐξέλθατε ἐκεῖθεν καὶ ἀκαθάρτου μὴ
ἅψησθε, ἐξέλθατε ἐκ μέσου αὐτῆς...
προπορεύσεται γὰρ πρότερος ὑμῶν
κύριος . . .

         2 *Kings* 7.14   *Heb.* 1.5*b*
ἐγὼ ἔσομαι αὐτῷ εἰς πατέρα, καὶ   ἐγὼ ἔσομαι αὐτῷ εἰς πατέρα, καὶ αὐτὸς
αὐτὸς ἔσται μοι εἰς υἱόν   ἔσται μοι εἰς υἱόν
(v. 8—τάδε λέγει κύριος παντοκράτωρ)

         Exod. 16.18
οὐκ ἐπλεόνασεν ὁ τὸ πολύ, καὶ ὁ τὸ
ἔλαττον οὐκ ἠλατόνησεν

         Ps. 111.9
ἐσκόρπισεν, ἔδωκεν τοῖς πένησιν,
   ἡ δικαιοσύνη αὐτοῦ μένει εἰς τὸν
   αἰῶνα

         Jer. 9.24   1 *Cor.* 1.31
ἀλλ᾿ ἢ ἐν τούτῳ καυχάσθω ὁ καυχώ-   ὁ καυχώμενος ἐν κυρίῳ καυχάσθω
μενος,
συνίειν καὶ γινώσκειν ὅτι ἐγώ εἰμι
κύριος . . .

Text	IF	NT
2 *Cor.* 13.1		2 *Cor.* 13.1
. . . In the mouth of two or three witnesses shall every word be established.		ἐπὶ στόματος δύο μαρτύρων καὶ τριῶν σταθήσεται πᾶν ῥῆμα
Gal. 3.6		*Gal.* 3.6
Even as Abraham believed God, and it was accounted to him for righteousness.	καθὼς	Ἀβραὰμ ἐπίστευσεν τῷ θεῷ καὶ ἐλογίσθη αὐτῷ εἰς δικαιοσύνην
Gal. 3.8		*Gal.* 3.8
And the scriptures, foreseeing that God would justify the heathen through faith, preached before the gospel unto Abraham saying, In thee shall all nations be blessed.	προϊδοῦσα δὲ ἡ γραφὴ . . . προ- ευηγγελίσατο τῷ Ἀβραὰμ	ὅτι ἐνευλογηθήσονται ἐν σοὶ

πάντα τὰ ἔθνη. |
Gal. 3.10		*Gal.* 3.10
. . . for it is written, Cursed is everyone that continueth not in all things which are written in the book of the law to do them.	γέγραπται γὰρ	ὅτι ἐπικατάρατος πᾶς ὃς οὐκ ἐμμένει πᾶσιν τοῖς γεγραμμένοις ἐν τῷ βιβλίῳ τοῦ νόμου τοῦ ποιῆσαι αὐτά
Gal. 3.11		*Gal.* 3.11
. . . for, The just shall live by faith.	(ὅτι)	ὅτι ὁ δίκαιος ἐκ πίστεως ζήσεται
Gal. 3.12		*Gal.* 3.12
. . . but, The man that doeth them shall live in them.	(ἀλλὰ)	ὁ ποιήσας αὐτὰ ζήσεται ἐν αὐτοῖς
Gal. 3.13		*Gal.* 3.13
. . . for it is written, Cursed is every one that hangeth on a tree:	ὅτι γέγραπται	ἐπικατάρατος πᾶς ὁ κρεμάμενος ἐπὶ ξύλου

LXX   NT Parallels

Deut. 19.15   *Matt.* 18.16 (cf. *John* 8.17)

ἐπὶ στόματος δύο μαρτύρων καὶ ἐπὶ   ἐπὶ στόματος δύο μαρτύρων ἤ
στόματος τριῶν μαρτύρων στήσεται   τριῶν   σταθῇ
πᾶν ῥῆμα   πᾶν ῥῆμα

Gen. 15.6   *Jas.* 2.23
καὶ   ἐπίστευσεν ᾿Αβρὰμ τῷ θεῷ   ἐπίστευσεν δὲ ᾿Αβραὰμ τῷ θεῷ
καὶ ἐλογίσθη αὐτῷ εἰς δικαιοσύνην.   καὶ ἐλογίσθη αὐτῷ εἰς δικαιοσύνην
                                     Rom. 4.3
                                     ἐπίστευσεν δὲ ᾿Αβραὰμ τῷ θεῷ,
                                     καὶ ἐλογίσθη αὐτῷ εἰς δικαιωσύνην

Gen. 12.3
καὶ εὐλογηθήσονται ἐν σοὶ
πᾶσαι αἱ φυλαὶ τῆς γῆς

Gen. 18.18
καὶ ἐνευλογηθήσονται ἐν αὐτῷ
πάντα τὰ ἔθνη τῆς γῆς

Deut. 27.26
ἐπικατάρατος πᾶς ἄνθρωπος ὃς οὐκ
ἐμμένει ἐν πᾶσιν τοῖς
λόγοις τοῦ νόμου τούτου ποιῆσαι
αὐτούς

Hab. 2.4   *Rom.* 1.17
ὁ δὲ δίκαιος ἐκ πίστεώς μου ζήσεται   ὁ δὲ δίκαιος ἐκ πίστεως   ζήσεται
                                       Heb. 10.38
                                       ὁ δὲ δίκαιός μου ἐκ πίστεως ζήσεται

Lev. 18.5   *Rom.* 10.5 (cf. *Luke* 10.28)
ἃ ποιήσας ἄνθρωπος ζήσεται ἐν αὐτοῖς   ὁ ποιήσας ἄνθρωπος ζήσεται ἐν αὐτῇ

Deut. 21.23   (*Acts* 5.30)
ὅτι κεκαταραμένος ὑπὸ θεοῦ   κρεμάσαντες ἐπὶ ξύλου
πᾶς   κρεμάμενος ἐπὶ ξύλου

N

Text	IF	NT

Gal. 3.16
He saith not, 'and to seeds', as of many; but as of one. 'And to thy seed.'

 οὐ λέγει . . .
ἀλλ' . . .

Gal. 3.16
καὶ τῷ σπέρματί σου

Gal. 4.27
For it is written, Rejoice, thou barren that bearest not; break forth and cry, thou that travailest not; for the desolate hath many more children than she which hath an husband.

γέγραπται γάρ

Gal. 4.27
εὐφράνθητι, στεῖρα ἡ οὐ τίκτουσα,
ῥῆξον καὶ βόησον, ἡ οὐκ ὠδίνουσα,
ὅτι πολλὰ τὰ τέκνα τῆς ἐρήμου
μᾶλλον ἢ τῆς ἐχούσης τὸν ἄνδρα

Gal. 4.30
Nevertheless what saith the scripture? Cast out the bondwoman and her son: for the son of the bondwoman shall not be heir with the son of the freewoman.

ἀλλὰ τί λέγει ἡ
γραφή;

Gal. 4.30
ἔκβαλε τὴν παιδίσκην   καὶ τὸν
υἱὸν αὐτῆς
οὐ γὰρ μὴ κληρονομήσει ὁ υἱὸς τῆς
παιδίσκης μετὰ τοῦ υἱοῦ τῆς
ἐλευθέρας

Gal. 5.14
For all the law is fulfilled in one word, even in this: Thou shalt love thy neighbour as thyself.

. . . νόμος . . .
πεπλήρωται ἐν
τῷ

Gal. 5.14
ἀγαπήσεις τὸν πλησίον σου ὡς
σεαυτόν

Eph. 4.8
Wherefore he saith, When he ascended up on high, he led captivity captive, and gave gifts unto men.

διὸ λέγει

Eph. 4.8
ἀναβὰς εἰς ὕψος ᾐχμαλώτευσεν
αἰχμαλωσίαν,
ἔδωκεν   δόματα τοῖς ἀνθρώποις

Eph. 5.14
Wherefore he saith, Awake thou that sleepest, and arise from the dead, and Christ shall give thee light.

διὸ λέγει

Eph. 5.14
ἔγειρε ὁ καθεύδων καὶ ἀνάστα ἐκ
τῶν νεκρῶν,
καὶ ἐπιφαύσει σοι ὁ χριστός

LXX   NT Parallels

Gen. 22.18 (cf. 12.7; 13.15; 17.7f)   *Acts* 3.25 (cf. *Luke* 1.55)
καὶ ἐνευλογηθήσονται   καὶ ἐν τῷ σπέρματί σου
ἐν τῷ σπέρματι σου   ἐνευλογηθήσονται πᾶσαι αἱ πατριαὶ τῆς
πάντα τὰ ἔθνη τῆς γῆς   γῆς

Isa. 54.1
εὐφράνθητι στεῖρα ἡ οὐ τίκτουσα,
ῥῆξον καὶ βόησον ἡ οὐκ ὠδίνουσα,
ὅτι πολλὰ τὰ τέκνα τῆς ἐρήμου
μᾶλλον ἢ τῆς ἐχούσης τὸν ἄνδρα

Gen. 21.10
ἔκβαλε τὴν παιδίσκην ταύτην καὶ τὸν
  υἱὸν αὐτῆς
οὐ γὰρ μὴ κληρονομήσει ὁ υἱὸς τῆς
  παιδίσκης μετὰ τοῦ υἱοῦ μου Ἰσαάκ

                                       Matt. 19.19; *Matt.* 22.39; *Mark* 12.31;
              Lev. 19.18   *Rom.* 13.9 (cf. *Luke* 10.27)
καὶ ἀγαπήσεις τὸν πλησίον σου ὡς   ἀγαπήσεις τὸν πλησίον σου ὡς σεαυτόν
  σεαυτόν
                                                  Matt. 5.43
                                       ἀγαπήσεις τὸν πλησίον σου

        Ps. 67.19
ἀναβὰς εἰς ὕψος ᾐχμαλώτευσας
  αἰχμαλωσίαν
    ἔλαβες δόματα ἐν ἀνθρώπῳ.

  (*Isa.* 60.1, 19, 20, ?)   (cf. *John* 5.25; *Rom.* 13.11)

Text	IF	NT

Eph. 5.31

For this cause shall a man leave his father and mother, and shall be joined unto his wife, and they two shall be one flesh.

Eph. 5.31

ἀντὶ τούτου καταλείψει ἄνθρωπος
τὸν πατέρα
    καὶ τὴν μητέρα
καὶ προσκολληθήσεται πρὸς τὴν
    γυναῖκα αὐτοῦ,
καὶ ἔσονται οἱ δύο εἰς σάρκα μίαν

Eph. 6.2-3

Honour thy father and mother; which is the first commandment with promise; That it may be well with thee, and thou mayest live long on the earth.

Eph. 6.2-3

τίμα τὸν πατέρα σου καὶ τὴν μητέρα,

(ἥτις ἐστὶν ἐντολὴ πρώτη ἐν
    ἐπαγγελίᾳ,)
ἵνα εὖ σοι γένηται καὶ ἔσῃ
    μακροχρόνιος   ἐπὶ τῆς γῆς

1 *Tim.* 5.18

For the scripture saith, Thou shalt not muzzle the ox that treadeth out the corn, And, The Labourer is worthy of his reward.

λέγει γὰρ ἡ
γραφή

(καί)

1 *Tim.* 5.18

βοῦν ἀλοῶντα οὐ φιμώσεις

καὶ ἄξιος   ὁ ἐργάτης τοῦ μισθοῦ
    αὐτοῦ

2 *Tim.* 2.19

... The Lord knoweth them that are his. And, Let every one that nameth the name of the Lord depart from iniquity.

(καί)

2 *Tim.* 2.19

(ἔγνω κύριος τοὺς ὄντας αὐτοῦ

καὶ ἀποστήτω ἀπὸ ἀδικίας πᾶς ὁ
    ὀνομάζων τὸ ὄνομα κυρίου)

LXX	NT Parallels
Gen. 2.24	1 *Cor.* 6.16; *Matt.* 19.5; *Mark* 10.7-8

ἕνεκεν τούτου καταλείψει ἄνθρωπος
τὸν πατέρα
αὐτοῦ καὶ τὴν μητέρα αὐτοῦ
καὶ προσκολληθήσεται πρὸς τῇ
γυναῖκι αὐτοῦ·
καὶ ἔσονται οἱ δύο εἰς σάρκα μίαν

ἔσονται . . . οἱ δύο εἰς σάρκα μίαν

Deut. 5.16

Matt. 15.4

τίμα τὸν πατέρα σου καὶ τὴν μητέρα
σου
(ὃν τρόπον ἐνετείλατο κύριος ὁ θεός
σου,)
ἵνα εὖ σοι γένηται καὶ ἵνα
μακροχρόνιοι ἦτε ἐπὶ τῆς γῆς

τίμα τὸν πατέρα καὶ τὴν μητέρα

Mark 7.10 (cf. *Luke* 18.20)
τίμα τὸν πατέρα σου καὶ τὴν μητέρα
σου

Exod. 20.12
τίμα τὸν πατέρα σου καὶ τὴν μητέρα,
ἵνα εὖ σοι γένηται καὶ ἵνα
μακροχρόνιος γένῃ ἐπὶ τῆς γῆς

Deut. 25.4

1 *Cor.* 9.9

οὐ φιμώσεις βοῦν ἀλοῶντα

οὐ κημώσεις βοῦν ἀλοῶντα

(cf. *Lev.* 19.13; *Deut.* 25.14-15)

Luke 10.7
ἄξιος γὰρ ὁ ἐργάτης τοῦ μισθοῦ αὐτοῦ

Matt. 10.10
ἄξιος γὰρ ὁ ἐργάτης τῆς τροφῆς αὐτοῦ

Num. 16.5
καὶ ἔγνω ὁ θεὸς τοὺς ὄντας αὐτοῦ

APPENDIX III

COMBINED QUOTATIONS IN THE PAULINE EPISTLES

1 MERGED QUOTATIONS

NT	OT	Section of Jewish Canon
Rom. 3.10-18	Ps. 13(14).1-3; 5.10; 139.4; 9.28 (10.7); Isa. 59.7-8; Ps. 35(36).2	Kethubim + Nebiim
9.25-6	Hos. 2.23(25); 1.10(2.1)	Nebiim
9.33	Isa. 8.14; 28.16	Nebiim
11.8	Isa. 29.10; Deut. 29.4	Nebiim + Torah
11.26-27	Isa. 59.20; 27.9	Nebiim
11.34-35	Isa. 40.13; Job 41.3	Nebiim + Kethubim
1 Cor. 15.45	Gen. 2.7; (?)	Torah + ?
15.54-5	Isa. 25.8; Hos. 13.14	Nebiim
2 Cor. 6.16-18	Lev. 26.11-12 (Ezek. 37.27) Isa. 52.11-12; 2 Kings 7.14	Torah + Nebiim
1 Tim. 5.18	Deut. 25.4; Matt. 10.10 (Luke 10.7)	Torah + *verbum Christi*

2 CHAIN QUOTATIONS OR *Haraz*

NT	OT	Section of Jewish Canon
Rom. 9.12-13	Gen. 25.23 + Mal. 1.2-3	Torah + Nebiim
9.25-9	Hos. 2.23(25); 1.10(2.1) + Isa. 10.22-23 + Isa. 1.9	Nebiim
10.5-8	Lev. 18.5 + Deut. 30.12-14	Torah
(10.11-13	Isa. 28.16 + Joel 2.32	Nebiim)
10.19-21	Deut. 32.21 + Isa. 65.1 + Isa. 65.2	Torah + Nebiim
11.8-10	Isa. 29.10; Deut. 29.4 (3) + Ps. 68(69).23-4	Torah-Nebiim + Kethubim
15.9-12	Ps. 17(18).50 + Deut. 32.43 + Ps. 116(117).1 + Isa. 11.10	Kethubim + Torah + Kethubim + Nebiim

APPENDIX IV

PARALLEL QUOTATIONS

Paul	OT	NT	Comment
Rom. 1.17 (Gal. 3.11)	Hab. 2.4	Heb. 10.38	vary from the LXX and from each other
4.3 (Gal. 3.6)	Gen. 15.6	Jas. 2.23	virtually verbatim with the LXX
9.7	Gen. 21.12	Heb. 11.18	verbatim with the LXX
9.33	Isa. 8.14; 28.16	1 Pet. 2.6-8	combined quotation; variations
10.13	Joel. 2.32	Acts. 2.21	virtually verbatim with the LXX
10.16	Isa. 53.1	John 12.38	verbatim with the LXX
12.19	Deut. 32.35	Heb. 10.30	vary from the LXX but agree with each other; a λέγει κύριος quotation
13.9 (Gal. 5.14)	Deut. 5.17ff Lev. 19.18	Matt. 19.18f Mark 10.19; 12.31; Luke 18.20	variations in order; Paul agrees with the LXX and is nearest Luke
1 Cor. 6.16 (Eph. 5.31)	Gen. 2.24	Matt. 19.5; Mark 10.7-8	virtually verbatim with the LXX
15.27	Ps. 8.7	Heb. 2.8	Paul varies, Hebrews agrees with the LXX
2 Cor. 6.18	2 Kings 7.14	Heb. 1.5b	Paul varies, Hebrews agrees with the LXX
13.1	Deut. 19.15	Matt. 18.16	Paul agrees, Matthew varies from the LXX
Gal. 3.16	Gen. 22.18, etc.	Acts. 3.25	Paul probably had several Genesis passages in mind
Eph. 6.2-3	Deut. 5.16	Matt. 15.4; Mark 7.10	slight variations

INDEX OF SUBJECTS

INDEX OF AUTHORS

INDEX OF REFERENCES

Old Testament*

GENESIS

1.26ff	50
27	63f, 153f
2. -	106
7	64, 73, 152, 154, 177, 186
17	58, 153
24	73, 97, 151f, 175, 185, 187
3. 4	154
6	154
13	153f
16	153f
17	58
19	58, 153
21	53
4.10	70f
25	71
5. 3	61
6. 2	62
5	59
11. 5	50
7	50
12. 3	105, 119, 124, 152, 181
7	152, 183
13.15	152, 183
14.14	53
15. -	106
5	150, 159
6	56, 93, 95, 105, 119f, 124, 150, 152, 159, 181, 187
16	154
16.11	97
15	154
17. 5	52, 150, 159
7f	152, 183
10f	153

GENESIS (contd.)

17.16	70
18.10	122, 150, 161
14	150
17	81
18	119, 124, 152, 181
21. 3ff	52
10	152, 183
12	95, 122, 150, 161, 187
13	71
22. 8	95
16	95
18	105, 119, 124, 152, 183, 187
25.23	150, 161, 186
26. 4	124
28. 9	46
14	124
32.28	52
35. 3	50
7	50
40. 9	51

EXODUS

4.21	153
7. 3	153
9.16	150, 161
12.21	153
40	56
13. 8	132
15.23ff	68
16.18	152, 179
29	41
17. 5f	68
19. 5f	137, 139
20. -	14
12	152, 185
12ff	73, 151, 171

EXODUS (contd.)

20.17	150, 159
22. 9f	41
14	41
27	47
24. 4	48
8	153
14	75
31.18	153
32. 6	55, 152, 175
33.15	70
19	150, 161
34.29ff	13, 153
40.34ff	66, 133
38	66

LEVITICUS

5.23	50
18. -	106
5	30, 74, 119, 123, 151f, 165, 181, 186
19. -	106
3	48
13	50, 185
14	153
18	73, 88, 93, 151f, 171, 183, 187
26.11f	90, 152, 179, 186
27. 7	41

NUMBERS

3.15	63
11. 4	153
21	68
34	153
14.11	117
16	153
16. 5	152, 185
20. 1f	67

* Ordinarily the Septuagint references are employed

APOCRYPHA AND PSEUDEPIGRAPHA

THE BABYLONIAN TALMUD

THE MIDRASH RABBA